Reciprocity

Reciprocity is the basis of social relations. It permits a peaceful and free society in which people and rights are respected. The essence of families and communities, it also enables the working of markets and organizations, while correcting their main failures. Reciprocity is also a basis of politics, and it justifies social policies.

Although the importance of reciprocity has been widely recognized in other social sciences, it has, until recently, been somewhat ignored in economic analysis. Over the past three decades, economic theorist and moral philosopher Serge-Christophe Kolm has been at the forefront of research into the economics of the deepest aspects of societies. In *Reciprocity*, he provides a unique in-depth analysis of the motives, conducts, and effects of reciprocal relationships. In doing this, he explains crucial functionings of society and its economy, and the ways in which they can be improved.

This book should be read by economists, sociologists, philosophers, and anyone concerned with understanding the economy of social relationships and its far-reaching consequences.

Serge-Christophe Kolm is Professor of Economics at the Ecole des Hautes Etudes en Sciences Sociales, Paris.

Reciprocity

An economics of social relations

Serge-Christophe Kolm

CAMBRIDGE
UNIVERSITY PRESS

CAMBRIDGE UNIVERSITY PRESS
Cambridge, New York, Melbourne, Madrid, Cape Town, Singapore,
São Paulo, Delhi

Cambridge University Press
The Edinburgh Building, Cambridge CB2 8RU, UK

Published in the United States of America by Cambridge University Press,
New York

www.cambridge.org
Information on this title: www.cambridge.org/9780521882651

First published 2008

Printed in the United Kingdom at the University Press, Cambridge

A catalogue record for this publication is available from the British Library

Library of Congress Cataloging-in-Publication Data

Kolm, Serge-Christophe.
Reciprocity: an economics of social relations / Serge-Christophe Kolm. – 1st edn.
   p.   cm. – (Federico Caffè Lectures)
Includes bibliographical references and index.
ISBN 978-0-521-88265-1 (hardback)
1. Economics.   2. Altruism–Economic aspects.   I. Title.   II. Series.

HB71.K57   2007
302'.1 – dc22   2007033194

ISBN 978-0-521-88265-1 hardback

"Give and you will be given to."

Luke

"Of all the persons whom nature points out for our peculiar beneficence, there are none to whom it seems more properly directed
than to those whose beneficence we have ourselves already experienced. Nature, which formed men for that mutual kindness, so
necessary for their happiness, renders every man the peculiar
object of kindness, to the persons to whom he himself has been
kind."

Adam Smith, The Theory of Moral Sentiments (VI, 2, 1)

"Reciprocity is the vital principle of society."

Leonard T. Hobhouse

"The principle of reciprocity is the basis on which the entire
social and ethical life of civilization rests."

Richard Thurnwald

"Reciprocity is the human rock on which societies are built."

Marcel Mauss, The Gift

"Social equilibrium and cohesion could not exist without the
reciprocity of service and return service. All contacts among men
rest on the scheme of giving and returning the equivalence."

Georg Simmel

Contents

Illustrations

Foreword

When the University La Sapienza, in Rome, did me the honour of asking me to deliver the Federico Caffè lectures of 2003, I thought this could provide a welcome opportunity to gather my work of more than three decades on a human conduct which turns out to be pervasive, basic and often crucial in social and economic life, the solution of many of its problems and the cause of some of them: reciprocity. Whether they are conspicuous or taken for granted, various conducts of reciprocity are necessary for the existence of a peaceful society in which people and their rights are respected; they are the main correctors of market and organization failures and sometimes their cause; they constitute the very substance of the life and economy of families and various communities; they are essential in various aspects of the working of the public and political sector; and they inspire both most of the policies of "welfare regimes" and farther visions of human betterment. Reciprocity is the conduct that can provide fairness in freedom, sustainable altruism and mutual appreciation of all types and intensities.

My analyses of reciprocity and its causes and consequences have appeared over more than three decades in various languages, including the 1984 book in French *La Réciprocité Générale – La Bonne Economie* (and are now generally out of print).

Introduction: nature, scope, forms, motives, and effects of reciprocity

Reciprocity is treating other people as other people treat you, voluntarily and not as a result of a binding exchange agreement. It concerns acts, attitudes or sentiments, and the tradition of social science restricts the term to favourable items (to which revenge and retaliation are only very partially symmetrical, as we shall see). When reciprocity is not the whole of a social relation – as with returning a favour, or liking people who like you –, it is generally a part of it, often necessary for the rest. For instance, a free, peaceful and efficient society requires the mutual respect of persons and properties – the police and self-defence could not suffice and are costly – and people would or could not so respect others if they were not themselves respected. This permits, in particular, the working of markets and organizations, which also requires a minimum of trust, honesty, promise keeping, or fairness – and mutual help in organizations –, which can only be reciprocal. These latter reciprocities palliate difficulties in information and coercion (in particular, they provide the main correctors of market failures). Communities of all kinds imply reciprocities of mutual help among their members and, often, between each member and the community as such. In particular, a family is primarily an intense reciprocity of services and affection. The political and public sector includes various relations of reciprocity, and the regimes known as "welfare states" add a few important ones concerning aid, health, pensions, and education. Good social relations in general, which are essential for the amenity and value of a society, are sustained by reciprocity. Indeed, reciprocity, when it is not supported by oppressive norms, is a balanced and fair set of free helpful acts, and sometimes it also results from reinforcing liking sentiments of all types and intensities. It is no surprise, therefore, that most social reformers have advocated a greater role for reciprocity as the alternative to coercive hierarchy, selfish exchange, and the utopia of unconditional altruism.

Reciprocity may seem to be a simple and unitarian behaviour – the simplistic tit for tat. On the contrary, however, reciprocity has several different psychological motives and various social structures, and most of these motives consist in a dynamic combination of a number of more elementary sentiments. However, these motives, dynamics, sentiments and structures are clear and neat when analyzed sufficiently.

The acts that constitute a relation of reciprocity are in the nature of gifts, by definition: each is freely chosen by an actor at some cost for herself, and it benefits someone else. They can in fact be transfers, help, aid, respect, favouring, being fair towards someone, and so on. These acts are not parts of an exchange of acts mutually conditional by external obligation – we will restrict the term "exchange" to this standard case (such as market exchanges). Note that some sentiment of "moral" obligation to "give in return" refers to another kind of obligation (it is not the implementation of a previous agreement or contract).

There are two categories of motives of reciprocity, plus an ambiguous third case, and two, three or four corresponding types of reciprocity (depending on specification), all this resulting from the interactions of thirty – or so – basic psychological phenomena.

In *balance* or *matching reciprocity*, the "return gift" is given with the aim of restoring some property of balance of the initial situation disrupted by the initial gift, and, therefore, establishing some kind of balance with the initial gift. This equality is sometimes related to a sentiment of fairness. More precisely, this can be either rewarding justice providing a reward to the initial giver, or compensatory justice compensating the initial gift or the situation of both agents. The motive may be a sense of duty or of propriety, often obeying a moral or social norm, and failure to provide the return gift may arouse a sentiment of guilt or shame, or at least of impropriety. This failure may arouse a sentiment of moral indebtedness, which can induce dependency (if the initial giver can choose to demand something "in exchange") and a sentiment of inferiority with respect to the giver or in general. These views may be shared by other people, who may elicit a social pressure for giving in return or redeeming this moral debt. These moral or social obligations are sometimes oppressive, but they are not always, and they do not always exist. In contrast, balance or fairness accompanying benevolent gifts are favourable to good social relations. Nevertheless, it may also be that all this indebtedness induces is a sentiment or a duty of gratitude, and such a situation may last and constitute an important social bond.

In *liking reciprocity*, giving a return gift is motivated by a positive affective sentiment towards the initial giver. This sentiment may be aroused by an initial benevolent favour: it attaches to the person responsible for this favour. It may also result from a direct reciprocity of sentiments, by which one tends to like people who like oneself – and both sentiments can induce altruistic gift giving. This reciprocal liking results from the fact that one benefits more from being liked by someone when one likes her more. Indeed, one then cares more for her view, and her caring about oneself is more favourable to one's sense of self and of social existence, especially since her caring is with kindness and affection. As a consequence, a process which is both conscious and unconscious, and voluntary (in paying attention to the other person) and involuntary, creates and allocates the attention and affection that constitute this sentiment.[1]

The ambiguous case is "sequential exchange": an agent replies to a gift with a return gift in order to be given another gift, and so on. The motives can be purely self-interested. The transfers or services are then no longer gifts proper, but simply parts of an exchange which are *de facto* yielded under the threat that later parts are not provided. However, sequences of favours commonly mix motives of interest, balance (or fairness) and liking. The last two are bound to be induced by the fact that the agents get to know each other, and they can provide a motive for the last gift.

Two other phenomena may intervene in reciprocities. One is gratitude, which is favourable to liking, but also has an aspect of balance or matching both in itself and by the return favour it may induce. The other fact is imitation, given that the beneficiary is particularly aware of an act aimed at her and benefiting her, and the initial giver is readily available as a beneficiary for the induced giving – this induces the strong mirror-image imitation. Similarly, a "contagion" of sentiments can induce reciprocal liking.

Concerning social structure, reciprocity between two agents extends into reciprocities involving a larger number of agents. Through "generalized reciprocity," having benefited from someone's help makes one prone to help still other people. This is the famous "helping behaviour" abundantly studied by social psychologists since the 1960s in observations and experiments. This extends further into "general reciprocity" based on a reciprocal sentiment towards

---

[1] Another phenomenon is that of giving for showing and proving one's liking. If the aim is to please the other person because she likes to be liked, the effect is like that of an altruistic gift. However, if the aim is to be liked in return, this aim is no longer altruistic, the giving is not genuinely benevolent, and, hence, this endeavour is largely self-defeating. Nevertheless, since the giver wants more to be liked the more she herself likes, this giving still generally reveals the giver's liking sentiment.

others in general, or "society" at large. For instance, the overall reciprocity of respect noted earlier is of the general type (you often do not meet again people who respect you, and your defecting in not respecting others in a large society does not change it – hence the motive is not sequential exchange either). The opposite of generalized reciprocity is "reverse reciprocity," by which people who help others tend to be helped by still others (they deserve it) – discussed notably by René Descartes, Adam Smith and Jeremy Bentham. Generalized and reverse reciprocity extend into longer chain reciprocities, such as various intergenerational reciprocities found in families, in pay-as-you-go pension systems, or in the public financing of education. These extended reciprocities are explained by some of the motives of standard reciprocities; by acting towards groups or on behalf of groups; and sometimes by relations of liking between the people one helps and who help oneself.

Understanding reciprocity is indispensable for understanding all social forms, such as communities, organizations, families, and political systems. In the economy, it is indispensable for understanding a number of essential facts such as the basic social conditions of a market system; why so many "market failures" do not induce breakdown in fields such as the provision of public goods or various externalities; the working of firms; the labour market and wage rigidities; productivity induced by reciprocity in trustfulness and trustworthiness; relations between political support and public services; the ethics of the welfare state; the economics of the family; the economics of small groups and of traditional systems (reciprocity is the basic concept in economic anthropology); processes of development which often destroy reciprocitarian relations, but also succeed thanks to them in very important cases; and so on.

Understanding reciprocity implies understanding what characterizes this conduct: its motivations. This is why strict behaviourism is of very little help. A reciprocal behaviour can a priori have a variety of motives, and hence observing one provides little power to predict others in situations which cannot be strictly identical. The simple observation of acts can provide only very rough indications as to what is happening. It generally cannot show all the psychological possibilities and cases that lead to this behaviour. Only reflective psychological analysis can do this, with a notable role for empathy. Observation (including in laboratories) has a role for showing behaviour to be explained, not for providing the explanation itself. The advanced psychological analysis is often helped by formal models showing the relations between the various psychological elements and between them and action, and for analyzing the interactions between the participants.

The outcomes of these interactions are then explained by analytic "games of reciprocity." These games, however, are very particular in several respects. The players' motives and sentiments determine the type of the social relation. They may be similar (more or less symmetrical) or not, and of one kind or associating several kinds. This type of the social relation (and hence the motives and sentiments) a priori affects the players' preferences, in two ways: They are an object of the preferences, and they affect the preferences about the acts or transfers. The sentiments may then be modelled formally or not (as an example in which they are, the intensity of liking the other person can be modelled as an ordering or an ordinal variable). The direct interactions among these sentiments can also be represented. Issues of fairness can intervene in three ways: between the acts or transfers of different agents, about the resulting situation of the agents, and about the process and the choice of "solution" of the game.[2] The game can be

---

[2] For instance, the so-called Cournot-Nash solutions have in general no valid justification for one-shot (two moves) games. However, they are justified as one type of games of reciprocity, when the first player wants to be fair with respect to the order of the moves (chapter 22). The classical argument that Cournot-Nash solutions are "self-sustainable agreements" is not generally sufficient – and in addition would not apply to reciprocities since they are not agreements.

one-shot (two moves), or constitute a longer and more steady relationship. These games explain the acts or transfers, and, more or less, sentiments, attitudes, and the type of relation (for instance, a type of reciprocity or an exchange). In particular, this explains important paradoxes observed in processes of social change and development.

Reciprocity can support important and durable systems of giving and altruism, because it implies that a giver also receives, whereas pure giving is limited because it is detrimental to the giver. This has two types of important applications. One is the existence and sustainability of groups of people related by altruism and the corresponding aid, from family love to solidarities typical of various communities. The other is the existence of voluntary actions, more or less costly in some way to the giver, that freely transmit goods, services or information to other agents, or consist in freely abstaining from hurting them or obeying some indication or previous agreement, when these other agents could not otherwise have obtained these benefits, or could have obtained them only at a high cost. This includes transmitting private information of any kind. The costs saved can include various costs of forcing or constraining the agent. An impossibility of excluding a specific agent from a specific benefit and hence of selling it is a particular case (an externality, and the case of "non-excludable" public goods). These impossibilities or costs can prevent decisions of command or of exchange from having sufficient information. They can prevent commands from being obeyed and agreements from being implemented – thereby preventing commands and agreements themselves in the first place. These are "failures" of exchanges, agreements, or systems of command. The noted conducts, which are in the nature of gifts, sustainable in a framework of reciprocity, constitute the main correctors of such failures (other than replacing an exchange by a command, or the converse, with the resultant possibility of similar problems). This is manifested by various aids, respect, truth telling, promise keeping, trustworthiness and trustfulness, freely contributing to public concerns, etc., which are vital to the working efficiency, or possibility, of exchanges and organizations.

Finally, its possible very important effects on social and economic efficiency, and on the quality of social relations, make reciprocity a central concern of moral sociology and normative economics. Institutional design, organizational choices, education, and other influences on the ethos of the society, cannot bypass this central issue.

-:-:-:-

Note: This volume is only partially a translation of my book of 1984 on reciprocity (and of the previous papers that prepared it). These two works are complementary. Reference: *La Bonne Economie, La Réciprocité Générale*, Presses Universitaires de France, Paris, 1984; 472 pages.

Part I

Facts and forms

1

Presentation

1.1 Evidence, scope, and motives of reciprocity

In his *Essay on the Gift* (1924) – one of the most influential founding works of social science – Marcel Mauss calls reciprocity "one of the human rocks on which societies are built." Reciprocity is treating others as they treat you, because of this very fact and not as the result of some agreed upon or expected exchange (this will be explained in detail). This basic, polymorphic and pervasive pattern of human social conduct is present in all social interactions and relations between individuals or groups that are neither overt violence nor based on threat of it, as the main fact or as a reciprocity of respect or attention that permits the other aspects of the relation. Nevertheless, reciprocity is not a primitive social fact; it results from some of three more fundamental ingredients – a duty of social balance or equity, the interaction of liking, and a mutuality of interests – which themselves result from a number of still more basic psychological elements. Of course, besides the reciprocity of favourable acts and sentiments – to which the tradition of social science restricts the concept of reciprocity –, there also is the negative reciprocation of revenge and retaliation for deterrence, which is only partially symmetrical to and does not have the fundamental role of ("positive") reciprocity.

The existence, extent, importance and forms of reciprocity are in fact obvious. Indeed, you tend to give in return when you receive a gift or favour, and to hit back when harmed. You tend to like people who like you (and you need to be positively considered, especially by people you consider). You tend to respect persons and properties if other people respect your person and your property. You tend to like people who benevolently give something to you or help you, and also to be grateful towards them, and this tends to induce you to aid them or give them gifts in turn. You may also feel morally indebted towards people who give something to you, or help or favour you, and this may induce you to give something in return, sometimes for relieving a situation felt as a burden – a motive thoroughly different from the foregoing one. You generally resent being hurt, and this may lead you to hurt back in revenge (you also tend to dislike people who hurt you, but mere disliking usually does not induce hurting, in contrast to giving because of liking; and in a similar contrast, being disliked does not induce disliking as being liked tends to induce some liking). You tend to trust people who trust you (trustful people tend to be trustworthy – because trustworthy people tend to think that others are like them), and you often want to deserve this trust and hence tend to be trustworthy.

It is well documented that you tend to be helpful if you have been helped – even by people different from those you help (this classical "helping behaviour" is "generalized reciprocity"). Symmetrically, the plea that offenders were themselves victims of crime in their youth is one of the most common lines of defence in court cases. Both the philosopher René Descartes and Adam Smith discuss the opposite fact that people who tend to help others tend to be helped by still others (at least, they deserve it) – this is "reverse reciprocity." This may be implied by "give and you will be given to" (Luke). Similarly, people often tend to treat fair people fairly and rude people rudely.

You may also give in return in order to induce further gifts in your favour, but since a new gift induced in this way is made in expectation of another reward, this has a priori to be the start of a foreseen endless "sequential exchange." This relation can be strictly self-interested, and it is indeed a type of exchange rather than reciprocity proper as the foregoing cases, because you only "give" under the de facto threat of not being "given" to later (then, the terms "give" and "gifts" are not really proper). You may also hit back in retaliation in order to deter further harms; this is motivationally similar to the former case but formally the opposite since it stops the relation rather than extending it.

Reciprocity as *a set of motivationally interrelated gifts or favours* has been considered and studied by a long and rich tradition in social science. Hence, the term *reciprocation* came to be used to also include revenge and retaliation which are only very partially the "harmful" mirror image of reciprocity (liking in return, or giving in return because one came to like the benefactor, have no such negative mirror image, as we shall see).

Adam Smith, in *The Theory of Moral Sentiments*, discusses reciprocity (and reverse reciprocity, as Descartes did). He also uses the terms reciprocity and mutuality, but whether this refers to reciprocity as understood since or only as self-interested exchange is ambiguous and a classical debate (Danner, 1973). Uses of the concept and term of reciprocity as understood nowadays with mention or discussion of the particular relation, sentiments, or motivations are found in Morelly (1775, the sentiment being gratitude), Proudhon (1853, in *The Handbook of the Speculator in the Stock Exchange* and in line with his normative social theory), and Leonard Hobhouse (1906). The emphasis on reciprocity as an economic system is basically due to Richard Thurnwald, the anthropologist student of Carl Menger, in *Die Gemeinde der Banaro* (1921) and a number of later books. This has largely been followed in anthropology. The concept of reciprocity is also much used in sociology (see, for instance, the works of Georg Simmel, Howard Becker (1956), or Alvin Gouldner (1960)). Forms of reciprocitarian conduct are favourite topics of social psychology which analyses them with a wealth of experimental and empirical studies (this was notably the case, since at least the early 1960s, with labour as a reciprocity to pay and with the reverse reciprocity of "helping behaviour"). We will point out that the analysis, modelling and applications of reciprocity in economics developed in the 1970s and early 1980s. Finally, the term reciprocity is, of course, used here as it is by the tradition in social science, namely a set of motivationally interrelated favours, a priori different from self-interested exchange, but less scientifically careful uses of terms have used them in all directions (for instance calling reciprocity a particular exchange or exchange a particular reciprocity).

1.2 Social scope and values of reciprocity

Attentive observation of life in society shows how pervasive, important, and often essential reciprocity is in it.[1]

A family is neither a *pater familias* (*à la* Becker) nor an exchange (*à la* Chiappori), but a dense and intense network of various reciprocities in sentiments and conduct, in which commands and exchanges are in fact embedded in larger relations of reciprocity.[2]

Communities of all kinds imply reciprocities among their members, and often among members and the community as such. A community is – notably – a society of mutual support, and this support is motivated largely by sentiments of reciprocity. Members of a community are *ipso facto* "closer" to one another than people who are "foreign" to one another

---

[1] I cannot but warmly recommend the excellent and very informed recent survey of the scope of the economy of reciprocity "Between the gift and the market: the economy of regard," by Avner Offer (1997).

[2] See Kolm 1984a and 2000b.

are in this respect. This is favourable to "positive" sentiments towards one another and to comparison and a sense of fairness between them. As a general rule, reciprocity and a sense of community are closely related. However, communities are varied, they are more or less tight or loose, and restricted or extended. The two limiting cases are the family, and the community of mankind encompassing and linking all human beings. One can also see the place of reciprocal support in the intermediate national, cultural, religious, professional, residential, and other, communities.

All working groups use reciprocities of mutual services of aid and information, and of trust, and often could not function without them. The most efficient teams, firms, and societies are often those in which reciprocities are the most developed. Firms have various types of reciprocities among peers and across hierarchies. Reciprocities at the workplace are pervasive and necessary.[3]

The existence of any peaceful and free society – one that is not only a balance of threats – rests essentially on reciprocity. People generally respect others and their rights and properties, even when these other persons are weaker and the police are absent (one cannot put a policeman behind each of us). However, they would or could not do this if they were not themselves so respected in their person, rights, and properties. In particular, such a general reciprocal respect of rights and properties is necessary for the existence and possibility of a working market. General sociality – politeness, small acts of assistance, and so on – also results from the same reciprocitarian motives: people would generally not so behave towards others if they were not treated similarly themselves. This is also the case for more intense aid: people help others in need more when they are so aided themselves (this is the much studied "helping behaviour," a classical favourite topic of social psychology).

[3] See Julio Rotemberg (1994).

When, for some reason, the market "fails," the most common correctors and efficient substitutes rely on a variety of reciprocitarian motives such as matching (or balance) reciprocity or reciprocal promise keeping for paying one's due in the absence of enforceable contracts, reciprocal trust for remedying a lack of information and incomplete contracts and markets, or reciprocal joint free contributions to public goods (reciprocity transforms a prisoner's dilemma into a coordination game with a preferred coordinated solution, and such a contribution is also a gift to the other beneficiaries of the good, with a possible reciprocity in these gifts).[4] In all such cases, owing to the social interaction of reciprocity, failing to pursue self-interest is favourable to self-interest, and, in this sense, it is rational to be irrational.

Vast public transfers are accepted to a large extent in some societies both because they manifest reciprocities in case of need and because they constitute joint contributions for helping the needy – a kind of public good. The same societies often strongly support the "chain reciprocity" of "pay-as-you-go" pension systems whereby one generation supports the ageing people of the previous generation, given that it will itself be so supported later (and pensioners have themselves paid for the pensions of others). The public financing of education is another chain reciprocity with a reverse rationale: each generation finances the young given that its own education has been paid for by the previous generation (and the young will finance the education of the next generation). However, there is also a direct intergenerational reciprocity of pensions for education.

Moreover, reciprocity is commonly seen as one type of economic system – along with market exchange and command –, given that most actual economic regimes are compounds of the three in various proportions and according to various

---

[4] These issues are analysed in chapter 12.

arrangements. Smaller societies work essentially as systems of reciprocity.

Finally, with regard to the overall quality of a society, of the relations in it, and of its members themselves, reciprocity is the only alternative to oppressive command, selfish exchange, and the utopia of widespread unconditional altruism. Although social control, social pressure and stringent or oppressive norms can impose one type of reciprocity (balance or matching) in small groups, such obligations are found neither for many cases of this type, nor for other types of reciprocity, and generally not beyond such groups. Hence, reciprocity is necessarily central to genuine social improvement. Indeed, all social philosophers and reformers with some breadth of vision have seen this for millennia. For this reason also, an ideal of a larger role for good reciprocity has been and is the inspiration and the hope (the "directing utopia") of important social and cooperative movements. However, normative social science can analyse the possibilities of this idea and of its implementation.

Reciprocity thus appears as a basic force of interaction that maintains a collection of individuals as a society. It relates closely to other aspects of the social bond. A common culture creates a community which favours reciprocity among its members. Reciprocal respect permits the development of mutual interest. However, all these aspects are structures made up of more primitive facts, such as personal interest, empathy, affection and liking, the values of being liked and the dynamics of mutual liking, responsibility, information and communication, interpersonal comparison resulting in status and fairness, merit, a sense of retributive and compensatory justice, moral indebtedness, a sense of propriety and duty, guilt or shame, and imitation and emotional contagion. In any event, the central and necessary role of reciprocity explains why it has been one of the few core concepts in social science, albeit with different emphases in the various disciplines. It has been the central concept of anthropology for almost a century. Social psychology has extensively studied important instances of reciprocity, essentially by means of a variety of experiments. General sociology has considered reciprocity. Economics has analysed the relation of reciprocity and applied the results for a long time, although this has not entered (yet) into the most commonly used tools of the discipline. In this field, the analysis of reciprocity and the applications of the resulting concepts constitute a major contribution to the much needed general progress towards a more realistic psychology than that of the caricature known as "economic man."

1.3   Equality and fraternity: the two, three or four types of reciprocity

This short list of manifestations of reciprocity provides a glimpse of the extent, properties and varieties of this phenomenon. This variety exists but is limited by the fact that reciprocity rests on basic types of motivations which are quite different from one another but are very few in number. There are, in fact, two types of reciprocity proper, *balance reciprocity* (or *comparative* or *matching* reciprocity) and *liking reciprocity* which is itself of two different types, *liking the liker* or *reciprocal liking* (a reciprocity of sentiments) and *liking the benevolent giver*. In addition, *continuation reciprocity* leads to the relation of sequential exchange and has retaliation for deterrence as its negative counterpart, and both reactions can be purely self-interested. These pure reciprocitarian motives can more or less be jointly present.

In *comparative, matching*, or *balance reciprocity*, you (and possibly other people) feel that a gift or favour you receive from some agent has broken the balance of some previous state of affairs, and that you should give in return a "return gift" of similar value so as to restore the balance. So long as this return is not provided, you may feel (or be reputed to be) morally indebted towards the initial giver, and this may induce in you sentiments in the nature of guilt or shame of various possible intensities (this indebtedness also sometimes elicits views and sentiments of your dependency with respect to the initial giver who may be considered entitled to demand a return of some kind, or even of inferiority in comparison with her or as a general status). A sufficient return gift redeems this moral debt (although there sometimes remains some of it because the initial help or favour was the first one).

This motive for returning a gift, favour or help is a norm of conduct. It is "deontic" rather than "consequentialist", although having followed the norm, or not, and the resulting judgments, are also consequences of the act. This norm is usually both social and moral. As a social norm, it indicates a proper conduct (the right thing to do), and failure may elicit shame. As a moral norm, this conduct is more or less a duty, and failure may elicit guilt. The strength of these sentiments depends on the case. The norm thus "transcends" the individual at two levels: at the level of society as a merely social norm, whereas a moral norm is seen as also transcending society.

The most basic aspect seems to be the moral nature. Because of this nature, the view of this duty can be held by anybody in society – and not just the initial beneficiary –, or, one can say, "by society," and this gives it its (other) social aspect. This moral nature is related to the aspect of equality – in some approximate evaluation – between the two gifts or favours. The equality of something is also the basis of sentiments of fairness and justice. Hence, such sentiments are not necessarily present in balance reciprocity, but sometimes they are. The return favour can thus be seen as rewarding the merit of the initial giver in rewarding-retributive justice, or as compensating all the (material) effects of the initial gift in compensatory justice.

In contrast, in *liking reciprocity* the motive for your giving to the initial giver is that you like her – with any type and intensity of liking, from caring about someone to love. However, you may like this person either because she gives something to you or because she likes you. These are two different cases called gift-induced liking and reciprocal liking, respectively. They can be quite intermingled, however. Indeed, first, the strongest case for liking someone as a result of receiving a gift from her occurs when a final aim of this conduct is to benefit you, which can notably result from her liking you. Second, a value of both being liked and receiving a gift rests in the attention towards yourself they manifest, which is favourable to your sense of self and of social existence, especially when it is appreciative and kind. Moreover, in reciprocal liking, giving can be a means to show and prove one's liking in order to be liked in return; benefiting the receiver is not the final aim of this gift which, as a result, does not induce much liking in return by itself; nevertheless, the simple desire to be liked tends to show and prove the liking, since one wants more to be liked by someone the more one likes her. These relations involve various types of liking, issues of responsibility, and questions about the formation of sentiments. They will be analysed in chapter 7, but can be summarized here.

In *gift-induced liking*, you like the giver as benefactor (and not only as you like a thing or a person for another reason) because she has given you something benevolently, i.e., with the final aim of benefiting you. Then, you may like to receive this gift or favour for several reasons. One is simply the gift or favour you receive. Moreover, you are bound to like the attention shown by the giving, especially since it is appreciative of you and kind: this fosters your sense of self and of social existence, a most essential sentiment. You may also like the kind interaction in the process of giving. Your liking these facts makes you like the giver who is responsible for them. Then, you are bound to give something to her because you like her.

In contrast, in *reciprocal liking* you tend to like people who like you (a priori irrespective of any giving), this may be reciprocal, and each liking can induce giving. This reciprocity is one of sentiments (liking). The process by which you tend to like people who like you is rather subtle. You generally like to be liked, especially by people you care about and hence, in particular, by people you like, because it is agreeable and, more deeply, because their implied attention towards you fosters your essential sense of self and of social existence, especially since it is appreciative of you and kind. This tends to make you like people who like you by two categories of effects.

First, you like the person who likes you because you like to be liked and you like the causes of what you like. This causal liking, in itself, is what makes you like the apple tree because of the apples and your coat because of its warmth. In addition, however, this cause is a person. Futhermore, causally liking a person for a fact makes a particularly large difference if this person both is responsible for the fact and intends to favour you in choosing it. Moreover, these conditions make it possible that you are grateful towards this other person for liking you, and your gratitude is favourable to your liking this person. Now, the responsibility of the other person for her sentiment of liking you is ambiguous because it depends on her possibility to avoid this sentiment or to get rid of it. The classical ways of wilfully influencing one's sentiments by focusing or diverting attention and by reasoning exist but have limits; in fact, the issue of responsibility in this respect is even conceptually thorny (for instance, *akrasia* or weakness of the will is a common obstacle to changing one's sentiments, and the extent of your responsibility for it is a special conceptual choice – akin to the issue of laziness, for instance).[5]

---

[5] The general question of responsibility for one's tastes, preferences, or sentiments, is analysed in Kolm 2004, chapter 6.

Moreover, insofar as the other person is responsible for liking you, hence can wilfully influence this sentiment of hers, she hardly does this because you like it since this presupposes her sentiment of liking you (she is bound to do it more because you like her through the various effects considered here in inverting the roles). Hence, your *directly* liking the other person because she likes you exists but is limited.

However, a second series of effects intervene in the same sense. As suggested above, your sense of self and of social existence induced by someone liking you is greater the more you care about this person's view, hence in particular the more you care about this person in general, and notably the more you like her. Moreover, a number of the pleasurable effects of being liked are the stronger the more you like the person who likes you. As a result, by a process which has both unconscious and conscious elements, and involuntary and wilful aspects, implying creation and transfers of attention and emotion, this tends to make you adjust your sentiments towards liking people who like you and – *ceteris paribus* – liking more people who like you more.

In addition, gifts are given not only directly because of liking, but also in order to show and prove liking. They do this because the giver wants all the more to make the other believe that she likes her more, in order to please her (who likes to be liked) and most importantly in order to be liked in return by her, as she actually likes the other in the first place.

There are, thus, three worlds of reciprocity, *comparison* (*balance, matching*), *liking*, and *continuation* (notably for *self-interest*). They can be jointly present with some restrictions; notably, strong liking precludes comparison and self-interest, but milder liking does not – compare the two dictums of folk wisdom: "good reckonings make good friends" (*les bons comptes font les bons amis*) and *l'amour ne compte pas* (love does not reckon – money, effort, time, etc. – see "love counts for all"). These three worlds also associate by pairs, each in opposition to the other world. The duty of balance is opposed to the hedonistic or interested consequences of pleasing oneself or people one likes. The altruism of liking is opposed to favouring the interest or the social position (balance) of the ego. And self-interest is opposed to the social concerns of altruistic likings and of balance.

In the end, the three reciprocities respectively relate to the three basic social relations: fairness, altruism, and joint interest.

1.4 Reciprocity and reciprocating good or bad

We have seen that behind the apparent symmetry between reciprocating favourable and unfavourable acts deep dissymmetries, in fact, lie. The similitudes and differences depend primarily on the type of reciprocity, and the most striking is the quasi-absence of negative sentiments, acts and relations that would be symmetrical to liking reciprocities, for two reasons: your disliking someone neither induces you to hurt her nor induces her to dislike you.

Disliking someone does not induce you to hurt her, at least as liking tends to induce you to give or to favour. It may have such an effect in the extreme case of hating, and even in this case the reason generally refers to a cause of the hatred felt and to the harm done that induces it, and the hurting has a dimension of balance such as revenge – which is a different rationale. Hence, you generally dislike someone responsible for some harm you incur, but this disliking *in itself* is generally not a cause for hurting in return. The balance motive of answering harm with harm is something else, although it is then intrinsically accompanied by disliking (this motive is not retaliation for deterrence, which is yet another reason).

Moreover, if someone dislikes you, or even hates you, this generally does not induce you to dislike (or hate) her. It may only induce you to wonder why she has this sentiment, if this is not clear, or to ignore this person or try to in order to get rid of the generally mildly disagreeable sentiment of being disliked. Neither does this induce her to hurt you, as with giving in the opposite case of liking.

Finally, the negative parallel to giving because of liking fails in all respects. It would first be, if you dislike someone, to hurt her because she dislikes it. But your disliking her does not a priori induce you to like her pain. You would not hurt in order to be disliked either, since you do not particularly enjoy this, even from someone you dislike. And hurting merely to show disliking – rather than disapproval – cannot be supported by possible effects of this information for the other person (in general, you do not care whether she knows of your dislike and about her possible resulting feelings – if any; this information would not induce her to dislike you; and, at any rate, you generally would not enjoy this, even from someone you dislike).

As far as sentiments are concerned, resentment towards people responsible for harm you incur has some symmetrical analogy with gratitude, but giving for showing and proving one's gratefulness has no symmetrical counterpart in hurting for showing resentment.

The symmetry is closer with balance reciprocity. The analogue to giving in return is revenge, with vengefulness being the analogue to the sentiment of moral indebtedness. The requirement of balance, of evening things out, and the sentiments of duty, deserts or merit, and justice, are present in both cases.

We have seen that retaliation for deterrence is in the family of continuation reciprocity and can have similar motives. However, successful continuation reciprocity expands the relation, a priori indefinitely, whereas successful retaliation for deterrence stops it (although peace can be seen as sequential gifts consisting of abstention from harming).

Our focus here will be on acts, sentiments or attitudes favourable to others, rather than on unfavourable ones, because of the importance of the topic, due to several reasons. Liking reciprocities have de facto no negative counterparts, as we have seen. Deterrence is certainly a very important topic, but retaliation for deterrence is more particular (and, indeed, it has, as we will see about punishment, a problematic logic). Moreover, deterrence is a priori a purely interested motive, symmetrical to exchange, and this is not reciprocity in its most proper and characteristic understanding. Then, only revenge remains, and, although it certainly is an important motive of human conduct, its overall importance comes nowhere near to matching that of reciprocity (of favourable acts, attitudes and sentiments). This reciprocity, indeed, plays a fundamental role in the constitution, cohesiveness and existence of societies. It can by itself be the main or sole relationship underlying some social or economic systems. It has a major importance in the working of the economy and of political systems. It has an essential normative role in various ways. It often has an intrinsic normative value related to fairness or rewarding merit for balance reciprocity, and to altruism and liking in various forms for liking reciprocity. Reciprocity is also very commonly a necessary condition of altruism, respect, helping behaviour, affection, kindness, truth telling, promise keeping, trustworthiness, and cooperation. Finally, the common use of the term reciprocity, notably as one of the central classical concepts of social science, is restricted to these favourable, pro-other, actions, attitudes and relations. We shall therefore follow this long-standing tradition here, and use the term *reciprocation* for covering both types of relations, favourable and hostile. Hence, reciprocation encompasses reciprocity plus revenge and retaliation for deterrence.

1.5 Understanding and explaining reciprocities

The outline of the social scope of reciprocity presented above shows its overwhelming overall importance. This will be abundantly confirmed by the analyses proposed in following chapters. Understanding and explaining reciprocity is therefore very important for understanding society, notably its economy, and hence for forecasting aspects of them and certainly for improving them by social design, regulation, institutional reform, and education in all its forms.

By definition, reciprocity consists of gifts or favours motivated by gifts or favours from other people, or by sentiments induced by sentiments of other people. Hence, understanding and explaining reciprocity requires understanding and explaining motives and sentiments. The motive is necessary for the very fact that a transfer or service is a gift. Observation of acts only – behaviour – may conclude that some act is not motivated by pure self-interest alone, but this constitutes only very limited information about the actual motive, this method prevents distinguishing among the various non-self-interested motives, and its conclusions are actually mistaken in a number of cases. This precludes explanation, understanding, most of forecasting, and improvement.

The very meaning of a term describing a sentiment or feeling can be understood only by reference to the own experience of the person who understands it. Communication using this term can only rely on the interpersonal analogy of these personal experiences and on our belief about this analogy. Relations between sentiments, feelings, reasons and cognitions, and between them and actions they induce, as well as their causes, are inferred from observation within ourselves, and from our observation of other people's actions, and hearing their explanations, which we think we understand – notably by comparison with ourselves.

In particular, we have seen that reciprocity comes in various types, and that reciprocities are dynamic structures made of a number of more elementary elements including the following: senses of balance, fairness, merit, propriety, duty, due, moral indebtedness, guilt, shame; liking or respect of various types and intensities, a sense of self and social existence, responsibility, pleasure, information, attention; gratitude; imitation, conforming, emotional

contagion; interest; expectation; and, for negative reciprocation, disliking, hating, resentment, vengefulness. The
meanings of all these terms and concepts refer to our personal
experience comforted by consistent and repeated observation of other people and hearing from them, in conducts and
explanations we think we understand largely by analogy with
our actual or imagined experience.

This understanding in the philosophical sense compensates for the limitations in the external observability of these
mental phenomena. Fortunately, we need not study human
psychology from the outside only, as chemistry (in laboratory experiments), or as animal behaviour. The permanent
contact with ourselves and with other people (whom we
think we largely understand), during the decades of our
life, has given us most of the information we need for this
reflective analysis. This field of information is much more
than simple "introspection", given this permanent observation and understanding of other people, the interactive relations, mutual understanding and shared meanings with them,
and the vast human capacity for empathy and compassion.
We understand the meaning of the noted psychological elements for ourselves and, we think, more or less as they are
experienced by other people, although we generally know
that thinking more about them can reveal more. We have
some knowledge of the relations between these elements, and
between them and their other causes and effects – notably
actions –, including the notion that we can know more by
thinking, remembering, and observing more.

To understand and explain any sentiment and conduct, and
in particular reciprocities, any relevant piece of information
should be used to know when the relevant sentiments occur,
under which conditions, why they appear – as much as one
can find out –, and what they lead one to do. The analysis then
applies to this information the relevant distinctions, discern-
ments, comparisons, and classifications, with thought experiments imagining oneself (or others) in the relevant situations,

and propositions of theoretical explanations. When the properties in question and the relations of the explanation reach some degree of refinement, a formal model representing them helps gathering the relevant items and analysing their interactions. A major concern, at this point, is that the model should keep the generality of the described facts. Short of this, the model is unwarrantedly specific and of correspondingly limited usefulness (except as a tool for providing counter-examples). The worst mistake, in fact, consists in describing a concept by a variable having properties that the notion in question cannot have by nature, and in using these properties in the model. A standard example would be to describe a notion for which relations of more and less are meaningful by a quantity – for which this is also true –, and to use other properties of quantities, such as addition, multiplication, ratios, level zero, etc., whereas these other properties are meaningless for the notion in question. For instance, concepts of satisfaction, kindness, liking, fairness, etc. happen to have been unfortunately mistreated in this way. The noted property says only that they might be represented by an ordering or an ordinal variable. Such mistakes simply make the model meaningless. Individuals' choice of actions – here giving or helping – are often fruitfully considered as resulting from some ordering or ordinal utility function of the alternatives, as the choice of a preferred element that they define. The analysis of the structure and of the relevant variables and parameters of this ordering or function raises relevant questions about the interactions between the relevant facts. These putatively maximizing individual conducts then permit the analysis of individuals' strategic interactions in the mode of game theory. However, concepts and structures usually absent from game theory will have a foremost importance in such "games of reciprocity," such as preferences about acts or transfers and not only about the resulting states; preferences about intentions, sentiments, attitudes and the type of social relation; effects of these items on preferences about the outcomes; or various aspects of notions of fairness in acts (e.g. transfers), outcomes, or other aspects of the process (e.g. concerning the order of moves). One can thus explain reciprocities and their effects, and evaluate their consequences (for instance concerning satisfaction, efficiencies, and equities). The obtained results can then be used for explaining and evaluating a number of social facts, in the fields of organizations, economic intercourse, the firm, labour relations, the family, political life and systems, social and economic change, and so on.

There is a long history of systematic observations of reciprocitarian behaviour, including statistical and experimental studies, which will be discussed in following chapters. There has been an upsurge in such studies since the early 1960s, as branches of social psychology. They often considered specific issues, such as labour performed as a reciprocity for pay (e.g. the famous experiments and the theory of "equity" or "fair pay" of Adams and others in the early 1960s), or "helping behaviour" by which people who have been helped tend to help even people different from those who helped them (a "generalized reciprocity"). These studies have taken various forms: enquiries, monographs, experiments *in situ* (e.g. inducing people's help), and laboratory experiments. A few other laboratory experiments concerning reciprocity have been carried out since the mid-1990s. These experiments took various forms, but they often only demanded people to react in very simple situations. This was indeed sufficient for the sole conclusion of some of the first of these experiments, namely that people do not always react as the strictly self-interested *homo oeconomicus*. This was sound and successful Popperian methodology for falsifying this behavioural hypothesis, but this brought in no information that was not already obvious (and this model may be adequate in the appropriate circumstances). Informative results came, however, when these studies showed proportions of the various types of reaction. This is a kind of anthropological information about the population that provides the sample of subjects submitted to the experiment. Other issues studied will be discussed later (chapters 2, 12 and 23). Much remains to be done, however, to distinguish the various sentiments that lead to different actions and reactions; in particular to distinguish reciprocity from other conducts and to distinguish the various types of reciprocity whose different motives lead to different behaviour; to take account that reciprocities among the most important ones occur among people who have particular and often steady relationships (families, workplace, communities of various types, etc.); and to represent the situation with models the variables and structure of which have the properties of the actual facts (for instance, again, the only fact that there can be more or less of something does not permit one to represent it by a quantity but only by orderings or ordinal functions, and operations of addition, multiplication, ratios, etc. are meaningless and introduce properties that do not exist in reality) – the proper modelling, with the generality and actual properties of actual facts, is generally as simple or simpler, and it permits drawing conclusions about actual facts. Our particular information about human thinking, emotions, and the resulting choices, in ourself and in others whom we understand, makes this topic thoroughly different from physics and chemistry. As we shall see, only the corresponding reflective analysis can show us the relevant facts, distinctions and effects, determine what further information we may need, and set up efficiently the ways of obtaining it.

Explaining is a priori an endless process since any proposition can be followed by the question "why?" The question of the relevant point where to stop is therefore posed. One possible answer is not to ask useless questions (this is the Buddhist epistemology), hence only to look for information which can be helpful for action – yet, future needs for action may not be known, and the issue of merely satisfying the mind may have to be considered to some extent.

Understanding in all its dimensions – and not only explaining – can also progress. Most types of knowledge about man and society can be used to further understand or explain reciprocity. This is in particular the case with the various types of psychology and psychological philosophy. A phenomenology of reciprocities would doubtlessly help us to understand them better. Psychoanalysis can certainly tell us much about the elements of reciprocities – liking, liking to be liked, liking in return, a sense of self and social existence, norms of fairness, unconscious processes, and so on. Various branches of sociology already consider reciprocity, but one can introduce its relation with the sense of community or its place in the constituents of the social bond. It may be interesting if neurophysiology told us how the zones of the brain stimulated by reciprocities relate to other stimuli and zones: for instance, are the various reciprocal conducts only related to the respective materials of the reciprocation – liking, harm, fairness, etc. –, or is there some common zone relative to the fact of reciprocating (whatever its specific object)?

The major contributions of reciprocity to the stability, cohesion and efficiency of society, which will be analysed at length, suggest that evolutionary processes can play a role in explaining existing reciprocal motives and conducts (see chapter 16). The process and the selection can be genetic or cultural and organizational. Genetic selection in humans can only suggest processes that might play a role in explaining very broad behavioural tendencies. It should, to begin with, consider that first, there are several very different kinds of reciprocity, and second, reciprocity is not a primary element of conduct but consists of structures of various more primitive elements noted earlier (thirty or so types of them, without considering all the variants which have no limit). Each of these elements intervenes in other types of conducts. Explanation should first of all explain these elements, and after, only, account for their structural organization. Cultural selection rests on transmission by norms, habit, education, imitation and conforming, and social pressures of various types. However, it also includes intentional – possibly rational – changes of modes of behaviour (this makes it very different from genetic selection). In the corresponding group selection, the most important competition is not between full societies but rather, in complex societies, between organizational forms in economic or political life (chapter 16 explains this process).

1.6   Outline of the content of this volume

The foregoing sketchy presentation of the issues raised by the social relationship of reciprocity explains the necessary content and structure of this volume. The economic theory of reciprocity, presented in the last part (part IV) is preceded by three parts. The crucial issue concerns the analysis of the various motives of reciprocity, presented in part II. The effects of the relations and motives of reciprocity on the main social processes – markets, organizations, politics, social policies, the family – are analysed in part III. This permits understanding the place occupied by reciprocity in the overall social interaction. In part II, the analysis of motives leads to the comparison with social relations based on different motives and with the basic social sentiments. The evidence is presented in part I which shows both the importance of reciprocity in the various social processes, and the structures of reciprocities and of their extended forms. Part I also presents a basis in the analysis of the types of giving and motives for it. After a much-needed warning about methodology, the economic theory of reciprocity (part IV) focuses on balance and liking reciprocities, on the various solutions of games of reciprocity, and on the comparison of these solutions between themselves and with other social processes with regard to the outcome and to the judgments of participants.

2

Evidence and scope

2.1 Scope and role

All social relations and interactions probably have a dimension of reciprocity. You are more favourable to other people when other people are more favourable to you. You are less hostile to them when they are less hostile towards you. This is the consequence of a sense of balance and equity (or a desire of revenge), of liking of all kinds and intensities, and sometimes of interest in pursuing the relation. Some relations are only reciprocity (such as actually providing a return gift). Reciprocity can also be an essential part of the relationship, as within families with emphasis on affection. It is more or less important in other cases, as with relationships within communities of all types and more or less tight or loose – nation, local community, kinship, culture, workplace, organization, class or caste and the general community of mankind. Moreover, all peaceful and free relationships are based on a basic reciprocity of respect of others and their property, if the expression "peaceful and free" excludes the protracted war of an exclusive balance of threats (a generally unstable state that tends to erupt in overt violence or to lead to the political agreement shortly discussed). This provides general sociability and permits, in particular, standard (market) exchange and cooperation, and the working of organizations of all types.

Let us make this later point precise. Thomas Hobbes told us that human societies are trapped in a dreadful dilemma. Either human life is a war of all against all, or we should submit to a dictator imposing his law and order. However, most societies are neither general aggression nor a police state. People use locks and there is some police, but there is not only that. Hobbes overlooked one possible form of conduct: voluntary restraint from harming others and wilful respect for their person and property. Yet, people would not – or could not – so respect others if they were not so respected themselves (and respectful people deserve respect). Hence, free respect rests on this extended reciprocity. This basic reciprocity is indispensable in a peaceful and free large society. Private and public force, constraint, and threat cannot rule everything, since people have very different forces and can gang up, and there cannot be a policeman behind each of us. They use resources, and they would often require information they cannot have. Freedom, the quality of social relations, and the efficiency of society are greater, the greater the share of this free mutual respect of reciprocal restraint. This respect of property permits standard exchange and markets since self-interest leads one to take, not to exchange. This restraint includes some restraint from lying and cheating, and hence some a priori tendency to truth telling and honesty. This basic generalized reciprocity underlies general sociability and helpfulness. It permits cooperation, work in common in all organizations, and collective action.

Living in society, you ceaselessly see, experience and perform reciprocities of various kinds of nature and importance. About some scholars who concluded that reciprocity exists from laboratory experiments, the philosopher Michel Foucault said: "there are maniacs of indiscretion who, when they have to look through a glass door, peep through the keyhole." As it happens, reciprocity has also been a central topic of social science for many decades.

2.2   Direct reciprocity

You like people who like you – most of the time. And you like to be liked by people you like – short of masochism. Being so considered and valued is essential to your sense of self and of social existence, the ontological need which is the most basic of basic needs.

"I will love him who loves me," an old song says.

You act favourably towards people you like and you like people who act favourably towards you when this effect is their final objective.

You are grateful towards people who help you. This makes you prone to help them in turn, and to like them.

You also often feel morally indebted towards people who do you a favour of any kind. You know that they and possibly others often feel that you are so indebted. You often feel like "paying your debt" to them. You also sometimes think you ought to. This commonly leads you to return a favour re-establishing the moral balance (moral indebtedness sometimes also morally entitles the benefactor to ask a favour in return).

However, you also like being aided or given to for straightforward reasons: for the result; because this manifests concern and interest about you and in particular benevolent ones – which is good for your ego; and because it establishes agreeable actual and symbolic social relations. Then, you tend to like the benevolent people thus responsible for your pleasure, your social existence or your dignity. Moreover, you want to favour people you like. You like their situation being improved, their pleasure, their satisfaction, often their gratitude, their liking you more, and the relationship between you. All this induces you to give or help in return.

Inuit wisdom, which is expressed in proverbs, has two about giving, one for each base of these two motives for reciprocity. One dictum, the nice "friends make gifts and gifts make friends," only points out the noted positive feedback of altruistic sentiments and action in reciprocity from liking. However, a harsh, cold life does not grind out naïve people, as shown by their second giving proverb: "the gift makes the slave as the whip makes the dog."

You don't like being exploited, but you often prefer a fair deal to a good deal. And you tend to be fair towards people who are fair to you, thus transforming conflictual sharing into consensual fairness.

Doubtless you forgive offences, love your enemy, present the other cheek, and return good for evil. But you know people who don't. You did not invent "an eye for an eye and a tooth for a tooth."

Many people can hardly avoid instinctively hitting back when they are hit. Balance, status, and deterrence are compressed into a spark of nervous influx. They are not so much unconscious as instinctual, although they are provided as explanation when asked. Even dogs bite back. Deterrence and status may have selected their genes for that (status gives a reproductive advantage, and there may also be selection of the trait of liking mates prone to self-defence who will defend their nearest and transmit this character to the common offsprings, etc.). On the other hand, it took Alexandre Dumas's Count of Monte-Cristo a whole life of refined strategies to obey this primitive instinct, to take revenge and to do justice. In another kind of sophistication, Axelrod (1981, 1984) shows experimentally that tit-for-tat strategies (plus an initial favourable act) entail efficient cooperation; this can probably be explained by strategic rationality with its informational limits, but the selection of behaviour of revenge and giving in return can also be imagined.

The return of favours or aid may be aimed simply at inducing more of them. The return of harm may be retaliation for deterrence. However these narrowly interested strategies are not the only motives for reciprocating. They are not the gut *social* feeling of man in society. The other motives are those properly called reciprocity and revenge.

2.3 Extended reciprocities

Moreover, you tend to be more polite towards polite people, more helpful towards helpful people, more carefully fair towards fair people – even if you are not the beneficiary of their virtue. This may be natural since they deserve it. This "reverse reciprocity" has been discussed for long. For example, both the philosopher René Descartes and Adam Smith thought that people who give are given to, even by people who did not benefit from their acts – they even believed that these people will benefit more than the cost of their gift in the end.[1]

You are also more likely to be kind if you have been raised by loving parents. The opposite relation is the basis of the psychology of crime and the argument that is heard most in courtrooms.

More generally, you tend to be more helpful if you have been aided (even if not by the people you aid). At least, this is the overwhelming conclusion of scores of experiments, systematic observations and inquiries by American social psychologists in the 1960s and 1970s. They focused on this relation which they called "helping behaviour" after the ordeal of the young Kitty Genovese who, in 1964 in Queens, was stabbed to death and raped in sight of 32 onlookers none of whom tried to intervene or even called for help. This launched a nation-wide self-deprecating and soul-searching collective analysis, and these studies were the social psychologists' contribution (there also was a "public good" aspect: several onlookers thought others would call for help).[2]

---

[1] R. Descartes, *Works*, IV, and A. Smith, *The Theory of Moral Sentiments*, VI, 2,1.

[2] See, in particular, the contributions to Macaulay and Berkowitz, eds. (1970), Berkowitz (1966, 1968, 1970, 1971), Berkowitz and Friedman

Hence, you tend to help others if you have been helped yourself, to be nice if others have been nice to you, and so on, even if the people you help or favour are not those who favoured or helped you in the first place. And this is probably not only by sheer imitation of a behaviour that you have closely watched. This "generalized reciprocity" extends into "general reciprocity" when you see this relation as one between yourself and society, the group of others, or the "generalized other" as George Herbert Mead (1934) puts it: you tend to treat them well because they (globally) have been nice or kind to you, no matter how instinctual or thoughtful, conscious or unconscious, this relation is.

Indeed, people in this situation commonly feel grateful or morally indebted towards society, the group of others, or the "generalized other." This gratitude accounts for their favourable attitude towards these entities, and both gratitude and indebtedness can account for their benevolent conduct.

Any dense society is a closely knit network of reciprocities. So is the family, an integrated complex of intense reciprocities of sentiments, givings and services (economists have often modelled "the household" as a single agent; but would you like to be married to those whose progress in analysis consists in seeing the family as an exchange contract between purely self-interested agents?).[3] So also is the workplace, and it would not work without the multifarious reciprocities

---

(1967), Bryan and Test (1967), Doland and Adelberg (1967), Frisch and Greenberg (1968), Gergen, Gergen and Meter (1972), Goodstadt (1971), Goranson and Berkowitz (1966), Greenglass (1969), Handlon and Gross (1959), Harris (1967), Hornstein (1970), Hornstein, Fisch and Holmes (1968), Latané and Darley (1970), Leventhal, Weiss and Long (1969), Midlarsky (1968), Pruitt (1968), Rosenhan (1969), Wilke and Lanzetta (1970), Wright (1942), and the more recent works of Hoffman and Spitzer (1982), and Kahneman, Knetsch and Thaler (1986a, 1986b). This includes many psychological experiments. In addition, studies have investigated the family background and life experience of people prone to help in actual situations (for instance on the roadside, or civil right activists).
[3] See Kolm 2000a.

of services, trust, respect, goodwill, and information active within it.[4] So is any organization, firms in particular, with reciprocities both at the same hierarchical level and across hierarchies.

2.4 Reciprocity and exchange and markets

Adam Smith was convinced by Parisian economists, if not to abandon the "moral sentiments" of his first major study (which included reciprocity), at least to propose that if you need meat, you should not expect it from your butcher's altruism but from his self-interest in an exchange. However, your best self-interest is not for you to buy his meat but just to take it away without paying, if you are stronger than your butcher (you can gang up for this with the next customer). Among the reasons you have not to behave in this way, your spontaneous tendency to respect the butcher's property is an important one. However, people would tend less to respect others and their property if they were not so respected themselves. You may even have to steal to survive if you are continually robbed. Hence, the general reciprocal respect of property is a necessary condition for a working market. As, more generally, general reciprocal abstention from harming in any way is a condition for a peaceful and free society, a most essential good. The war of all against all interspersed with fragile and unreliable truces based on diffidence and suspicion, or a police state, are the two ugly and costly alternatives to the overall reciprocity of respect of others' lives, quietness and property. Moreover, if your butcher gave you the meat you need, as a gift, you would probably want to give him something in return, and each of you will have what she needs, plus the valuable bonus of a friendly and warm social relationship.

---

[4] See Rotemberg (1994).

The market thus has essential and ambivalent relations with reciprocity. As a set of purely self-interested agreements, it opposes the usual reciprocitarian sentiments based on liking or a sense of duty. By the same token, giving destroys the logic of markets, and possibly its reasons for implementing economic efficiency (however, people then also care about the nature of the relationship, and a single gift giving is a priori Pareto efficient since it maximizes the giver's utility). However, pure self-interest leads one to take, not to exchange. Self-defence and the police deter that, but self-defence cannot stop organised predators, and the police would hardly suffice if there was not one policeman behind each (other) individual. Hence, some voluntary respect of others and their property is undoubtedly necessary. And a person would not or could not respect others if she is not similarly respected. Therefore, reciprocity of giving is an alternative to the market in the proper conditions, but reciprocity of respect is a precondition for a general working market. Moreover, purely self-interested exchanges are also impeded by a number of impossibilities and costs – the classical causes of "market failures" –, which are overcome by reciprocities of various types: reciprocity of transfers, trust, or promise keeping replaces missing contracts or impossible complete contracts; reciprocity of voluntary contribution permits the free production of public goods; in exchanges of items provided alternately, reciprocity motivated by duty or benevolence elicits the provision of the last transfer and hence also the previous ones; and so on.[5] Furthermore, bargaining that is uncertain and costly is often ended and solved by reciprocal concessions seen as fair and which save time, cost of information and of threats, and the risk of seeing threats carried out. Hence reciprocity, sometimes an alternative to exchange and markets,

---

[5] Reciprocitarian corrections of "market failures" are analyzed in chapter 12.

or an impediment to them, also permits or improves them both in general and on specific important and widespread occasions.

2.5   Reciprocity and organizations and labour

Reciprocity is no less widespread, important and necessary within organizations of all types, including firms, administrations, offices, political parties, and associations of all kinds (even that paragon of hierarchical command, the army, needs to stress spontaneous mutual support among its fighters). In all organizations, mutual goodwill, help, support, or information are common and widespread. Some amount of them is indispensable to the working of the organization. They are often a major factor of its efficiency and productivity. And they also often provide some of the most important amenities of life in such a structure. These reciprocal services occur among employees or members of the same category, or of different categories, and in particular across hierarchical levels. They concern not only the work, the objectives of the organization, but also the individuals' position and benefits in it. Moreover, reciprocities are also often common and important between members and the organisation itself. Employees receive various non-contractual favours such as bonuses, promotions, or special personal services, and they provide effort, goodwill and loyalty. This is quite general but more or less important according to the specific organization and type of it (it is, for instance, particularly important in the classical model of the "oriental firm").

Indeed, the influence of norms, fairness and gratitude in exchange is particularly frequent in the provision of personal services and its reward, notably as a result of the fact that these "goods" are directly attached to persons. Tipping, a return gift for the quality of service, shows at least how widespread this view is. However, the tip is usually only a fraction of the pay. The reverse case, when labour reacts to pay, is much more important. You often want to – or think you should – provide labour matching the wage you receive, which you want to deserve (or to feel you deserve). This reaction and sense of balance have been studied in many experiments – the famous ones of Adams (1963, 1965) and Adams and Rosenbaum (1964) raised intense discussions – and empirical studies (this has become a rich and important branch of the fields of labour relations and labour economics, which is reviewed, discussed, and used in Kolm 1990).[6] The employer may have similar motives or this may not be the case, and the outcome can be any of the solutions of reciprocity games presented in chapter 22.[7] When the employer is strictly self-interested (which may be imposed by competition or by shareholders), she exploits in this way the return-gift behaviour of the employee. The "efficiency wages" described by George Akerlof (1982) are determined in this manner and they can explain deviations from the competitive equilibrium that resemble involuntary unemployment. However, the issue is in fact qualified not only by the possible prevalence of other solutions of the reciprocity game, but also by the fact that individuals' preferences are affected by the type of relation (see chapter 13).

2.6 Established groups, cooperatives, associations

In fact, both some sets of transfers and services, and some organizations, not only include a part of reciprocity, but are essentially kinds of reciprocities in themselves. This is common in the economy of small groups, notably with face-to-face steady relations (even beyond the family), as in villages

---

[6] For relatively recent discussions of the empirical evidence of behaviour of this type, see Bishop (1987), Baron (1988), Simon (1991), Levine (1991, 1993), Rabin (1993), Rotemberg (1994), Bewley (1995, 1999), and the works reviewed by Fehr, Gächter and Kirchsteiger (1999).

[7] Also presented in Kolm 1984a and 1984b.

or other small societies. This is a reason why reciprocity has been the central concept and concern of economic anthropology. The processes of modernisation in "development" often largely imply the replacement of relations of reciprocity by market exchanges or public administration. This changes social relations and the people themselves, with consequences which are often dramatic in various ways through the loss of cultures and civilizations and of traditional solidarities – not uncommonly, the transformation of proud tribesmen into the down and out of industrial society (who, then, do need "development").[8] It is possible to select positive aspects of modern technology without such social and personal destruction, but this kind of development is a delicate process which, precisely, has to rely on – rather than replace – traditional reciprocities permitting efficient cooperation, trust, solidarities, and local democracy, and which can thus often outperform standard markets and external administration in all respects.

In the field of organizations, the ideology – both a moral standard and an ideal – of cooperatives and of a number of associations is precisely reciprocity. They claim, and are proud, to be "more" than just groups of self-interested exchanging associates and to establish, among their members, a reciprocitarian solidarity with the corresponding attitudes and sentiments (cooperatives often do not have this dimension, and, in some of them, it has been reduced to mere decorum; however, it is important in other cases).

2.7 Reciprocity and community

Finally, a community of any kind importantly implies reciprocities of sentiments and acts between its members, and also, often, between members and the community as such

---

[8] This is the process of *clochardisation* analyzed by the anthropologist Germaine Tillon (about the example of Algeria).

which can be an object of sentiments and an actor through its institutions. A community is not just a collection of individuals or an association of purely self-interested individuals. It implies some commonness and communion among its members (for instance, it is Tönnies's *gemeinschaft* as opposed to *gesellschaft*). Communities are very varied in scope, in the nature of what is common to their members, and, importantly, in the intensity of the links and relations that they imply. They extend from the nuclear family to all mankind (if you see someone as a person, you feel you have at least a common humanity). A member of a community to which you belong is someone you tend to like – more or less and prima facie – , about whom you have some particular information (at least that concerning the community), whose opinion you generally tend to care about, and with whom you tend to compare – with, therefore, a sensitivity to issues of equality and inequality if you have the same relevant status. Now, these relations happen to be the basic elements that generate the two pure reciprocities in the strict sense. Hence, reciprocitarian relations are largely characteristic of a community, and their importance is related to the intensity of the sense of community of the members. Moreover, reciprocities in communities take place not only among members but also, more or less, among each member and the set of others and the community as such, through sentiments and conduct of "general reciprocity."

National communities are important instances. No doubt you "ask what you can do for your country rather than what your country can do for you" (as President Kennedy proposed). But it helps if the country also helps you. In fact, you receive for free benefits from public services which use a large part of GNP. Conversely, apart from your readiness to die for your motherland if necessary, most of us vote for parties that demand only relatively small changes in the system, and hence, notably, most of us vote for the correspondingly high taxes. Note that reciprocities, which are intrinsic if the collectivity is an organic community with a common culture and history, are no less present if the nation is seen as an association as in eighteenth-century or liberal political theory. Indeed, "social contracts," either between citizens or between citizens and the state, have often been found to be a powerful reason for mutual support or services; however, they are not actual contracts of exchange but only hypothetical or putative ones; therefore, their being felt as more or less compelling probably rests basically on sentiments of reciprocity by which each individual finds it normal to provide her contribution given that the others, or the government, provide their contribution.

2.8 Public aid

In particular, the general concern for the welfare and dignity of other people and for justice need not be pointed out in countries where the people either have some sort of socialist ideal or draw similarly their moral inspiration from Christianity or Buddhism – and which, in the end, redistribute a large part of income. Pure and direct altruism by which several people care for the needs, welfare, situation or income of the same persons can induce "joint or collective giving" which is not reciprocity, but a case of contribution to a non-excludable public good (the beneficiary's situation) which can be sustained by a reciprocity among the contributors.[9] More specifically, however, many of us vote for public transfers towards people who earn little or have particular needs, not only in exchange for our receiving transfers when we are in their situation – which is just standard insurance –, but also when we will certainly never be in their

---

[9] As explained in chapter 12 (including the paradoxical and important case of obligations that are necessary even though they are not actually binding).

situation – this becomes altruism –, and often with the reasoning that, had chance put us in this situation, other people would have similarly helped us – a reasoning of putative reciprocity (or of putative "fundamental insurance" reciprocally accepted among contributors).[10] For this reason, Europeans overwhelmingly vote for a public system of social insurance that includes redistributions of this type towards people a priori endowed with poor health (contrary to the pure actuarial exchange of private insurance with differentiated premia).

2.9 Intergenerational reciprocities

The same people, generally, vote for the collective support of individuals who earn no income because of their stage in the life cycle: they favour a system of pensions "by distribution" or "pay-as-you-go" and the public financing of education. However, this is justified not only by helping people in need, but also by a rationale of open-ended "chain reciprocities," forward and backward. That is, working people pay for the pensions of the older people given that they will be paid their own pensions by the next generation, and the older have paid the pensions of the previous generation. Similarly, people at work finance the education of the young given that their education has been paid for by the older generation, and the young will in turn finance the education of the generation to come. These chain reciprocities are particular structures of

---

[10] See Kolm 1985. A "fundamental insurance" is a hypothetical self-interested exchange or agreement of mutual insurance about a risk that, in reality, has already occurred, such as, for instance, the natural endowments of individuals or their education induced by the family. This is a theory of the compensation for these facts, justifying and determining it by the imaginary free agreement. It can be shown that this theory is a priori morally dubious from the point of view of justice, because a self-interested choice in uncertainty – that of the persons agreeing about the insurance contract – does not have, a priori, the same structure as a choice of justice – for compensating for the relative handicaps. However, this theory has to be accepted if all the individuals accept it, and one may accept it given that the others also accept it, hence from a type of reciprocity among people who give (see Kolm 1985, 1996a, 2004).

"extended" ("reverse" and "generalized") reciprocity. However, one could also note that people so pay the pensions of
the financial purveyors of their education. All these transfers
are interrelated collective gifts and are not exchanges in the
strict sense.

  These structures correspond in fact to some of the six intergenerational reciprocities at work in families, among which
are four open-ended chain reciprocities: you take care of your
ageing parents given that they have taken care of you and of
their parents and that your children will take care of you, and
you take care of your children given that they will take care
of you and of their children and your parents took care of
you. More distant relations enrich the network (you take care
of your grandparents who took care of your parents, and so
on) – this is relevant for pensions since the system of some
countries (Italy, Belgium) is in debt and so people are in fact
paying for the pensions already distributed to the generation
of their grand-parents.[11]

2.10 Evidence and history

These are but a few samples of a case of conspicuous evidence. You do not need a laboratory experiment to know that
reciprocity exists, or to know which factors a priori influence
specific reciprocal conducts, and such experiments could
hardly analyse the essential steady and complex social relations and strong interpersonal sentiments (not to mention the
"total social facts" that Marcel Mauss sees in reciprocities).
However, experiments can inform you about the frequencies
of elementary reciprocal reactions, if not in "human nature"
(if such a thing exists), at least in the particular subculture
from which the sample is drawn, and this may be an interesting piece of statistical anthropology. They can, moreover,
elicit reflection about these relations, and, since the issues

[11] See Kolm 2000a.

are sometimes rather subtle and not obvious, no help is to be discarded.[12]

If, moreover, you are the kind of person interested in the perceptive observations and elaborate reflection of other people, you will find thousands of pages to satisfy your curiosity about reciprocity. Mutual love, the cases where it fails to be

[12] Reciprocity has been the object of numerous laboratory experiments (and of other empirical studies) in the framework of social psychology since at least the early 1960s – as noted above. Recently, a number of such studies have been added in the framework of economics. They are discussed in chapter 23 along with remarks concerning the modelling that generally accompanies these studies (whether they are classified in social psychology or in economics), about the generality of the models and the nature of their variables. Let us simply note here a few remarks about the relations between experimental analysis and reflective-conceptual analysis for the study, understanding and explanation of reciprocity and similar conducts (not just behaviour!). These experiments present specific instances and cases of the more general phenomena in question. They raise at least three kinds of epistemic issues. Their incontestable success as scientific endeavour in the strictest sense is that they do falsify a hypothesis, namely that of the non-existence of the phenomena they study. However, nobody ever suggested this hypothesis in the first place (except, sometimes, a handful of ideologists of self-interest talking tongue in cheek who were not expected to be taken seriously). The existence of these phenomena is obvious to all from numerous observations in life (the fact that these phenomena are absent from a number of theoretical economic models which purposefully simplify reality is something else, the issue being only if and when the models choose the wrong simplification for their purpose, which requires a discussion including this purpose). The other, deeper, contribution of these experiments consists of providing frequencies of the phenomenon in question in the specific case of the experiment. However, there are also often commentaries about what can be concluded from such figures, in relation to the various specific aspects of the experiment. Now, in generally presenting and considering these reflections as second and subsidiary to the experiment and the figures rather than the converse, these discussions, feeling secure about precision, distinction, and rigour because of the experimental figures they consider, may not find it a priority to, in addition, much emphasise carrying over these characteristics to the concepts they mention. Showing this for all these studies would be too long and beyond the present scope, and may meet exceptions, but, for example, "reciprocity" may not be used with the discernment one may wish, its various very different types may not be distinguished when this may be relevant, it is sometimes confused with fairness (only one type of reciprocity may relate to fairness and much of fairness is something totally different), or again with altruism (reciprocity is only a specific cause of altruistic conducts), and so on. Moreover, is the relative importance of prior reflective analysis and of chance and haphazard

mutual, revenge, and gratitude or the lack of it, provide a large part of news headlines and still more of fiction. Reciprocity is one of the few main topics of social science. It has dominated anthropology for ninety years, whether it explains the economy, the polity, rituals, or kinship (marriages).[14] It has been importantly considered in sociology for one century.[15] It has been a main topic of social psychology – about labour relations, "helping behaviour," and other types of relationships – and it has been considered in numerous socio-psychological laboratory experiments for half a century. It has been analysed with economic models for several decades. In the classical theory of comparative economic systems, reciprocity is one of the three pure types along with exchange (markets) and command. Finally, reciprocal mutuality of services has been the main hope of thinkers about the good society for centuries and even millennia, since it is the only alternative to oppressive command, selfish exchange, or the utopia of widespread unconditional altruism.

discussions for choosing the topic to submit to laboratory experiment always the right one? The interested reader is sometimes tempted to suggest an inversion of priority, emphasis and importance of methods, which could be presented as an application, to experimentation, of the famous mathematicians' dictum about efficient sequencing: "first think, then compute." However, considering the set of such studies rather than a single one does show progress in this direction. But how far and how fast compared with different possible uses of means? As far as economics as a whole is concerned, the analysis of reciprocity and of its consequences is an old story. There have been models of reciprocity since the early 1970s, a meeting on this topic in Athens in 1974, a session about reciprocity at the meeting of the Econometric Society in Oslo in 1975, the consideration of a semi-reciprocity creating wage rigidity by George Akerlof in 1982, a book on reciprocity, its analysis, evidence and applications, and a number of related papers, by Kolm in 1984, a paper on a special reciprocity for contributing to a public good by Robert Sugden in 1984, an application of the same issue to the facing of a "tragedy of the commons" in the depletion of a free common resource by Swaney in 1990, before more recent studies related shortly.

[14] See, among many others, the works of Bronislaw Malinowski, Richard Thurnwald, Marcel Mauss, Raymond Firth, or Claude Lévi-Strauss.

[15] In particular in the works of Leonard T. Hobhouse, Georg Simmel, Howard Becker, George Homans, or Alvin Gouldner.

3

Giving and exchanges

3.1 Concepts and distinctions

3.1.1 Person, agent, actor, individual, etc.

We consider entities with these names who can act, perform actions, engage in conduct resulting in behaviour, be
responsible, have feelings, emotions, sentiments, reasons
and motives of all kinds, have information, expectations
and memory, have attitudes, preferences and desires, have
social status, and so on. They will usually be individuals,
but they can occasionally be constituted groups or institutional entities (whose consideration as persons in these
various respects requires an extended discussion omitted
here).

3.1.2 Action, conduct, behaviour, motives, preference

An action is a set of acts (possibly a single act) with an intention (or joint intentions) and a meaning for its actor (and
generally also for other members of the society). An action
manifests some freedom (although it can be more or less con-
strained and induced). Hence, it implies some responsibility
of the agent. The intention results from motives, which can
be reasons or sentiments of various possible types. A set of
acts is behaviour. A set of actions is conduct. Hence, conduct

is behaviour plus the corresponding motives (and meaning).[1]
Desires and drives are types of motives. Preference evaluates
several alternatives comparatively with respect to some values. Applied to action, it describes the choice of one of the
possible alternatives (economists' "revealed preferences"), as
a result of the corresponding motives.

3.1.3 Gift giving

We consider actions that are intended to benefit someone else
and are in some way costly for the actor. A transfer of a good,
or a service, can be such an action. This action is gift giving, and its result is a gift, if it is not a part of an exchange.
"Exchange," here, will denote, and be restricted to for clar-
ity, a set of acts from various actors, accepted by all these
actors when this exchange is free, and such that the acts of
each actor are compulsory by external obligation when the
others are implemented. An obligation is "external" when
it is not a pure sentiment of moral duty or norm following
alone. It can be enforced by constraint which is then seen
as "legitimate" because it has been a priori accepted by the
person's agreement (and which is often lawful), or under the
threat of such a constraint. However, the person can also perform her acts agreed upon – pay her due – voluntarily from
a moral sense of abiding by the agreement or promise keeping. Market exchanges are the paradigmatic exchanges. In an
exchange, the basic and primary (free) action of a participant
is not her doing her part; it is, rather, the previous decision of
accepting this binding agreement. Hence, an act that is part
of such an exchange is not gift giving. Note also that since
gift giving is an action, it is by definition free, not thoroughly
imposed (although it may be induced). However, several gift
givings can be related not by such conditionalities but by

---

[1] This is why the expressions will be "a motive *for* behaviour" and "a motive
of a conduct" (meaning a type or an instance of conduct).

motivations. When you have received a gift (by definition
without condition), you sometimes want to give something
"in return", or feel or think you have to, out of gratitude, to
please your benefactor, or to establish a balance and not carry
a moral debt. But you are not obliged to perform this act by an
"external" obligation such as a contractual one or an equivalent sense of duty or propriety to abide by an agreement. This
is the classical basic gift/return gift relationship, the proto-
type and archetype of reciprocity, and the building block of
more complex relations of reciprocity.[2]

Moreover, the cost of gift giving can have a compensation
for the giver, but it is not a conditional compensation as in an
exchange. For instance, the giver may be pleased to please the
receiver, to conform to a duty, norm or custom, to display generosity or a superiority over the receiver – in others' eyes or
in her own –, and so on. In fact, one can always explain a gift
trivially by the fact that the giver enjoys some sort of compensation exceeding the cost she incurs, since it is a free action.
The advantage can occasionally be quite material and self-
interested, as with givings that elicit a return gift (for whatever reason) that the initial giver values more than the cost of
the gift for her – this is the "half-reciprocity" of exploitation
of return-giving conduct and motives by the initial giver –,
rewards of various possible other origins, or indirect effects
through markets or other social processes.

The case of sequential exchanges is specifically considered shortly. They are sequences of free transfers or services

---

[2] Hence, two possible kinds of norm, duty or propriety for performing
actions favouring other people who perform actions favourable to you can
intervene here. One leads to return giving for reasons of balance, matching
or fairness. The other is abiding by an exchange agreement, doing one's part
as agreed upon, possibly keeping a promise to act given in this agreement.
These conducts are, respectively, one reason for giving in return and one
way of implementing an agreement. One can, moreover, freely abide by an
agreement or keep one's promise given that other people do the same, in
a reciprocity about these conducts – a reciprocitarian implementation of
agreements which can save the costs of constraints. In an ongoing relation
or a sequence of agreements, this latter reciprocity can in fact be a sequential exchange (each freely abides by agreements or keeps her promises in
order that others continue doing the same).

both ways between agents and extending in time, in which each transfer is provided in order to receive further ones. Hence, each transfer is provided independently freely. However, each full sequence of transfers from one agent to the other is provided under the condition that the other such sequence is also provided. Hence if the motives are self-interest only, the full process belongs to the category of self-interested exchanges (although other motives can also intervene in addition). One can also simply consider that each transfer is provided under the threat that next ones in the other direction are not.

3.1.4 Types and effects of gifts, refusing gifts

Hence, a gift from an agent to another can consist of anything done by the former and favourable to the latter or favoured by her, which has the properties just noted, and can be, for instance, bestowing a gift in the strict sense or a favour, approving or expressing a favourable judgment (if it has some cost, perhaps by its effects or compared to alternative opportunities), and so on. The former agent is the giver or benefactor, and the latter is the receiver or beneficiary.

Besides providing the gift, giving implies a couple of facts that sometimes play a part in its appreciation. It generally shows that the giver acknowledges the existence of the receiver, pays attention to her, gives her some kind of consideration. This can in itself be valuable for the receiver, notably when it is a benevolent gift, and notably when it shows that the giver likes the receiver. This appreciation generally results from the fact that this concern is favourable to the social existence and the ego of the receiver, in her eyes or in those of others whose opinion matters to her. This effect can result from the mere consideration or attention of the giver, but it is reinforced by her favourable attitude or sentiment towards the receiver, and still more by additional affects of kindness. The valuation and affection can be proven and even more or less measured by the cost incurred for providing the

gift. Moreover, giving, receiving, accepting or refusing constitute in themselves a *social intercourse* which is sometimes
important. In addition, the very facts and acts of giving and
receiving can constitute, or be the occasion of, a *factual social
intercourse*, which is sometimes appreciated in itself by any
of the participants and which sometimes has opposite effects.
Most gifts actually benefit the receiver, but *symbolic gifts* are
symbols of the relation between the agents, or of the giver's
favourable sentiments towards the other, and they may or
may not have other values. A particular gift can have several
effects, roles, or functions jointly. However, any one of these
effects is sometimes the main or sole reason for giving.

A gift can sometimes be refused, or restituted, but this also
is sometimes not possible, for two very different types of reasons. The reason can be factual: the service has been provided, the judgment made public, or the act has involved an
irreversible physical transformation. However, the reasons
are also often social, in that refusing or sending back the gift
is thought improper, "is not done," or is grossly offensive
towards the giver. A gift received may also sometimes be sold
(some consist directly in money income), or given as a gift
(the ceremonial gifts of the Melanesian *kula ring* have to be
given in turn to other people), but these uses are improper for
other gifts. Symbolic gifts are often submitted to constraints
of this type: returning the gift so received means refusing the
relation or the homage, but providing a return gift can mean
accepting them, on the contrary.

3.2 Motives for giving, notably in reciprocity

3.2.1 *A wide variety of motives, from best to worst*

Many motives elicit giving.[3] They include liking, compassion and pity, moral conduct and duty of various types, social

---

[3] A full analysis of this topic is presented in Kolm, 1984a. Only a short
summary is presented here.

value, following a moral or social norm, seeking praise, self-esteem, or an image of oneself in others' eyes or in one's own, the desire to produce various possible social effects, and simple self-interest, all with their various modalities. They combine, associate and relate in various ways. For instance, you give to your family because you like or love its members, and to someone in need because of compassion or pity, but giving to these persons is also morally and socially valued or praised or is a duty, and you may seek the approval, or the absence of disapproval, of others or of your own conscience by these acts. Moral and social praise or requirement even attach to the sentiments of liking and compassion or pity themselves. Other norms and traditions lead you to other kinds of giving. We will also discuss shortly giving for inducing other social effects. The reasons to give in return in reciprocity both can mobilize most of these psychological and social phenomena and are more focused. Apart from the possible interested desire to elicit a further gift, which leads to "sequential exchange" (see section 3.3), there are two properly reciprocitarian types of motives. Liking the benevolent giver, possibly because she likes the beneficiary, refers to one of the most common motives for giving, liking. In contrast, giving in return for maintaining some sort of balance or equality is a motive proper to reciprocity (it relates to the revenge aspect of negative reciprocation). On the other hand, another main motive for giving, namely compassion or pity, is a priori absent from reciprocity. However, this balance or matching motive uses – according to the case – a variety of common simple motives for giving such as morality, duty, following a moral or social norm or a tradition, the effects of approval or disapproval, seeking esteem or self-esteem, caring for one's self-image appraised by others or by oneself, and so on. Finally, the classification of general gift giving that is relevant for understanding reciprocity is according to the social sentiments and attitudes they manifest.

There are three kinds of giving in this respect: it can be benevolent, or neutral towards the receiver, and even hostile towards her in some way, and each category itself encompasses various types. An instance of giving can have several joint motives, but the various motives are more or less compatible. Moreover, besides giving to specifically known people, giving can be aimed at more or less anonymous receivers as with giving through the intermediary of charities, or "general giving" to the group of others or to society as a whole. In these cases, many motives can be the same as those of giving in general, but there are also differences – in particular, some motives cannot be present in anonymous givings (notably the worst ones noted shortly).

3.2.2 Benevolent giving

3.2.2.1 Liking and compassion. Benevolent giving is giving that results from a sentiment of benevolence towards the beneficiary. This is to be distinguished from giving accompanied by benevolence towards the receiver but provided for another reason – notably the neutral ones shortly to be noted – (and a gift can have several joint motives). Benevolent giving can have two different types of motives since this benevolence results either from *liking* the receiver – *affection* towards her – or from a *general motive of helping people in need*, which includes solidarity, charity, pity and compassion. Often, only one of these types of motives is present. They can also both be present, but only if the liking sentiment is in a mild form. Indeed, if you help someone whom you sufficiently like and who needs help in such a way that this would elicit help for a motive of compassion, pity, charity or solidarity, then your motive for helping is your affection for this person and the resulting pain that her pain induces in you, and not the other altruistic motives. Affection tends to drive away pity and related sentiments.

The psychological phenomena of empathy and emotional contagion can support the two types of motives of benevolent giving.

Moreover, if the aim of giving may indeed simply be to *please or satisfy the receiver*, because liking someone implies liking the pleasure, the satisfaction or the joy she feels, it may also be to *do something good* for the receiver independently of the receiver's tastes or preferences (then, it would often not please the receiver as much as it could, or it may even displease her – the possibility or impossibility of refusing the gift is then relevant) – this is often called "paternalism." This type of distinction even occurs sometimes for pity or compassion, which usually induces reducing the other person's pain, but sometimes consists in regretting some other aspect of her situation deemed inappropriate by comparison with some norm and may induce trying to remedy it.

Of course, the gift or favour can benefit or please the beneficiary in a variety of ways: by the gift or favour received, by showing appreciation of or respect for the receiver to her or to other people – which sometimes enhances the receiver's social status –, for the social intercourse in the relation of giving, and so on.

Finally, giving as a result of liking the receiver in general itself has three possible motives, which are closely interrelated, as we shall see: doing something deemed to be good for the receiver and in particular something she likes; giving in order to be liked by the receiver; and the demonstration effect of showing and proving one's liking sentiment.

3.2.2.2 Giving for eliciting the receiver's liking. The objective of gift giving is sometimes to induce the receiver to like the giver. However, this aim is in part self-defeating because of an opposition between the central motive for the giving and the main reason why it could have this effect. Indeed, the aim in question of the giver is not to please the receiver – or to do something good for her – as an end, because she likes the receiver. Rather, the aim is to be liked by her. The pleasure or appreciation of the receiver, or the improvement in her situation, is then a means to this final aim. However, the receiver of a gift tends to like the giver in a particularly specific and genuine way as a consequence, only if the final objective of this giving is to benefit her, which is not the case here. Nevertheless, the giver a priori likes more to be liked by the receiver, the more she likes her (for a reason to be explained in chapter 5), apart from peripheral reasons such as the status one can derive from being liked (even in one's own eyes). Then this giving, accompanied by benevolence if not made directly because of benevolence, and made for a reason (being liked) which practically requires liking the person whose affection is sought, nevertheless elicits some forms of liking the giver, although of an inferior nature and intensity (this will be presented in chapter 7). Moreover, since the giver likes the receiver, she enjoys doing something that benefits her, even if this motive, by itself, would not suffice for eliciting giving. In fact, these two objectives are not inconsistent, and they are often jointly present: giving then aims both at favouring the beneficiary and at inducing her to like the giver.

3.2.2.3 Showing and proving liking.   Moreover, the object of giving may be to *show or prove* to the receiver that the giver likes her. The giver does this for two possible reasons. First, she may think the receiver will like to know she is liked, and she enjoys the receiver's pleasure or satisfaction because she likes her. Second, the giver may expect that the receiver's knowledge that the giver likes her will induce her to like the giver ("I will love him who loves me") – a reciprocity of sentiments explained in chapter 7. And the giver likes to be liked, especially by people she likes. In all this description, "like" can also mean "like more." Giving, then, is a signal of liking. The sacrifice of the cost of the gift measures the intensity of the liking sentiment. It is chosen for showing and proving this intensity. However, this favour only shows and proves that the giver wants the receiver to think that she is liked with this intensity. It does not directly show or prove the actual liking. Nevertheless, for the first effect of pleasing the receiver who likes to be liked, the giver wants more the receiver to think that she is liked, and she wants her to think that she is liked more, the more she herself likes the receiver. Hence, the giving finally reveals the liking, and its cost reveals the intensity of this sentiment. For the second effect of eliciting the receiver's liking by the reciprocity of sentiments, the giver wants more to be liked, and she wants to be liked more, the more she likes the receiver. Hence, the giving does again reveal the liking, and its cost reveals the intensity of this sentiment.

Moreover, the receiver tends to be grateful towards the giver for actions and choices of the latter that aim at benefiting the receiver as an end – and for which the giver is responsible (which is implied by an action or a choice). This includes such gifts – and the corresponding sacrifices – because the giver likes the receiver, and also gifts or aid for a reason of compassion, pity, charity, or solidarity. It also includes directly the giver's liking sentiments towards the receiver in so far as she can influence this sentiment of hers.[4] Now gratitude can pave the way to liking if other relevant facts intervene, and it can elicit a kind of return giving for showing and "proving" it.

3.2.3 Neutral giving

The second category, that of giving with sentiments and attitudes that are neutral towards the receiver, includes very different types of motives.

---

[4] There also exists sometimes the particular sentiment of being grateful for something one enjoys and that is not caused by an agent's action. This can, for instance, be experienced in the presence of "gifts of nature" of some kind. This kind of gratitude is a manifestation of the general tendency to anthropomorphism which is a basis of religions of all kinds. However, it can in particular apply to someone else liking oneself while this liking does not depend on her will, or insofar as it does not. This particular gratitude is not for an action, yet it is addressed to a sentiment of a person which is an intimate part of her, and hence to this person for her very existence.

3.2.3.1 Interest. In *interested giving* the only objective of the giver is to favour her own interest in a strict sense. Such an effect can have many causes (rewards, economic or other social indirect effects, and so on). However, one type of them is directly related to the issue of reciprocity: the intention to benefit from a *return gift* elicited by the gift. This sometimes includes appreciation of the attention manifested by the return gift or of the corresponding symbolic or factual relation. Since this giving not motivated by liking does not elicit or increase the receiver's liking of the giver (if the receiver does not mistakenly believe that this giving results from her being liked), the motive for this return gift (or increase in it) is not this liking but another motive. There are two possibilities (see chapter 5). One is comparative or balance reciprocity which elicits a return gift counterbalancing the original gift. The other is that the return gift is motivated by a desire for the gift to be repeated, a case that leads to the sequential exchange described in the next section (the return gift may also attract giving from third parties interested in engaging in such a relation). However, an interested giver may also hope to receive something from *imitation* of her giving by any agent, or from a *reverse reciprocity* by which a giver is given to by someone other than the receiver, possibly as a reward for her merit (see chapter 4 – this is a "Descartes effect").

3.2.3.2 Duty and propriety. A second type of "neutral" giving is that of giving motivated by *duty* or by the conception that it is *proper* or appropriate. Duty generally refers to a moral judgment, whereas propriety only refers to a social value or norm that is not moral. Several types of such motives for giving are noteworthy. One is giving to people in need, as charity or solidarity. This attaches to the needs of the receiver and the means of the giver, or to their relative status. There need not be any corresponding benevolent sentiment of the giver. However, the conception that having sentiments of compassion, charity or solidarity towards the people in need is a duty also exists. This implies that the person has some possibility of influencing her own sentiments (this issue will be discussed in chapter 7 about other sentiments).

Duty to help is sometimes supported by moral reasoning of various possible types. A most common one is "generalization" of the type elaborated by Kant: "I help (in a category of circumstances) because the result would be very bad if nobody helped in such cases." Another reasoning is that of "putative reciprocity," of the type: "I help her because she would have helped me if our situation were reversed"; or, in a "generalized" extension, "because I would have been helped" (by anybody).

In fact, actual comparative, matching or balanced reciprocity is another type of duty-bound or proper giving.

Finally, there are gifts to particular people or relatives in particular occasions, induced by tradition, sometimes routinely performed, sometimes in a particular social setting (often a feast). In all cases, duty or propriety is not just a sentiment of the individual but also a social normative view. Hence, all givings from duty or propriety are bound to be more or less demanded as a norm, and can be more or less induced by social opinion or other forms of social inducement or pressure.

3.2.3.3 Being generous, wanting to be or to appear generous. Other categories of motives involve further-order desires and judgments. You give because you *are generous* (or acting properly or from duty). You also give sometimes because you *want to be generous.* Then you are generous in acts (this is generally all you want, but if you also want to be generous in sentiment in addition, you may know or have the intuition that the best way to acquire a sentiment is to act as if one had it and acted for this motive – this is explainable by the reduction of a kind of cognitive dissonance). At any rate, wanting to be virtuous is often more praised than acting from a natural, given, effortless generosity. For Kant, for instance, only this type of conduct is moral – spontaneous generosity is only an "inclination," as any other taste is. However, some people also act generously because they want to be *praised*, or *praiseworthy*, for so acting, or for being generous in sentiments (possibly mistakenly assumed by observers, or induced by the action), or for wanting to be generous. This may be their own judgment about themselves,[5] or the judgment of others about which they care. They thus try to build an image of themselves in their own view or in the view of others (reputation) as someone generous in acts, in sentiments, or in intentions. However, this can be for two reasons. Such givers may want to be praiseworthy or praised in this way because they value generosity, a homage to virtue which is in itself half a virtue, and hence they like to appear to be generous in their own view or in the view of others, whether they actually have generous sentiments or not. Or else these people may want to be praised or praiseworthy in itself, and then they choose the virtue of generosity (in acts, sentiments, or intention or appearance of sentiments) because generosity is valued by a common social sentiment, by other people, or by society. They may also desire various possible benefits entailed by this reputation or society's judgment in terms of honour, status, interest, and so on. However, in so far as the person's aim is to be praised or praiseworthy, this cannot be for an actual sentiment of generosity.

The case in which people give because they care about the approval or disapproval of other people who value this giving because it would be moral and hence for a moral reason presents a particularly interesting social structure of sentiments and action which can apply more generally to all moral conducts. In such cases, indeed, some people value giving and do not give, while others give but do not value giving in

---

[5] The case of self-judgment about the act of giving – in fact, the gift – is what Jim Andreoni labels the "warm glow" (see Andreoni 1989, 1990a).

itself. More generally, some people are moral in judgment but not in action, while others act morally but have no moral judgment. This nice division of labour is quite common. There is no moral actor, and yet there are actions the form of which is moral, in this society. However, a priori the general situation is that each individual both praises giving by anyone – herself or others –, and gives because of praise by anyone – herself or others. The praise of others may be necessary for her to give (even if she also morally values her own giving). In the end, society as a whole may be much more generous, or moral, than each individual's motives are for her own actions (this society may be any small or large group of persons so interconnected by such judgments).[6]

3.2.4 Giving, inequality and status

3.2.4.1 Status. The third type of giving and of motives for it concerning the effect on the receiver emphasizes the inequality between both parties. The relevant inequalities are of roles, means, wealth, freedoms, positions and, importantly, status in hierarchical relations. Besides the material effects of gifts, the symbolic function of giving will be particularly important. Inequality, status, moral indebtedness, and the like, are a priori social views. They can be so conceived by the receiver, by the giver, or by other members of the society. These views of others may matter for the giver. They can also be enforced on her by the various forms of "social pressure." Most relevant sentiments will be relational and positional, such as sentiments of inferiority and superiority, of subjection and domination or power, of humiliation, or the corresponding pride and shame, or again sentiments associated with an attitude of condescension.

Giving, an asymmetrical relation by nature, is often in itself seen as an inequality. Avoiding or suppressing this effect is

---

[6] See an analysis of this situation in Kolm 1996a, chapter 14.

a main reason for refusing a gift or for returning a compensatory return gift. However, this is an inequality of roles, of acts, and in the transformation of situations and in particular of holdings for a material gift. In this latter case, however, the inequality in wealth can be diminished – on the contrary – by a gift from a richer person to a poorer one.[7] Moreover, this decrease in inequality is obtained in a way that respects freedom and, indeed, thanks to a free act. By the same token, however, this gift makes this inequality in wealth conspicuous, and, since it is voluntary, it shows the giver's generosity. Giving can thus display wealth or means, possibly obtained with effort, or generosity, in absolute terms or comparatively to other people – in particular the beneficiary. This can thus provide the giver with a desired reputation or status. This status can be in absolute or relative terms. By the same token, the gift can attract attention on the poverty of the receiver and endow her with the corresponding status. Giving is sometimes aimed at showing a superiority of the giver over the receiver. This gift, and the receiver's acceptance if she has the choice, may, moreover, elicit a particularly unfavourable image of the receiver. For example, it may suggest that she is unable or too lazy to cater for her own needs (or those of her family). This is sometimes received with severe social judgments which can arouse shame, guilt or humiliation. There exist vicious givings that aim specifically at this result.

3.2.4.2 Power and moral credit. If the gift is important to the beneficiary, she may become dependent on it, and hence dependent on the giver's will, which is a loss of freedom. Correspondingly, this is a power of the giver, who may specifically seek it. This is before the gift is given, but that is often a recurrent situation.

Moreover, receiving a gift often creates a *moral debt* of the receiver towards the giver. Refusing the gift – when this is

---

[7] This diminishes the inequality between these two people, but perhaps not the overall inequality in a larger society (see Kolm 1999).

possible – or providing an adequate return gift, often aims at avoiding such a situation. This indebtedness is often disagreable for the receiver, in itself or as a result of the judgment of other people (possibly including the giver) or of society. Redeeming this debt by a return gift is often proper and a norm. This moral debt is sometimes seen as attributing some form of social superiority of the giver over the receiver. The time and manner of redeeming the debt by a return gift are often the choice of the initial beneficiary. However, the moral creditor can sometimes ask the debtor to do various things in appealing to this situation ("you owe me something"). The receiver is the "*obligé*" of her benefactor. In some societies and situations, norms can make such a situation very oppressive, often with the help of other people's judgment and sometimes of social pressure of some kind. Giving sometimes aims at such a moral domination or enslaving, by giving more than the receiver can ever return. This power may be sought for its actual possibilities or in itself, notably as superiority. Giving in return redeems the debt and erases its effect, but sometimes this is a further occasion for showing that the initial gift or service and the ensuing indebtedness have existed. Recall the Inuit proverb: "The gift makes the slave, as the whip makes the dog."

3.2.4.3 Hierarchies. The giving relationship constitutes one of the main social bonds, but it uses this property in a great variety of ways. Being both a voluntary sacrifice for a person and a benefit for the other, giving is an adequate ingredient for tightening other bonds. Indeed, gift giving often accompanies an agreement, to seal it by showing goodwill. Established statuses also often use gifts of various kinds. Sometimes they require them. These cases are sometimes neutral obedience to tradition. However, statuses often use required giving to remind of and confirm the relation. Sometimes they tend to erode when this is not done. This can induce more or less balanced gifts between equals. However, such gift giving is also often an important vector of unequal and hierarchical relations. Gifts either way are used for this purpose. A very common case is that of a gift from a superior to an inferior. It shows this relation and the comparison, and it produces the corresponding moral indebtedness. In fact, acknowledging the superiority and superior status of the giver is often, for the receiver, an implicit way of "paying her debt." The superior thus "buys" her status in some sense – although this is not an exchange in the strict sense. However, there are also cases in which the inferior gives to the superior. This is also a way of acknowledging acceptance of the status. And yet, when the status corresponds to relative force, such payments are commonly de facto forced, although in a steady relationship both parties often find it convenient to pretend that these transfers are free, voluntary gifts or tributes.[8] There may thus also be transfers both ways, especially when the nature of the services or gifts differs, in a kind of unequal, hierarchical and hierarchy-strengthening reciprocity.

3.2.4.4 The variety of moral differences. Hence, giving is the vector of many types of social sentiments, attitudes and relations. Liking the other and generosity constitute its central domain. Even this field encompasses quite different cases, however. Solidarity is in the sphere of fraternity, but charity is often tainted with condescension, and we have met gifts used for establishing or maintaining superiority or domination, even for humiliating or de facto enslaving. However, the important thing for normative uses concerned with the intrinsic quality of social relations, attitudes, and persons, is the existence and the possibility of the former cases.

---

[8] History records many instances when a tribute is called a voluntary gift (for instance from proud Arabic tribes to the Persian king, or from the "Franc-Lyonnais" who took a toll on all items of merchandise moving into and out of the city of Lyon to the king of France). Sometimes this transfer is also a price for protection, but the same force can protect and threaten, and, in fact, it protects its own source of income – which is a good way to make sure that the protection is provided.

The foregoing analysis of the variety of motives for giving, and of the sentiments and views related to it for the actors or onlookers, have shown that there are essential differences between the case where the receiver is specifically known, notably by the giver, and the case of giving to anonymous beneficiaries. This latter situation is notably the case of giving to or through charitable organisations, or of "general" giving to the group of others or to society as a whole performed in general pro-social behaviour (which can extend, for example, from abstaining to pollute public places to dying for the motherland). Most motives or sentiments that are present in the "anonymous" case can also exist with identified beneficiaries and givers, but many that are present in the latter case do not exist with the former, or exist only in a quite different form. In particular, giving in order to show a specific superiority, or to humiliate, does not exist in the case of gifts to anonymous beneficiaries. The superiority that can be exhibited in being generous through charities is different; it is more superiority over other givers or possible givers than superiority over the beneficiaries. For general gifts, the corresponding possible pride or competitive devotion to the public good is something rather different. In particular, the noted particular relational vices in giving are impossible or much less possible for gifts to anonymous or general others, or to society.

3.3   Sequential exchange

In an important type of situation, there are two agents each of which performs actions favourable to the other and costly for herself, either alternately or when the relative need of the beneficiary or the relative means of the actor are high, or, again, as a sequence of simultaneous actions (possibly a continuous relation), with purely and narrowly self-interested motives. That is, the motive of each action is that the process should continue and hence that the actor benefits from later actions of the other. It is purely "consequentialist." Each action is performed because it is thought to be a condition for later actions and, except for the first gift, its expectation was a condition of former actions, and it generally has former actions as conditions in spite of its consequentialism. Hence, on the whole each actor provides her set of actions only under the condition that the other provides hers. Therefore, this is in fact an exchange in the retained sense, as shown by the exclusively narrowly self-interested motivations (in spite of the fact that each step can be considered an action, with the continuation of the process as its intention – although this can also be seen as acting under the *de facto* threat that later acts of the other party are withheld or less interesting). This is not reciprocity in the proper sense, although it may look like it if one considers partial gestures only rather than also their motives and the whole process. However, omitting motives leads to the superficial consideration of "behaviour" only (which may be proper for studying animals but misses the essence of social science). Now, there can indeed also be a similar sequence of similar actions that are actual gift giving. In particular, each gift can be influenced by the gifts received by the actor, by the gifts she gave, and also by the set of gifts both ways she expects, in a steady reciprocity. The overall motivations are not the same, however. In the former, exchange, case, the motive of each other-gratifying action is: "I do this in order that she gratifies me later – and she will be motivated by the same reason." In contrast, in the latter case of genuine reciprocity, the motive rather is: "I gratify her because she has gratified (and will gratify) me." The two cases may present similar behaviour but consist in deeply different and opposite conducts – but behaviour is superficial while understanding and explanation refer to conduct. The difference will in fact a priori show in the specific acts – for instance, quantities handed out to the other –, which have no reason to be the same with the two kinds of motives. This difference, however, is not necessarily large if the reciprocity proper is motivated by a sense of balance (see chapter 6), since self-interested handing out will be sufficiently high to induce the next steps but not higher than necessary for that[9] – however, reciprocity proper can also have another motivation, mutual liking, for which the relation between the gifts can a priori be much looser. In addition, however, these types of motives are often both present and associated, in various possible proportions. They even tend to be, as a consequence of the protracted interaction of the sequential exchange. Indeed, in this process each pays attention to the other, is aware of her. This may elicit some sentiment of duty or fairness towards her, and possibly some sympathy for her. All the more so as this person benefits from the relationship, and, hence, from the existence and cooperation of the other person. These sentiments of fairness, with the corresponding sentiment of balance between what each person yields to the other, and of sympathy with the satisfaction from the other's satisfaction it may entail, constitute the two basic motives of properly reciprocitarian conduct. Moreover, reciprocity may be more sustainable if the participants are aware that it also benefits their self-interest.[10] Of course, the motives may differ for the two participants: one may be self-interested and the other reciprocitarian of one kind or the other, and they also may have several motives in different proportions.

However, even the simple self-interested sequential exchange is far from something simplistic. If on one occasion one participant provides less than the other expected, the other may react by providing more in order to draw the attention of her partner to the interest of the relationship, or by providing less for the same reason, or because she thinks that her partner has become less interested and wishes to exchange smaller amounts, or because this decrease makes

---

[9] Remember, however, that the so-called "folk theorem" suggests that the case of sequential exchange can have any solution that is jointly preferred to the absence of this relation. Actually, the specific actions or transfers depend on participants' preferences, needs, alternative possibilities, strategies, information and beliefs about the other, intelligence and mental capacities, and other circumstances.

[10] However, non-self-interested motives are also sometimes valued more when they are pure, not tainted by self-interest, or even opposed to it.

her less confident about the pursuit of the relationship (she may think that her partner has lost interest), or, finally, in order to punish her partner. However, a purely self-interested agent is only forward-looking or "consequentialist." For her, therefore, punishing can aim only at showing the other that punishment will occur again if she fails again. If this partner does fail again later, however, the threat has not worked, and hence the punishment for showing a threat does not work. Therefore, the agent does not repeat it with the same intent anew. The other agent foresees this logical reasoning, and hence the threat is ineffective. The agent understands that, and hence she has no reason to threaten and to punish for this reason in the first place. Hence, this initial punishment is not performed. Then, however, the other, failing agent receives no message and has no reason to stop failing. Unless the agent gives less or not at all for the other noted reasons, either a lowering of the expected objectives of the self-interested sequential exchange, or the introduction of non-directly self-interested motives, such as punishment as retribution for failing to maintain what was considered an implicit arrangement. This may induce the failing agent to give again sufficiently. But this is no longer the effect of an action chosen as a punishment for a simply and strictly self-interested motive. Note that this reasoning is not affected by the idea that the failing and punished agent will abstain from the second failure because she would believe that "the same situation entails the same effect," because the situation is not the same since there has been the threat;[11] the reasoning can also be extended to the case in which there can be several successive punishments as a learning process for carrying the message of the threat.

However, if the punishment nevertheless occurs and is intended as a punishment (not just a reminder to draw

---

[11] For a finite process, the passing of time modifies the future prospects at each moment, and hence the conditions, but this often does not affect the noted effects.

attention), the defector can only conclude that the punisher is not rational in the sense of persuing her interest with all the required reasoning. This suffices for her to conclude that, a priori, this irrationality would again be manifested at the next defection and result in the same punishment. Hence, punishing in order to show a threat and deterring from future defection can work in the end. This is a case in which, from the point of view of the punisher's interest, it is rational to be irrational. This irrationality can have several causes, with the possibility that several of them might be present jointly. The punisher may not perform the computation noted above – this is a rationality and interest of dumbness. She may assume that the other does not do her part of the assumed reasoning – an advantage of assuming that the other party is dumb. Or, again, the punisher's motives are not only her self-interest, she is not only consequentialist, she is moved or also moved by motives such as revenge for not being treated as expected, or a sense of duty to punish someone who breaks an implicit contract, or a moral principle of promise keeping for carrying out the threat (even though this is not a promise of something agreeable) – at least, it suffices that the other believes that she has such motives. This is one of the various cases in which self-interest is best served by not solely pursuing it.

The simplest case is that of the last action favouring the other person at some cost for oneself. It cannot be motivated by self-interest. Hence, it will not exist if self-interest is the only motive. However, if there is no last action, there can only be no action at all. Hence this process cannot exist. Or else it should last indefinitely. But you don't need a Keynes to tell you that in the infinitely long run, we shall all be dead – even meta-individual institutions such as nations, governments or firms. In fact, both agents can foresee that any considered last action will not take place, hence that the last but one, becoming the last, will not occur either, and so on, and they do not begin or they stop. This is sometimes also described by the complicated mental process of "backward induction."

That is, the agent who would be last but one foresees that the would-be last one will not act in fact, and hence she will not perform the last but one action either; the would-be last one guesses this rational thinking of the other, and deduces that she will not take the previous step either; this is understood by the other; and so on; and hence no one acts in the first place.[12] Actually, however, sequential reasonings of this type are not made beyond two or three steps – a case of "bounded rationality." What exists in people's mind in this respect is "unknowledge" (absence of knowledge, which is not uncertainty which refers to a clear and conscious lack of certainty between rather well-defined possibilities). It can work here as uncertainty, however, and the uncertainty of one agent (at least) about the end of the process or about the other's behaviour can suffice for sustaining the existence of the process.[13] Another solution is a binding contract with an enforced last move, but this is another type of situation and it may not be possible. And an unconditional imposition by force of the last move pushes back the problem to the last but one, and so on. Finally, the only other solution is that the last action would be provided for another motive. It would be a gift. If it is a simple unconditional gift, however, the same question as before is raised for the previous actions, which will not be provided. Hence, this last action has to be motivationally conditional on the previous actions. That is, it would be a move of a genuine reciprocity. This cannot be liking reciprocity or gratitude, however, because this return gift should then react to a previous liking or to a benevolent gift it induces. Hence, the motive should be balance or matching reciprocity (for instance, there should be the same number of actions favourable to the other person from each side, or

---

[12] See, notably, Peter Hammond (1975) and Mordechai Kurz (1978a, 1978b), whose description delights thus in showing that "altruism" is in fact self-interested.

[13] See Basu (1977), Radner (1980), Smale (1980), Kreps, Milgrom, Roberts and Wilson (1982), and Axelrod (1984).

some equivalence in value). Nevertheless, if such motives exist, there is no reason why they should not exist during previous actions. Then, some liking may also be present before the end. The process is in fact actual reciprocity, including self-interested motives as usual. Note that the non-strictly self-interested last move requires this motivation for the last actor only; hence one actor only needs to have this motivation and behaviour; the other can remain strictly self-interested. Finally, it is remarkable that sequential exchange can exist only if there is uncertainty, irrationality, or non-self-interested reciprocity. However, mechanics also tells us that there would be no walking without friction.

4

Forms and structures of reciprocity

4.1 Facts and relations

Reciprocity takes a variety of forms which are more or less close to or distant from the core meaning of the concept. It consists of relations between facts such as actions, sentiments, attitudes or judgments, each belonging to one person and concerning another or others, that are directly related by motivations. In standard cases, these facts concern two agents, they are from one to the other and vice versa. In extensions of the concept, however, only one person is concerned in the two facts, or both original agents are replaced by two different ones (as explained shortly). The agents are often individuals, but they can also be groups or institutions of various kinds. The various cases depend on the nature of these facts and people, on the structure of the relationship and the number of people and of facts involved, and – most essentially – on the types of motives that induce the relation.

These facts can be of various natures. They can be actions favourable to the other person, as with the basic gift/return-gift relation, or unfavourable to the other, as with revenge (and retaliation for deterrence). There are also reciprocities of sentiments, as with liking people who like you (explained in chapter 7). There are reciprocities of attitudes, which are induced by sentiments or reasons and may denote propensity to action. You can, for instance, be benevolent, kind, polite, fair, hostile, rude, unfair, and so on, towards people who display a similar attitude towards you, or possibly towards others, or again only because yet other people have manifested such an attitude towards you. Reciprocity can also apply to judgment, to saying something about someone, and so on.

The facts the relation between which constitutes the reciprocity must have something in common in their nature and in some concept of their intensity. These relations depend on the specific motives of the reciprocity (balance, liking, or continuation) and on the particular application. The natures of the related facts should have something in common, but they may have to be more or less similar according to the case. For instance, sometimes the facts have to be of the same nature, while in other cases it is sufficient that they are all favourable or all unfavourable. The "intensities" of the acts or sentiments are also related in various ways. Some sort of equality in intensity is often directly favoured with matching reciprocities motivated by comparison and balance, while other motives lead to different relations – with generally the same sense of variation – or indirectly to some sort of equality (the relation in the case of sequential exchanges has been noted – give enough for the desired continuation but no more than is needed for it).

4.2 Reciprocal structures

4.2.1 Basic structure

The structure of the relations between the oriented facts (each from one person towards another) and the number of people and facts involved depend first of all on two dichotomies: there are two facts or more, and there are two people or more. Let us denote the different people involved as A, B, C, etc., and a fact of person A towards person B as $A \to B$ (A gives to, likes, favours, hurts, is fair or kind to, praises, etc. B). The influence between facts is that one elicits the other. With just two people and two facts, the only case is $A \rightarrow B$ elicits $B \rightarrow A$. The gift/return-gift relationship is such a case, as are liking people who like you, returning benevolence, kindness or fairness, and, on the dark side, revenge. The theory of reciprocity will show how this relation is sometimes associated with the converse one, $B \rightarrow A$ elicits $A \rightarrow B$, in various possible ways (chapter 22). There are also cases of longer sequences of motivationally related givings between the two agents A and B. In fact, the most typical reciprocities are of this type. Each act can be influenced by several past acts in either direction, and possibly by expected ones. Thus, there can be a dynamics and equilibria of the relation. A set or a sequence of such elementary acts in one direction can also be considered to be one act of giving.

4.2.2 *Extended reciprocities*

There are also cases of "extended reciprocity" in which more than two actors are involved. They are of various possible types. With only two acts, $A \rightarrow B$ can elicit $B \rightarrow C$, or $C \rightarrow A$, or $C \rightarrow D$. The former ($B \rightarrow C$) is called "generalized reciprocity" and the second ($C \rightarrow A$) is "reverse reciprocity." The basic question, of course, is the motivation of the second act – whatever it is – in relation to the former. Several types of cases have to be distinguished. They depend on the relation between the agents who change from one act to the second, or on the absence of such a relation.

With the closest relation, a receiver is replaced by someone she likes or a giver is replaced by someone who likes her: the second act $B \rightarrow C$ can be motivated by the fact that the initial giver or offender A likes the new beneficiary or victim C; the second act $C \rightarrow A$ can be motivated by the fact that the new actor C likes the initial receiver B; and the second act $C \rightarrow D$ can be motivated by the fact that the new actor C likes the initial receiver B and the initial actor A likes the new receiver D.

In another type of case, possibly associated with the former, the participants consider the relevant actors or objects of the act to be in fact social groups: one person is considered as receiving or giving for the groups she belongs to and, possibly, represents (as with inter-clan *vendetta* for revenge).[1] If (AB) denotes the group of persons A and B, the three cases are in fact seen by the deciding participants as $(AC) \rightarrow B$ elicits $B \rightarrow (AC)$, $A \rightarrow (BC)$ elicits $(BC) \rightarrow A$, and $(AD) \rightarrow (BC)$ elicits $(BC) \rightarrow (AD)$. Moreover, the relevant groups usually encompass a larger number of people than the two directly involved in a specific case. Then, the scope and size of these groups, hence the set of persons who are the potential objectives of actions or actors of an extended reciprocity, constitute an essential issue. In the limiting case opposed to that of simple reciprocity, this is a relation between one individual and all the others, or society as a whole.

In all cases all the basic reciprocitarian motives can be at work, that is, liking, balance, or inducing continuation, singly or in association with others, with all the more specific motives such as gratitude, moral indebtedness, deservingness and merit, imitation and conforming, and so on. However, particular aspects of or reasons for these motives are emphasized in each structure, and the various types of extended reciprocities are quite different in this respect.

4.2.3 Generalized and general reciprocity

The cases in which $A \rightarrow B$ elicits $B \rightarrow C$ constitute *generalized reciprocity* (or *generalized reciprocation* to include cases of harmful acts). Examples are the noted famous *helping behaviour*, or the fact that people tend to treat their children as they were treated by their parents. When the reason is that person B sees persons A and C as belonging to the same relevant group, and this group extends in fact to all other people in the society under consideration – possibly the "generalized other" of G. H. Mead –, or, even, is seen as "society as

---

[1] *Vendetta* is the Corsican term (see, for instance, the beautiful short novel *Colomba* by Prosper Mérimée for a very perceptive rendering of the relations, rationales and sentiments involved).

a whole," the case is *general reciprocity*. Generalized reciprocity consists of a "transfer of reciprocity" (from A to C, for B), and general reciprocity results from a "generalization of reciprocity" (from A to the group, for B). Sentiments and relations of general reciprocity between a person and a community she belongs to constitute a very important element of a sense of community (which can also rest on a common culture or history, common interest, neighbourhood, kinship, and so on). The largest general reciprocity extends to all mankind and is not inexistent. A specific generalized reciprocity is a result of general reciprocity when person C is helped by the reciprocating person B because she is a member of the relevant group. However, general reciprocity can take two polar forms and be any combination of them. In one type, the reciprocal attitude is a general helpfulness or kindness, a general tendency to aid others and, possibly, to like them. In the second case, the sentiment and attitude is more focused towards the group itself, with a propensity to make efforts or incur sacrifices on its behalf, from sentiments of duty or of liking (as with nationalism, for instance, or analogous sentiments with a large variety of other social entities – down to the lineage and the extended family who can have "honour," in some cultures).

4.2.4 Reverse reciprocity and the Descartes effect

Reverse reciprocity, in which $A \rightarrow B$ elicits $C \rightarrow A$, is the case formally opposed to generalized reciprocity ($A \rightarrow B$ elicits $B \rightarrow C$), and it extends more generally to *reverse reciprocation*. The philosopher René Descartes regarded this favouring favourable people to be an important social fact, and Adam Smith emphasizes this idea in almost the same terms.[2]

---

[2] Descartes, *Works*, IV, and Adam Smith, *The Theory of Moral Sentiments*, part VI, section 2, chapter 1. Both Descartes and Smith, and also Bentham, even thought that the initial giver will gain in the end, in terms of her

The reasons for reverse reciprocity are found in all types of reasons for reciprocity in general, but in a particular application which is partial and dim for the most typical motives, liking and balance. The standard motives for person C giving to person A who has given to person B have two faces. First, person A's generosity classifies her as a good person, notably in the field of giving and helping, and this is in itself favourable to helping her. Second, person A's good action can be thought of as deserving a reward, and person C volunteers to provide it. Person C's gift also has an aspect of compensatory justice concerning person A. Person C's gift can also be intended to induce person A to give again – the continuation motive. However, if receiving such a gift becomes person A's motivation, she is no longer generous and a priori deserving, and these possible motives for giving to her disappear (the generous person becomes person C who helps person B through person A's self-interested gift). Of course, if a priori person C particularly likes person B, her giving to person A may simply be a substitution to a return gift of person B, for all possible motives.

Finally, there is also a reverse negative reciprocation, but, as usual, for motives of balance or justice but not of disliking: if person A hurts person B, person C may want to punish person A, or avenge person B, or deter person A from doing it again, in hurting person A (but she does not hurt simply because she dislikes person A for her conduct).

4.2.5 Chain reciprocities

Generalized reciprocities and, much more rarely, reverse reciprocities, may induce chain reciprocities $A \to B \to C \to D \ldots$ in which each relation is induced by one or several

---

self-interest, from the whole process (she finally receives more than she gives). She may, therefore, have this non-altruistic objective. However, the other people may not give to her if they are aware of this motive (see the discussion in Kolm 1984a).

others. The chain can be finite, open-ended at either side or both, or closed (coming back to *A*). A gift in a chain reciprocity can be motivated by the generalized reciprocity of a gift received by the giver, by the reverse reciprocity of a gift provided by the receiver, or by both. The influence can even be more general, with gifts influenced simply by the existence of the whole chain they are a part of (this can for instance be seen as a tradition). A gift can react to a gift in present time, or in the past in a delayed reciprocity, or expected in the future in an anticipated reciprocity. All cases of reciprocity combining the motives – balance, liking, continuation –, the structures – direct, generalized, reverse – and the timing – present, delayed, anticipated – can be found.

4.2.6 The case of intergenerational reciprocities

Reciprocities among generations provide the best examples. They can more or less apply in two domains: for support and transfers within families; and for approving, supporting, or accepting pay-as-you-go pension systems and public education implemented by public finance. In the following, the terms "children" and "parents" of someone will mean the generation of the children and of the parents in the case of the financing of public finance.

A person then helps her children and her ageing parents. This makes six types of reciprocities, two direct ones and four chain reciprocities, with both delays and anticipations, and, for chain reciprocities, both generalized and reverse reciprocities, as indicated below.

I   – Self aids children, given that:
  1) children will aid self: direct, anticipated,
  2) children will aid grandchildren: reverse chain, anticipated,
  3) parents have aided self: generalized chain, delayed.

II — Self aids parents, given that:
  1) parents have aided self: direct, delayed,
  2) parents have aided grandparents: reverse chain, delayed,
  3) children will aid self: generalized chain, anticipated.

4.2.7 Why extended reciprocities?

Reciprocity is explained in full in the coming chapters. All the psychological mechanisms of its causes and reasons are presented, for the various types of reciprocity. The same broad types also a priori explain extended reciprocities: balance reciprocity, with its possible dimension of fairness; liking reciprocity, which is liking the benevolent giver or direct reciprocal liking; gratitude; continuation reciprocity, which can largely be strictly self-interested; and also imitation. However, there are important differences due to the fact that some mechanisms that play an important role in the various reciprocities are absent in extended reciprocities, either because of the substitutions of people, or because "the group" or "society" is a priori not an individual person comparable with oneself, endowed with a specific will, intention, responsibility, and capacity to like.

In generalized reciprocity, having been helped induces you to help someone else. This establishes some balance between you and the group of others, but this does not also provide a balance for each of these other people. You are not being fair towards any of them. Having been benevolently helped or given to may induce in you some liking for other people in general. This may favour your giving to some other. Nevertheless, this other person has a priori no affection for you and is not responsible for the benefit you received, and hence you are not likely to like her as you like your initial benefactor. The transfer of the reciprocal relation lowers the intensity of the sentiment, and more or less changes its nature. Moreover, an important cause of direct reciprocal liking (liking the liker) does not work for generalized reciprocity. This is the largely involuntary process that makes you like more someone who likes you more – through the creation and allocation of attention and affects – because you benefit more from being liked more by people you like more, notably because this sentiment towards you fosters more your sense of self and of social existence.[3] Finally, helping someone other than the initial benefactor does not a priori induce the latter to reiterate.

Reverse reciprocity can restore some balance in the initial giver's situation. It rewards her merit. It may be fair towards her. Yet, there is no individual balance for the other participants. Someone who benevolently helps others and likes them may be likeable as a good person and be helped or given to for this reason, but the main mechanisms of liking reciprocity, giving in return as a result of liking the benevolent giver to oneself or directly the liker of oneself, are absent. Finally, helping someone who helps someone else may induce her to help again, but not a priori the rewarder who, therefore, cannot give for the sake of her self-interest.

General reciprocity differs most from generalized reciprocity when the person's sentiment is directed towards the group of others, society, the collectivity or the community, for the society in question. She may have benefited from help or liking received from other people in general, from some specific others whom she considers to be representative of the group or social entity, or from institutions of the society. The return actions may aim at benefiting society in general, or they may help specific others because they are members of this society. A general sentiment of indebtedness towards society, leading to pro-social actions paying one's due in some sense, is rather common. This general matching reciprocity is a basic bond relating individuals to their group or society. We will see its role, for instance, in the relations between citizens and public finance. However, it differs

---

[3] See chapters 7 and 19.

in various ways from matching reciprocity between individuals. The balance is generally a vague concept, without the more or less precise comparison that is sometimes the case in ordinary reciprocities.[4] Fairness towards society or the group is seen as inadequate when the ultimate values are seen as referring to individuals. For the same reason, one can hardly conceive of merit or deservingness of the society. Moreover, one usually cannot compare an individual and a society or a group. Gratitude or resentment towards society as a whole are also not uncommon sentiments. This corresponds to the notion that society has some responsibility for one's situation being good or bad. However, this use of the concept of responsibility is particular because this effect may not result from a clear action. Affection for a social entity, or more or less a priori liking other people – two very different sentiments – are also usual and lead to pro-social actions. This may be fostered by having benefited from benevolent favours from "society," its institutions, or its members. However, if there is not a clear and direct will and responsibility for benefiting the person, her liking the benefactor entity as a result is only of a milder and inferior kind. Moreover, if you are only a rather anonymous member of the society, you are hardly liked by society or its institutions even if they are favourable to you. Hence, liking them (largely involuntarily) because you benefit more from being liked by someone you like – a central mechanism of reciprocal liking – has a priori no place here. In addition, "society" hardly likes to be liked by you and does not help you for this purpose – although political rulers use institutions precisely in this way when expecting liking, gratitude and moral indebtedness that will induce your vote or support. Finally, although a social atmosphere of benevolence

---

[4] This is not always the case, though. In various societies there is a careful accounting of individuals' voluntary contributions to the group (for example in the awards of public honours in our societies, or in the representation of pigs given in collective feasts by the wooden pieces of the chest necklace of Papuan highlanders).

(or its opposite) is bound to influence individuals and favour sentiments and acts in the same mood, this differs from the direct imitation of other individuals.

In addition to the basic reciprocitarian motives of balance (including fairness) and induced liking, there is the reciprocitarian form of inducing repetition and continuation – notably from a motive of self-interest. A priori, this does not work in a generalized reciprocity in which the beneficiary of the return gift is not the initial giver – unless the initial giver wishes to favour the beneficiary of the return gift. Moreover, in a general reciprocity the information that a particular individual gives in return tends to be lost. However, there are general continuation reciprocities with rewards for pro-social acts or for contributions to the collectivity, provided by institutions or otherwise. Finally, giving in return to a giver to induce another gift can have this effect on onlookers expecting such a reward as well as on the initial giver. Hence, this can be a reason for a reverse reciprocity as well as for a direct one in the next round (the expected reiteration then is a gift to the new giver and not to the initial giver), with the following logic. An onlooker C who sees that $A \rightarrow B$ induces $B \rightarrow A$ can give $C \rightarrow B$ in the expectation that this will similarly induce $B \rightarrow C$. Then, this $C \rightarrow B$ appears in a sense as a reverse reciprocity to the return-gift $B \rightarrow A$. Individual B may thus give in return $B \rightarrow A$ not – or not only – for eliciting another $A \rightarrow B$, but – or but also – for eliciting this gift $C \rightarrow B$. Moreover, if individual C thinks that any $A \rightarrow B$ is motivated by A's desire to establish a sequential exchange, this may induce her to establish such a relation with A in giving $C \rightarrow A$, which appears as a reverse reciprocity to this $A \rightarrow B$.

Imitation, and doing what "is done" and proper to do, commonly play a role in giving and helping, and watching help can constitute a reminder of the duty to help. $A \rightarrow B$ can thus induce $C \rightarrow D$. If the identity of the beneficiary of the act is included in the object of such an imitation, then $A \rightarrow B$ induces $C \rightarrow B$. Another fact has the reverse effect: the beneficiary is also a particularly close watcher of the act, and this is favourable to her imitating it; thus, $A \to B$ induces $B \to C$. Moreover, the initial actor is, for the beneficiary, readily available for the reciprocation and, thus, $A \to B$ tends to induce $B \to A$.

4.3   Larger reciprocities

Reciprocities also often involve larger numbers of facts or people. The most standard concept of reciprocity in social science does not, in fact, refer to an individual's *reaction*, but to a steady *relation* between people or groups, with a rather large number of acts favourable to the other or to others. For instance, individuals or groups give to others or work for them in turn, or they provide others with their particular type of products or services, or each is aided by others when she particularly needs help and aids others when they need help, or each shares with others exceptional benefits she receives. This can happen between two people or groups or between a larger number of them. This relationship can consist of many types of transfers or services provided as a series of gifts in reciprocity rather than as elements of an exchange (in the strict, strictly self-interested sense of exchange defined above). They can be services to the community provided in turn (chores, work, watching over, organizing festivities, and so on), a division of labour, mutual "insurance" against particular needs the nature of which arouses more benevolent motives than the exchange of commercial insurance does, the sharing of the product of hunting or crops favoured by chance, aid for exceptional building, providing wives to other groups, and so on. One recognizes here the very stuff of social life in groups or communities, such as in durable dyads, families, village societies, many associations, the workplace, as well as, for a part, larger communities, and general sociality.

In such steady relations of reciprocity, each transfer or service is jointly a return gift of past or anticipated others, and

a gift that will initiate others as return gifts in the future or
the previous anticipation of which has elicited other gifts
in the past. When there are more than two people, the process generally also includes generalized and general reciprocities, reverse reciprocities, and various chain reciprocities.
Of course, a single action can result from several motives
intervening jointly, often in a more or less dim or instinctive way. The essential difference with exchange (in the strict
sense) concerns the motivations, and, from them, the attitudes towards other people and the types of social relations
that go with them, but this will also induce a difference
in the acts and transfers performed towards others. Each of
these transfers or services is first of all a voluntary free gift.
There is no explicit or implicit binding contract. Nevertheless, a number of motives different from those that induce
this giving can also be present, although the free giving gives
the relation its particular nature. Self-interest in the benefit of
gifts, aid or services is generally present. Indeed, apart from
exclusively symbolic or relational gifts, a gift should have
some value and some cost, in terms of self-interest, for the
receiver and the giver respectively. However, being helped or
given to in the future can be one of the reasons for giving or
helping. That is, the relation may also be, in part, a sequential exchange as described above. By definition, though, this
is not the only motive. In particular, the quality of the social
relation is very important. It results from mutual voluntary
caring for one another, common appreciation of the facts,
results and processes of giving and receiving, at least some
mutual affection, a sense of balance and fairness in the gifts
or services yielded and received – which is less important
the larger the affection is –, and sometimes the festive aspect
of the interaction.

In limiting cases, the relational values are the main or
only thing, for the interchange in itself or its symbolic
value. This is shown in particular when people give each
other the same gifts they could use for themselves, as with
successive treats of drinks, meals, entertainments or feasts.

Durable gifts, notably reciprocal ones, are often valued only as reminders or symbols of the relationship. An external, purely "behaviourist" observer could hardly explain why people mutually transfer to each other identical wedding rings. But, of course, all the motives proper to reciprocity can be present, hence not only mutual liking and a collective high mood but also duty and a sense of fairness, moral obligation or indebtedness, the relevant equality or balances (which may be strict equality or according to need, means or merit), and social opinion, reputation, maintaining or acquiring status, and social pressure of all types.

The use of money or its absence is sometimes relevant. Money is not characteristic of exchange (in the strict sense) since barter – that is, moneyless exchange – does not use it. Gifts may be in money, for helping or sharing, notably in reciprocities. However, the giver means more if she chooses specific goods or services. This sometimes means that she cares for the specific desires and tastes of the receiver, or else the nature of the gift obeys a custom or a norm. In both cases, this is bound to make for a stronger social bond (norms that have not degenerated into mere routine are rich in meaning). The receiver can a priori sell the gift in turn, if this is materially possible, but often she ought not to because this would impair the relational value.

4.4 Reciprocity as social or economic system

Reciprocity is also the name of a social system, and in particular of an economic system. It has become usual, in particular after Karl Polanyi,[5] to distinguish three types of economic systems: exchange, redistribution and reciprocity. Exchange refers notably to market exchange. Redistribution consists in a political central power taking products and redistributing them, or deciding allocations of goods and services. In modern times, this describes the public sector (and possibly,

---

[5] *The Great Transformation* (1944).

when extended to most of the economy, central planning). The third system is reciprocity as a set of interrelated givings. Of course, the actual economies of whole societies are *regimes* which encompass these three pure *systems* in various proportions. These systems are thus more generally modes of transfers of goods or services: exchange, force and reciprocity. The various relevant properties or aspects of these modes will be compared in chapter 10. Their relative importance in a society constitutes an essential feature of this society. They can be measured by the proportion of goods or services transferred using each mode. Of course, such measures require many specifications of what is taken into account and what is not. They can nevertheless be very interesting for comparing societies and studying their evolution. These proportions can in particular be represented in a triangular diagram by a point in an isosceles triangle with these proportions as the distance to each of the three sides. This is sometimes quite enlightening for comparing economies and representing their evolution. Clusters of points show economies of the same type in this respect. Some show economies with a dominant system (points close to the corresponding summit).[6]

Finally, Marcel Mauss, whose *Essay on the Gift* (1924) durably shook social science and launched its analysis of giving and reciprocity, dubbed giving and reciprocity a "total social fact." Although Mauss emphasized the great ceremonial givings and return givings of traditional societies, this characterization also often applies to more modest levels of reciprocity, given the variety of relations and motives that can be involved (as pointed out in chapter 3, section 3.2).

---

[6] Discussion, development and application of this analysis can be found in Kolm 1984a, chapter 1.

4.5 Reciprocity, revenge, reciprocation

Favouring and harming give rise to actions and sentiments with symmetrical counterparts, to some extent. We thus have: gift or favour *versus* harm; return giving for maintaining some balance *versus* revenge; gratitude *versus* resentment; liking benevolent givers *versus* disliking responsible harmers; moral indebtedness *versus* vengefulness; and rewarding giving for eliciting another *versus* retaliation for deterrence. The grand tradition of social science restricts the term reciprocity to the case of gifts or favours.[7] This is natural since it wants to explain a more or less extended social system of transfers of goods and services, the social bond, the primary integrative forces of society, with sometimes an emphasis on the intrinsic values of social relations. Revenge is of limited relevance in this respect (and punishment as purposeful harm by society not for deterrence only is another topic – although it is a case of general reverse balance reciprocation). Moreover, as soon as the facts are observed with a minimum of perceptiveness and precision, the symmetry crumbles and the parallel appears to be only very superficial, approximate, and rather misleading. The structures turn out to be basically different, and essential phenomena, sentiments and relations on each side have no counterpart on the other.

This appears for all three pure motives for reciprocity (see chapter 5).

The self-interested return gift which rewards giving in order to receive another gift resembles retaliation for harm incurred, as a punishment in order to deter further harm. In both cases, the reaction is self-interested (or it is made by a third party who wants to favour the future beneficiary or victim), it is favourable or harmful according as to whether the action is favourable or harmful, and it intends to show

---

[7] The expression "negative reciprocity" has occasionally been used. However, its most famous use is by Marshall Sahlins who basically uses it for fighting.

and prove an intention and willingness to be repeated if the action is repeated (since, in the case of giving, it assumes that this reward will induce another act of giving to obtain another reward). In both cases, the reaction can also be a message to third parties, for inducing them to give or deterring them from harming. However, the return act intends to induce similar acts in the positive case, and to stop similar acts in the negative case. Consequently, the effects are formally the opposite. Rewarding giving to receive another gift develops into a sequence of givings (the initial giver gives again to receive again). This sequence should even be a priori considered endless if this motive is the only one, that is, it should be a pure sequential exchange (see the analysis of this process in section 3.3). In contrast, successful retaliation for deterrence is only one-shot. However, the situation after retaliation can also be seen as becoming a type of positive reciprocity, a positive reciprocity of restraint, characteristic of armed peace: the retaliation has shown the possibility, capacity and willingness to hurt back, and, then, the "gift" of not hurting is rewarded by the return gift of not hurting back, with continuation as in a sequential exchange. However, if hurting provides an advantage of any kind to the offender (as with stealing, for instance, or avoiding the inconvenience or cost of taking care not to harm or hurt the other as a side effect of some desired action – in the appropriate circumstances –, or pure malice), and if hurting back is costly to any extent for the other person, the issue of the last restraint is raised as with the last gift of a sequential exchange, with similar theoretical detrimental effects on the whole relation, and similar solutions (uncertainty about duration or about the other agent's behaviour, or other motivations inducing respect – but, then, these motives should also have existed before). Finally, since retaliation is punishment for not respecting peace, the logic of punishment discussed above also applies to retaliation (a difference is that retaliating may be costly whereas punishing in giving less is in itself beneficial).

The motives that lead to reciprocating for establishing or restoring a balance are also superficially parallel but quite different in reciprocity and in negative reciprocation. The possible embarrassment of being "morally indebted" for having received a gift or a favour is usually much milder than the possible anger, humiliation (or shame) that may lead one to hurt back. Anger for being morally forced to give in return is much more rare and indirect. Furthermore, the instinctual hitting back has no proper equivalent in giving (except, perhaps, in smiling back in many cultures, but this usually entails no cost).

The superficial similarity and deep difference in the result are the most pronounced for the effects of liking and disliking (and love and hate). You tend to like people who benevolently give to you and to dislike people responsible for harm you incur, especially if harming you and your resulting suffering is their final, vicious objective. Note that there is already only an imperfect symmetry, and that such vicious harming is rarer than giving to favour the receiver as a final objective (because simply disliking someone induces less enjoying what is bad for her than liking makes one enjoy what is good for her, and it induces even less causing this harm, as we will soon see). A parallel can also be made between resentment and gratitude, and resentment is favourable to disliking the person who is the object of it, as gratitude is favourable to liking (however, for a reason shortly to be pointed out, there is no harming for the purpose of showing resentment – and disliking – as there is giving in order to show and prove gratitude, and when there is harming in such a situation it rather comes from a motive of revenge and balance stemming from an initial previous harming). Now, liking someone who gives to you can induce you to provide a return gift, since liking someone implies liking what is good for her, and generally her satisfaction, pleasure or happiness. Disliking someone may similarly lead one to like the misfortunes or pain she endures. If the disliking comes from having been hurt, this satisfaction is revealed by expressions such as "it serves her right" which, however, refers to a concept of balance. However, liking what is bad for people whom one dislikes is in itself bound to be much more restricted than the converse liking what is good for the people one likes, except in the strong case of hatred. Relatedly, *schadenfreude* in general is usually considered a morally condemnable sentiment, and this may tend to limit its extent and its effects.

The main difference, however, lies in the next step. Enjoying things favourable to people one likes can lead one to create such things by favouring or giving. In contrast, if you dislike someone and – perhaps reluctantly – like her pain or misfortune, this usually does not in itself lead you to endorse responsibility for creating this pain or any other bad situation for her. Such conduct would rather be abnormal. Inflicting pain for the pleasure of it – sadistic conduct – is a pathology. However, this no longer tends to be the case in the strong case of hatred, but here the sentiment tends to have an aspect of revenge, with a close relation to the harm received in the first place. Moreover, you tend to give because this shows and proves your liking, which enhances the other person's liking of you – something you appreciate because you like her. There is no symmetrical hurting just for showing your disliking. This hurting may elicit or increase the other person's disliking you, but you are often indifferent towards this sentiment, or you may evaluate it any way. Finally, liking someone directly because she likes you – the essential "reciprocal liking" that will be explained in chapter 7 – has no real counterpart: you certainly do not dislike someone because she dislikes you, at least to the same extent (this disliking may puzzle or trouble you, or be disagreable because it affects you ego, and attract your attention or make you try to neglect or ignore it, but these are other matters).

Yet another difference is that punishing harmful actions is more easily socialized (and institutionalized) than rewarding free favourable ones. There are other differences, and, when closely looked at, all the items of the symmetry in fact have notable differences and the symmetry appears to be only a rough and rather superficial approximation.

Reciprocity is at the intersection of two fields of social conduct. Return giving – the elementary reciprocity – is both giving and return. It is a case of giving, along with giving of other types and origins. It is also a case of reciprocation, along with revenge and retaliation. We have just seen the asymmetries between positive and negative reciprocation – reciprocating good or bad. There are also common structures, however, and part of the theory of reciprocity developed below also applies to revenge and retaliation. Nevertheless, our topic will be reciprocity, with only occasional remarks about other reciprocation, essentially because – without neglecting the role of revenge in human affairs – reciprocity is much more important, since it constitutes the basic structure of the social bond and covers the whole field between the joint interest of exchange and the other-oriented attitudes of all kinds. Reciprocity is also present and sometimes essential in various parts of the economy (and it even constitutes a classical type of economic system by itself).

Part II

Motives

5

The three worlds of reciprocity

5.1 Three basic reasons

If you look attentively within yourself, or draw on your synthesis of the thousands of relevant experiences you have incurred and felt, watched and understood in others, or been told about and explained, during the decades of your life, you see that being favoured by someone – say receiving a gift – can elicit a large number of various sentiments. But you also see that providing a return gift can result only from a much smaller number of types of sentiments, albeit ones that are very different from each other (and which can be present jointly or not).

Indeed, the most important thing about reciprocity is its motives. And the most important thing about the motives of reciprocity is that they belong to three fully different classes, which can be labelled a sense of *propriety*, induced *liking*, and seeking *interest*. The third motive consists only in giving in return in order to elicit another gift, and, in fact, is barely worth the label "reciprocity." The second type of motives rests on sentiments of induced mutual liking between the partners. The motives of the first type rest on a sense of social balance and include particular types of fairness. The motives of propriety or fairness and of liking have sub-motives of different kinds. The various motives and sub-motives can more or less be jointly present.

Very briefly, in *comparative, matching, compensatory,* or *balance reciprocity,* your return giving or favour aims at establishing some balance between what you benefited from and what you provide in return. It "evens out" some inequality in the relation. You think that you ought to do this, that this is the proper thing to do, and you often feel you have a kind of moral debt towards the initial actor as long as you have not "paid your debt" by this return action.

In a second case – call it *liking reciprocity* –, your providing a return gift or favour results from your liking the initial benefactor. This liking can itself result from two kinds of reasons. On the one hand, you like a giver whose final objective in giving to you is your good as you see it, which can happen from the various advantages you receive from the giving: the gift or favour itself, the appreciative and kind attention towards you which supports your sense of self and of social existence, and possibly the very process of receiving the gift. On the other hand, if the giver likes you, you tend to like her for this very fact as it is kind and appreciative attention towards you with the effects just noted, especially insofar as she can be held responsible for this sentiment. Then, the gift has (also) the effect of revealing, showing, and proving the giver's liking. Moreover, since the giver knows this, she tends to give for this very demonstration effect because she likes to be liked, particularly by people she likes. Such an informational giving, then, is not altruistic, and yet it nevertheless does show and prove the liking, and this in fact is its intention. Moreover, being given to with the final purpose of favouring you, and being liked, both elicit gratitude, which in turn favours liking the giver and the liker, and may also elicit giving as a "proof" of gratitude. These effects are considered at greater length below.

In the third case – call it *continuation reciprocity* – the return gift is a reward intended to induce another gift. This assumes that this latter gift will be motivated by the expectation of another similar reward, which – with the same

motives – can be given only to induce still another gift, and
so on. Hence, the agents logically should foresee the full
sequence of an iterative exchange. The motives may be anything appreciated in receiving the gift. This may simply be the
item received (as in the standard sequential exchange), but
one may also appreciate the mere attention of being given
to (favourable to one's sense of self and social existence), a
certain status derived from the relationship, and the relation
in itself or the very process of receiving. Pure interest can
be a motive of (apparent) reciprocity only in this way. However, motives of the other two types – liking and balance –
can also be present in addition. The two parties may have
different reasons for appreciating each act of giving. Their
expectation of the whole sequence is implicit in and implied
by their choice, although it is generally not clear in their mind
(as we have seen, this sequence has to be infinite, or else with
uncertainty about the end or the other agent, or it can be associated with reciprocitarian sentiments of the two other types
which can put an end to a sequence of gifts). Moreover, such
a return gift may be provided as a reward for inducing third
persons to give to the giver with the intention to also receive
a corresponding reward.

Revenge is akin to balance reciprocity and retaliation for
deterrence to continuation reciprocity – the differences have
been pointed out.

In addition to these motives aroused by effects or causes
of the initial gift that specifically concern the receiver, the
latter's reaction can also be motivated by judgments about
the initial gift or harm that do not depend on who benefits
or suffers from it (as is the case for the general motives of
reverse reciprocity or reciprocation). She can thus notably
in general reward merit, like good people, induce to pursue
the relation, punish for a reason of deserts and retributive
justice or of deterrence, and also imitate and conform, and
she applies these motives, in particular, to the gift or harm
of which she happens to be the beneficiary or victim. These

motives are usually much less intense than those induced by being the beneficiary or the victim of the action, but they can have a social importance because they can reflect the opinion of many people, who, therefore, judge the return action favourably, and the receiver may be sensitive to their opinion. All these various types of motives can be jointly present (either for favourable or for harming actions) in various possible proportions.

We will shortly analyse in detail the specific modalities, workings and reasons concerning these various motives, and the relations between them, but we should first emphasize that on the whole they belong to three very different regions of the mind in society.

5.2 An overview of the general structure

Thus there are three categories of reciprocitarian motives: *liking, comparative* (*matching, balance*), and inducing *continuation* which will be associated with *interest.*

There also are three kinds of dichotomies in the categories of motives: **pleasure** *from satisfying one's interest or that of people one likes* versus **duty** (or honour, norm, fairness); **altruism** versus sentiments based on the *interest or the social situation of the* **self**; and **self-interest** versus **socially oriented** *sentiments in altruism or comparison.* These classifications and remarks require some explanation shortly provided. They do not tell everything – one can also focus on the fields of manifestation of reciprocal conducts, or on the association of varied sentiments or motives. However, they seem to be indispensable to avoid confusion in the consideration of reciprocitarian and reciprocal conducts. They lead to the structure represented by figure 5.1.

A particular giving or favouring in return can be motivated by one or jointly by several of the noted relations. That is, its motives can be pure or mixed. Denoting the initial gift or favour as g, the return act as r, and the types of motives as

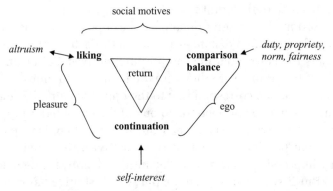

Figure 5.1 The three spheres of reciprocitarian motives

respectively *a* for *altruism, b* for *balance*, and *c* for *continuation*, the return act, determined by *g* and by these motives, can be written as the function

$$r = r(g; a, b, c).$$

These motives have different effects on the return act, and in particular on its relation with the initial gift or favour, denoted as *g*. For instance, balance alone directly tends to elicit some sort of equality between *r* and *g*. Continuation implies bounds on inequality, for an indirect reason: giving too little may not suffice for the inducement, while giving more than necessary for it is a waste. As for the effects of altruism, mutual likings often tend to be not too dissimilar and each can induce giving. However, a return gift induced by liking a benevolent giver tends to vary in the same direction as the initial gift (if relations of more and of less are defined), but with no a priori tendency to an equality.

Moreover, if, in a very rough and impressionistic but possibly suggestive way, one dares to express the relative importance of the three types of motives as proportions, the set of motives at work in a particular reciprocity can be represented by a point in the isosceles triangle represented in figure 5.1:

the distance of the point to each side roughly represents the proportion of the motive denoted at the opposite summit (the sum of these three distances is constant). Each summit represents the corresponding case of pure motives. Points on a side of the triangle are those at which one of the motives is absent (the one corresponding to the opposite summit), and hence each side corresponds to one of the considered properties of motives (pleasure, ego and social). Of course, apart from the possible absence of some motives, this device is only impressionistic since no "quantity" of motive is defined yet. But it sometimes has a qualitative illustrative value for analysing particular reciprocities or their evolution, for comparing them, and for analysing or comparing various groups of reciprocities, notably by the clustering or dispersion of the points.

However, these motives in fact interact. Some are incompatible and others mutually favourable, depending on the motives and on their intensity. For instance, love as very strong liking is not consistent with seeking balance in giving in return, and with attributing too much importance to one's self-interest in the relation. On the contrary, the milder liking of amity and moderate friendship is both favourable to the fairness of balance and favoured by it. As we have already suggested, compare the two dictums: "Good reckonings make good friends" and "Love counts for all," which means that love does not reckon the rest (in French: *L'amour ne compte pas*).

5.3   The graph of reciprocity

These motives, and a few other relevant ones, are analysed in the following chapters. The graph on figure 5.2 gathers the resulting effects in showing how the motives that can be induced by a gift in turn induce a return gift. The first three groups of relations correspond to the motives of balance, of

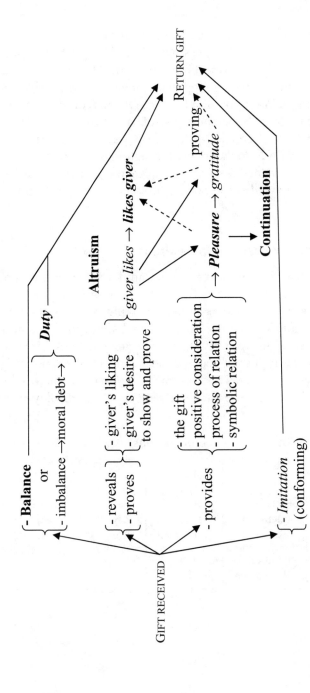

Figure 5.2 The logic of reciprocity

induced liking, and of seeking the continuation of pleasure. A fourth link shows the possible effect of imitation (which is also discussed later). Gratitude has a particular place because it is for the pleasure and appreciation (of various kinds) provided, it can induce both liking the giver and, directly, giving in return, and it also has an aspect of balance both as a "return sentiment" in itself and by the return gift it can directly support (in addition to this effect through liking). The places of moral indebtedness and of the informational roles of giving are noted, as well as the various reasons for liking to be given to.

5.4 The six basic reciprocations

If we now add "negative" or harmful reciprocations, the most conspicuous fact is the practical absence of negative parallels to reciprocities based on liking, because the tendency to dislike someone because she dislikes you, or to hurt someone because you dislike her, are generally absent (or, at least, without possible comparison with the corresponding "positive" sentiments and actions). This gives, on the whole, the six basic or pure types of reciprocations displayed in table 5.1.

Table 5.1 *The six pure reciprocations*

		interest	balance, matching	affects	
positive		sequential exchange	balance reciprocity	gift reciprocity from liking	reciprocal liking
negative		retaliation for deterrence	revenge	✕	✕

6

Balance reciprocity

6.1 The propriety of reciprocity

Balance reciprocity results from the urge or desire to reciprocate the gift or favour with a return gift or favour that has a certain relation of equality with the former, and, in some sense,
matches or compensates it. The balance sometimes takes the
form of pure tit-for-tat reciprocation; in limiting cases, the
reaction can be instinctive or almost so, with no conscious
motive. However, the answer is more often conscious and
weighed, sometimes carefully. Then, the action is pushed by
a sense of propriety or duty, rather than directly pulled by
desire – although one can always consider a desire to restore
a balance, and even speak trivially of a desire to act properly
or to do one's duty. The balance-reciprocal action is "deontic"
rather than "consequentialist" – although this motive induces
one to want consequences of one's act, namely the resulting
balance and even, one can say, to have behaved properly or
morally, and it is often also supported by a desire for social
approval (or non-disapproval). At any rate, the motives for
balance reciprocity are thoroughly different from those of
other reciprocities: they have nothing to do either with liking
or – consciously – with seeking interest (although they can be
associated with some motives of these types to some extent
and in various ways). These other motives for reciprocity
are consequences of other sentiments or desires – liking and

interest. The demand of balance reciprocity is a particular application of the rationality of equality – which is explained shortly. This rationality is also the origin of sentiments of comparative fairness. Hence, the demand for balance reciprocity can elicit a sentiment of fairness, although this specific judgment does not necessarily arise. The other reciprocities may lead to some relation in the family of equality, but this relation is not primitive and its reasons are very different. For continuation reciprocity, the self-interested return gift should be sufficiently close to the initial gift in value so as to induce another gift, whereas giving too much is a waste; the very approximate equality is a consequence and not a primary value. With regard to liking reciprocities, a priori the return gift or the return in liking only increases with the gift or with the other person's liking; and a desire to be liked as much as one likes applies to a sentiment of the other person. Finally, the equality or balance of balance reciprocity is sometimes qualified for some differences in the two agents that is deemed relevant, such as different means, needs or relative status. Pure balance or equality is required or proper only when there is no such difference deemed to be relevant. In the other cases, the equality is relative to the relevant characteristic (means, needs, status, etc.).

The motive for balance reciprocity rests on several more basic and elementary sentiments or reasons. They can be present jointly, and each can be more or less intense, or absent. Some of these sentiments directly induce giving in return. Other sentiments exist when the return gift is not provided or is insufficient, and avoiding them is one of the motives for giving in return. They can include sentiments of failing to do what is proper or required, of moral indebtedness with the possibility of dependency on the initial giver's future demands, and of inferiority. Moreover, all these sentiments are properly social sentiments in the sense that they are not proper to the beneficiary of the initial gift but represent opinions that are bound to be shared by other people and are "objective" in this sense. The initial giver can be one such person. The initial beneficiary may care for these opinions, and for the judgment about her behaviour that they entail. This may influence her (it may even constitute her only motive).

6.2   The basic motives for balance reciprocity

A sentiment that can entail balance reciprocity may focus on several items: the overall situation disturbed by the initial gift, the two transfers or services, and the situation of either of the two agents or of both jointly. The fact that the initial gift is a free and voluntary act – with its implication of responsibility – may or may not be relevant. With regard to the overall situation, the sentiment is that the initial gift has disrupted the existing order of things and the *balance* it includes, and the return transfer or service aims at restoring this balance. This return gift then matches the initial gift and compensates for its effect with respect to this balance. The focus can also be on the situation of the initial giver: the initial gift constitutes a cost or a loss for her, which the return transfer compensates for. This concern for maintaining a person's situation in some sense belongs to the realm of *compensatory justice*. Similarly, the initial receiver has benefited from a windfall profit that, a priori, may not be justified by a new particular merit, need, or right. This makes her situation a legitimate source for the transfer compensating the initial giver. Moreover, the required equality in value of the two transfers or favours also results from a sense of equality which results from rationality in its most basic sense, as presented shortly.

None of the foregoing considerations rests on the fact that the initial transfer is a gift, hence a free and voluntary act. This fact can have two opposite effects. On the one hand, since the cost of the initial gift is incurred voluntarily, there may be no moral requirement to compensate for it. On the other hand, one may think that having voluntarily incurred a cost or a loss for benefiting the other person is a praiseworthy action that deserves a *reward*. This is a concept of *merit* or *just deserts*, with this possible consequence in the field of *reward justice*. This reward can be provided by the initial beneficiary. It can also be provided by another agent, thus inducing a "reverse reciprocity" (a "Descartes effect").

However, when the freedom and will of the initial giver intervene in the motives for the second transfer, her intention is also bound to matter. If, for instance, the initial giver aims only at inducing a return gift for a purely self-interested reason, there can be a compensation for the cost she has incurred, but no reward for kindness or benevolence, or from gratitude. If, on the contrary, the initial gift is motivated by the benevolent desire to benefit the receiver, this kind of reward is justified. Then, in particular, the receiver is bound to feel grateful, and gratitude can be a motive for giving in return, alone or along with some other motive. Nonetheless, this situation is also bound to induce the receiver to like the benevolent giver, and thus elicit the corresponding motive for liking reciprocity.

However, taking the intent of the initial giver into account may, on the contrary, prevent giving or favouring in return. If the initial giver wants only to obtain a return gift, her selfish behaviour may lead to the conclusion that she does not deserve one, and that she does not even deserve a compensation because she voluntarily parted with what she gave with no benevolent concern for others. Then, self-interestedly trying to extract a return gift is self-defeating. If, on the contrary, the initial giver intends to benefit the receiver as an end in itself, she certainly deserves praise, but giving in return would diminish the favour she provides to the receiver, hence go against her intention, which may have to be respected – all the more so that it is praiseworthy. Then simple thanks are the appropriate return.

6.3   The basic rationality: a case of equality

The basic motives noted above all refer to a sense of propriety or requirement of equality, between some value of the two transfers or services, viewed either in themselves or as they concern any one of the two agents. The most basic rationale for this view rests, therefore, on the rationale of equality, applied here to the particular situation, circumstances and items in question. Considering any one of the two agents, this equality simply means a compensation that maintains the initial order disturbed by the first gift or favour. Considering the two transfers or favours, the equality in their value also results from a very basic and general principle of rationality, the "principle of insufficient reason" (also at the basis of the theory of probabilities, for instance): if there is no valid or relevant reason why one agent should yield to the other more than she receives from her, the two transfers or services should be equal in value. In fact, this principle can itself be derived from a still more basic reason which is the determinacy of a reason for choice. That is, if transfers of unequal values were recommended, the absence of relevant discriminant characteristics of the agents implies that a reversal (permutation) of these values could equally be required; then, there would be two different requirements, whereas a full principle of choice among mutually exclusive alternatives should be unique;[1] this failing is absent only if the two values are equal, so that the permutation yields the same solution.

The most basic rationale of balance reciprocity, therefore, is a principle of rationality in the most basic sense of providing a reason, applied as indicated. This application has the characteristic that it is not from the point of view of any of the agents, but takes an "objective", impartial view

---

[1] A random choice is not a solution. Indeed, what would the probabilities be? Presumably equal. Then one is taken back to justifying equality. Moreover, the lottery introduces an extraneous element. Such a solution is justifiable as a second best only when equality is impossible, and equality in probabilities is then justified in the way that equality in general is.

of the situation. This is also, in a sense, an a priori equality of consideration of the agents. This impartiality gives balance reciprocity its moral value. The reason that has been described is akin to, or a particular case of, the general reason for the morality of the relevant equality, which is a basis of the concept of justice, fairness, or equity (equity is simply the latin word for equality). Aristotle remarked that "justice is equality, as everybody thinks it is." However, equality can be of many things (including rights or freedoms), and these items characterize the various concepts of fairness. Balance reciprocity applies to the particular items that are the gifts or favours. This is why it sometimes raises a sentiment of fairness.

This reason for balance reciprocity has to be somewhat specified. One issue is the comparison of the two gifts or favours and of their "value." It is straightforward when they are identical, which can occur when some situation of the people is reversed (notably a need of the receiver or means of the giver). In other cases, the comparison often comes to be made by some social norm, habit, or tradition, when the noted basically moral view is adopted as a social norm as will shortly be pointed out (approximately equal money value – hence market value – plays a role, but this equality cannot be strictly required in general because the services or transfers are in the field of gift giving rather than of purely self-interested exchange). Moreover, the two agents may not be identical in the relevant way. A difference in situation or status of some kind may be considered to be relevant for comparing the two favours or gifts. This may be, for instance, a difference in wealth and means, in needs, in social status of some sort, or an asymmetrical relation between the two agents that is deemed relevant for this issue. Then, the relevant balance is qualified, possibly an equality between weighted values, and this difference is also sometimes deemed relevant for demanding gifts or favours of different nature from each person.

6.4   A moral and social norm

The particular moral aspect of balance reciprocity tends to make this reciprocation a moral norm and a duty, and to elicit a sentiment of guilt if the proper return fails to be provided. Since the moral judgment in question is based on impartiality and objectivity, it is bound to be shared by all members of the society who know and understand the relationship in question. This tends to make the demand of balance reciprocity a social norm as well, and not just a moral norm, with a value of propriety, and to elicit a sentiment of shame for a beneficiary who fails to provide a proper return. These judgments are "social" judgments, endorsed by the actor and by other people in the society, including the other party to the interaction and still others. They judge the receiver, who may be sensitive to this opinion, and sometimes they are accompanied by social pressures of any type and intensity.

Moral and social norms in the field of reciprocity also attach to sentiments (and not only to the gifts). Two kinds of sentiments are relevant here, concerning gratitude, on the one hand, and shame or guilt, on the other. It can be held that you should be and feel grateful for having benefited from a benevolent favour, and that you should be and feel somehow ashamed, and even that you should feel guilty, if you do not return the favour properly. Injunctions that you should have these sentiments generally assume that they can themselves induce this effect in fostering your awareness of the situation. Gratitude is particular in that it consists in a sentiment favourable to the benevolent giver. This is not liking because it remains closely dependent on the benevolent favour one is grateful for, but it goes in this direction, and it is favourable to liking the benefactor. It can thus help inducing liking reciprocity, and sometimes it also induces a return gift by itself, from affection or for showing and proving gratefulness. Gratitude thus belongs to both realms of comparison and of liking. In the end, all these norms about sentiments and feeling can induce reciprocal action. However, return giving induced by gratitude does not have much of a relation of balance or equality with the initial favour: the effect through liking implies only a positive relation, whereas giving for showing gratitude need not reach balance and is often merely symbolic.

6.5 The inconveniences of imbalance

When the return gift is not provided, or is considered insufficient to match the initial gift, the initial beneficiary may be regarded, by herself and other people, as having a moral debt towards the initial giver. This can entail disagreeable sentiments and judgments, and the desire to avoid them can motivate the return gift. These sentiments can have very varied intensities. At the lowest level, the beneficiary may be no more than ill at ease because of the situation. With higher intensities, the beneficiary may feel guilty for not giving (or giving sufficiently) in return. When she refers to the social judgment about herself – even when this judgment is only interiorized and imagined by her – she may feel ashamed. The situation can lead to a state of dependency towards the giver, which can be quite material when it is admitted that this moral debt entitles the giver to demand reimbursement in return in the form of services or goods the nature and timing of which she can more or less choose. Depending on the case and the society, this tends to create a situation of inferiority towards the giver, and also sometimes in comparison with other persons who are not so indebted, with a corresponding lower social status. This lower status and inferiority, and particularly the dependency, can offend the person's pride and, most importantly, her dignity. The saying "I don't owe anything to anyone" expresses the dignity of being free from this dependency. Correspondingly, when the gift is not counterbalanced by a return gift, the giver often sees herself as a moral creditor ("she owes me something"). This sometimes arouses in her sentiments of superiority, of power and domination, and occasionally of pride, although they tend to be less intense than the symmetrical sentiments of the receiver. The Inuits' dictum "The gift makes the slave as the whip makes the dog" denotes an extreme form. In the case of harm, vengefulness consists of various sentiments that parallel those of moral indebtedness, often with more intensity as with anger and sentiments of humiliation, shame, or being the victim of an injustice.

However, lasting situations and sentiments of moral indebtedness, often accompanied by gratitude, constitute one of the most common social bonds – which, then, requires the absence of a balancing return gift.

6.6 Refusing and revenge

A situation of balance reciprocity can be accompanied by most other effects brought about by gifts. The gifts or services received and the costs of providing them matter for the self-interest of the parties. There can be other sentiments between the parties, although not all sentiments are possible. Notably, strong altruism, and in particular strong liking tend to exclude the accounting comparison of the gifts and moral indebtedness. Yet, the balance is consistent with mild liking and even favourable to it. The total self-interested effects may be favourable or unfavourable to any of the participants. A participant for whom they are unfavourable may accept the relation because of other effects. However, a participant may find the relation undesirable when taking all aspects into consideration. If she is the initial giver, she can avoid the relation in not giving in the first place (this sometimes implies going against some norm of giving). If she is the initial beneficiary, this avoidance consists in refusing the gift.

Refusing a gift is sometimes possible, and sometimes impossible or costly because the gift cannot be reversed materially or for a social or moral reason which can be more or less compelling: refusing the gift may be impolite, or offensive, or go against a norm which may be supported by social opinion or, possibly, by social pressure of any possible kind. The initial receiver may have any possible preference between remaining with this unique giving, refusing it, or providing a return gift, according to the possibilities and everything being considered (the gifts or favours received and provided, the balance or imbalance, the moral indebtedness, and other aspects of the relationship). This may lead her to refuse the gift in the first place, if she can. If she accepts the gift when refusing it is possible and costless, she is responsible (co-responsible) for the whole situation, including her moral indebtedness. Similarly, if the initial giver freely refuses a return gift, the beneficiary's moral indebtedness often vanishes. Then, it suffices, to cancel the moral indebtedness, that the beneficiary be ready to redeem this debt.

Refusing the gift can sometimes be identical to returning the gift received, or providing an identical item or service as return gift. However, a matching return gift can generally differ from the initial gift, and the initial receiver generally prefers this case. A similar gift or favour on another similar occasion is often suitable, however. With unfavourable acts, taking back something stolen, or compensation for harm received, is not balance reciprocation, but revenge or the law of talion are – with a new equilibrium with about equal losses for everyone. In this case, providing an identical harm is a possibility and is often favoured ("An eye for an eye . . ."). The parallel of identical gifts with identical situations of both parties in the "positive" case can only occur for services that one cannot provide to oneself (e.g. praise, recommendations, endorsement); or when the gifts are ear marked for their giver and their "exchange" symbolises the relation and the sentiments (as with wedding rings); or again when the acts of giving are valued for the social relation that occurs during their process (e.g. meals, drinks). Punishment for a reason other than to deter future misdeeds is a type of balance reciprocation, in the family of generalized or general reciprocation (defined as it has been for reciprocity) if the punisher is not the initial victim (as with lawful punishment "in the name of society").

Being angry with some person, or simple resentment towards her, results from this person being responsible for harm or prejudice that disrupts some state of affairs considered as fair, or expected, or hoped for. These sentiments therefore often accompany balance reciprocation of harm, and anger is a common direct inducement to it. Resentment presents some symmetry with gratitude. It can induce disliking the person who is its object, as gratitude is favourable to liking. There is no norm of resentment, however, whereas there can be moral and social norms of gratitude, and a social norm of revenge. Moreover, neither of the two possible effects of gratitude on return giving – through liking and as a direct demonstration of the sentiment – has a parallel in resentment since it induces revenge neither directly nor through disliking (which does not have this effect), although it can accompany vengefulness. All this shows again that the "symmetry" between "good" and "bad" reciprocation is only very superficial.

7

Liking reciprocities

7.1 Introduction

"Friends make gifts and gifts make friends", an Inuit proverb says. This pair of relations proposes a reason for reciprocity in giving when taken in reverse order, and in friendship, or liking one another, when taken in this order. However, not all gifts make friends, only friendly ones. Hence, one may in fact only have "friendship makes friendship", a direct reciprocity in sentiment, plus the easily understandable "friends make gifts" and a possible role of giving for informing about liking. Staying with folk wisdom, this is what a beautiful old song expresses in saying *J'aimerai qui m'aimera* (I will love him who loves me). Nevertheless, although folk wisdom epitomizes respectable experience, it is no substitute for explanation. If "liking elicits giving" is rather straightforward, "receiving a gift elicits liking the giver" requires closer explanation and analysis of its conditions, and "liking elicits liking" still more so.

These reciprocities based on liking constitute one of the main fields in the realm of reciprocity (along with balance reciprocity and self-interested continuation). Moreover, reciprocity in liking is a main social bond, with essential manifestations from general sociality to family love, the constitution of groups, and the nature of communities. Liking reciprocities also have a major direct normative value for the quality of society and of the relationships and people in it. Hence, understanding and explaining liking reciprocities is a major task.

We will thus, successively, point out giving because of liking; emphasize the distinction between reciprocities in giving and in liking; present the basic relevant phenomena; analyse the various types of "causal liking" and notably "benefactor-liking"; consider gratitude and its various types (for favours or gifts and for sentiments); point out the existential value of being considered (and approved and liked); discuss whether sentiments are given to their holder or can be influenced by her; show how and when receiving a gift entails liking the giver; analyse the mechanisms of reciprocal liking; present the property of the complementarity of mutual liking; analyse informational giving; point out the role of imitation, "contagion," or conforming; consider the consequences of such mutual interactions; observe that there is practically no counterpart in negative reciprocation; and note the factual and normative importance of reciprocities based on liking.

The sentiments of liking considered here can be of various intensities, from simple respect to love.

A basic and characteristic fact of liking reciprocity is that liking someone is a standard, direct reason for giving to or favouring her. This is, indeed, the main motive for giving. The reason is simply that if you like someone, you like what you deem to be good for her, and you bring it about if it is not too costly otherwise (this is often liked by the receiver – in particular, you are bound to like her satisfaction –, but not necessarily so in the cases called "paternalism," and then the gift depends on whether the receiver can refuse or resell it, which depends on material and social considerations).

7.2   Reciprocities in giving and in liking

A crucial point is that there are two kinds of liking reciprocities: one kind of reciprocity in giving and reciprocity in liking. The former is reciprocity of giving from a motive of liking. The second, also called reciprocal liking, is a reciprocity in sentiments, the sentiments of liking. These likings can then induce givings. These two reciprocities are quite different, although they are related in various ways.

Liking reciprocity in giving is your giving in return for a gift you received because you like the initial giver, and this liking results from her giving. This latter relation requires that the initial giving has particular motivations such as liking you, as we shall see.

The other type, reciprocal liking, consists in the fact that you tend to like people who like you (*j'aimerai qui m'aimera*). However, the reason for this tendency is a complex of inter-related effects which will be explained shortly.

7.3 Basic phenomena

Understanding and explaining these facts require understanding a few basic facts and relations. Some of these basic issues are present in both types of liking reciprocity. They are the questions of causal liking (i.e. liking the causes of what one likes), the reason for liking to be the object of attention and consideration, the question of responsibility for one's sentiments, and the issue of gratitude. Liking reciprocity in giving also rests on the general reasons for liking to be given to. Reciprocal liking also rests on the issues of the allocation of one's capacities for liking, and of giving for informing about liking.

7.4 The various reasons for liking to be given to

Remark, to begin with, that you have various different possible reasons to appreciate receiving a gift or benefiting from a favour. You may, first, enjoy the gift or favour in itself, of course. Moreover, the very fact of being an object of attention – which is implied by this situation – can be very valuable *per se*, for reasons that are discussed shortly. If the giving results from the giver liking you, it shows and proves this sentiment directly and, possibly, also because the giver wants this giving to show that she likes you. Indeed, the giver may want to inform you about her liking you because she knows you like to be liked and favours what makes you happy because she likes you. Even if she wants you to know, or to believe, that she likes you in order that you like her in return (by processes shortly explained), she wants this essentially when she likes you and she wants this more, the more she likes you. Hence, this giving again reveals that she likes you. Note that these informational effects can be obtained by simple communication, but the cost incurred in giving proves the intentions and sentiments. And you indeed generally like more or less this liking and the kind attention towards you that it implies (one reason is that they enhance the effects of simple attention towards you). Moreover, in all cases the giver's sacrifice of the cost of the gift reveals the intensity of this attention and liking. The process of giving is also often a type of relationship, a positive or even warm one if liking the beneficiary is the reason, and this is often appreciated in itself. The giving and the gift can in addition have various other effects related to their symbolic value or to establishing or confirming statuses.

7.5   Causal likings

The various types of liking the causes of what one likes have an important role in the analysis of liking reciprocity. *Causal liking* is the fact that you tend to like the causes of what you like. However, three types of causes have to be distinguished here in this respect. (1) In *simple causal liking*, the cause can be anything. For instance, you can like the apple tree because of the apple and your coat because of its warmth. (2) *Agent-liking* refers to the cases in which a cause is an agent's free (freely chosen) act, that is, a part of an action in the proper sense of the term (inaction is a particular case), and hence something this agent is responsible for. This act is a cause of something you like, and this agent (and, notably, her will) is a cause of this act and hence of the item you like. (3) *Benefactor-liking* is agent-liking when the final motive of the act is specifically to benefit you. Note that this latter case does not include the cases in which the giver provides you with a benefit as the result of another motive, even if the final end of this motive is a consequence of your being pleased by the gift and the giving (these other motives can be, for example, inducing a return gift, eliciting liking in return if the giving could have this effect, being or appearing generous and benevolent, or even showing one's liking as is soon to be discussed).[1] The required benevolence of the final objective of the giver can result from any altruistic sentiment towards the receiver. However, the focus here is in the family of liking the receiver, which is essentially affection of various possible intensities (sympathy in the common sense of the term is a mild form of it), but can also be one kind of pity or compassion that is accompanied with liking, and can

---

[1] A common case is when the giver gives in order to be liked in return by the receiver, because she likes the receiver, and she likes to be liked by people she likes – for a reason that will be explained shortly. The giver may then rely on two possible reactions. Her giving may directly elicit the receiver's liking; or her giving shows her liking to the receiver, and this liking elicits the receiver's direct "reciprocal liking" shortly explained. In this latter case, the receiver likes because she is liked and not because she receives (the gift merely shows and proves the liking, either directly or in showing and proving the giver's desire to be liked which may result from her liking). This is not benefactor-liking. However, since benefactor-liking the giver requires a motive of benevolence for the gift, and this can result from the giver liking the receiver, these two reasons for liking the giver are not easily disentangled. Benevolent giving in fact commonly obeys all these motives jointly: benefiting the receiver, showing liking from this effect and possibly from showing a desire to be liked, and hence eliciting returns of benefactor-liking and of reciprocal liking. More straightforwardly, note that giving for being praiseworthy or praised elicits no benefactor-liking. The question of giving in order to be liked implies impossibilities and relations that will be considered more closely in chapter 19.

include – as a borderline case – appreciative attitudes leading to respect.

7.6   Gratitude

The conditions for the existence of the sentiment of benefactor-liking are also those of the sentiment of gratitude towards the benefactor. Moreover, both these sentiments belong to the same field of sentiments carrying positive affects towards this person. Their intensities can be quite different, however. Gratitude is a priori favourable to liking the person one is grateful to. At least, it seems difficult both to be grateful towards someone and to dislike her. Since benefactor-liking and gratitude are sentiments in the same field of positive interpersonal sentiments and with the same cause, reason and protagonists, gratitude tends to induce liking through a kind of classical "halo effect." Gratitude in itself can motivate some giving in return for the particular motive of showing or proving it. However, these sentiments are quite different and distinct in themselves, and they have different positions as social sentiments. Indeed, there is a social value and norm with regard to having a sentiment of gratitude towards benevolent benefactors, and, correspondingly, blame for ingratitude. In contrast, liking one's benefactor is not a normative requirement, although it can be somewhat socially approved. This difference is as if being grateful were considered to be more amenable to voluntary choice than liking. The sentiment of gratitude, and any return giving it can motivate, have an aspect of deontology and of balance reciprocity. In a sense, they constitute a bridge between the two proper types of reciprocity, liking reciprocity and balance reciprocity.

Moreover, there also exists a particular sentiment and mental attitude of "existential gratitude," of being grateful just for the existence of something one likes or appreciates, a sentiment that is not addressed to a particular person. This can in particular apply to the existence of someone's favourable sentiments towards oneself, or to the existence of someone one likes or who likes oneself (one could be grateful in the standard sense for the other person's sentiment only insofar as she wilfully chooses her sentiment for the purpose of benefiting oneself, a case which usually has only a limited scope).

7.7   The existential value of being the object of attention, approval, and liking

You can be the object of attention and consideration, to various possible degrees. This attention can be accompanied by a judgment or evaluation of yourself. Moreover, this attention and evaluation can be accompanied by affects towards you (e.g., liking, disliking, hating, loving. despising, and so on).

Being the object of attention is favourable, and probably to some extent necessary, to your sense of self and ego and of social existence. This is enhanced by appreciative judgments or evaluations of yourself that may accompany this attention. It is still more when, in addition, it is accompanied by positive affects towards you. Moreover, these effects increase with the intensity (including the duration) of this attention, positive judgment and affection. Such effects are thus elicited by being the object of attention, possibly by being "known," by being the object of consideration, especially if it is with approval such as being esteemed or admired, and particularly if it is with affection (which implies some sort of approval), such as being liked or loved. Kindness implies attention, some approval, and some favourable sentiment in the direction of liking.

This benefit that you derive from these facts is something you may like, favour or prefer; its nature, however, is in fact deeper than is usually implied by these terms, in the realm of existence, being, and "ontology." A lack of these attentions and of their qualities is the most common cause of suicide.

Now being given to implies being an object of attention. Being liked implies being an object of attention with some favourable evaluation and with positive affects.

7.8   Slave or master of one's passions?

The extent to which one can be held responsible for one's sentiments, and the dynamics of sentiments, are crucial facts in liking reciprocity.

Sentiments tend to be given to their holders. David Hume expresses this in saying that we are "slaves of our passions." In contrast, a figure in a play by Jean Racine proclaims: "I am master of myself as of the universe." Few of us are Stoic Roman emperors, however. The reality is often in between, with the largest part on Hume's side. However, we sometimes wilfully, consciously and purposefully influence our sentiments. This is done by reasoning or by more or less indirect devices such as focusing attention or "forgetting about it," or in trying to get used to something. However, these effects and their possibilities are limited. Even if we are not thoroughly "slaves of our passions," they do have an important hold on us. Insofar as one can voluntarily influence one's sentiments, and to this extent only, we are responsible for our sentiments, as implied by the very meaning of the concept of responsibility (although defining this possibility can lead to a lengthy analysis).[2] All this applies in particular to liking.

Moreover, it is not uncommon for sentiments to adjust more or less involuntarily to interest or other advantages. This mental process involves a number of well-known phenomena such as attention, habit, oblivion, halo effects, reward, conditioned reflexes, compliance, and so on. It is parallel, in the field of sentiments, to cognitive dissonance in the domain of cognition. In fact, both the conscious and unconscious, and the voluntary and involuntary, are often closely interwoven

[2] See the discusion in Kolm 2004, chap. 6.

in this process (for instance, a phenomenon such as attention can be both voluntary and involuntary, and it can even be unconscious). Although *l'amour est aveugle* (love is blind) and Cupid is blindfolded, the blindfold is not thoroughly opaque (people generally happen to fall in love with persons of the appropriate social class).

7.9   Liking the giver

You can appreciate receiving a gift or favour for this gift in itself, for the attention towards you that this constitutes, and possibly for the relationships established in the very process of giving and receiving and as a result of the gift, or for an effect on your social status. Since giving is a free act, this makes you agent-like the giver. If, moreover, the giving is made with a motive of benevolence towards you, this fosters the positive effect of the attention and possibly of the relationship or status, and it makes you benefactor-like the giver and can induce your gratitude towards her. This latter liking may in turn elicit a gift to the initial giver, which appears as a return gift motivated by the process described. However, this initial giver's liking of the receiver can also have an effect in itself, a priori irrespective of the giving.

7.10 Reciprocal liking

7.10.1 General presentation

After liking the benevolent giver – and hence, possibly, giving to her – the second type of liking reciprocity is reciprocal liking. This is a direct reciprocity in the sentiment of liking. It consists of the fact that the relation "person A likes person B" tends to entail the relation "person B likes person A." This occurs with any of the possible types or degrees of the relation of "liking." The reverse influence normally also tends to occur, and, therefore, these two relations entail a dynamics of these two sentiments with states of equilibrium. Moreover, there may also be giving which can notably have the effect of informing about liking in various possible ways.

A notable number of psychological phenomena cooperate in a few psychological processes that can lead to reciprocal liking. Although people generally appreciate being liked as they appreciate a gift they receive, reciprocal liking can only be very different from balance reciprocity for several reasons: people do not choose their sentiments except to a limited extent; liking has no direct cost as a gift has (at most, it can have a kind of opportunity cost in allocating attention or affection); people's effort is more for being liked than for liking; and the issue of balance in sentiments, although not thoroughly absent, cannot have the same property as that of gifts and return gifts (notably for the comparison).

The main process inducing reciprocal liking rests on the fact that people benefit more from being liked the more they like the person who likes them – as discussed shortly. This is the *complementarity of mutual liking.* This benefit, indeed, induces, in the sentiments of the person liked, adjustments that make her like her "liker," by a process which is largely involuntary but can include some voluntary elements. This both enhances and allocates the person's "liking capacities" of attention and affection.

Another phenomenon inducing reciprocal liking is that people, who generally like to be liked, like *ipso facto* the main cause of this sentiment towards them, that is, the person who likes them – a "causal liking" of the "liker." However, this liking cannot be of the strong benefactor-liking kind – as with liking a benevolent giver – because the original liking is only limitedly voluntary (if at all), and, at any rate, when it has a voluntary dimension, its intent is not to benefit or please the liked person. This causal liking can only be simple causal liking, and, to the (small) extent to which the liking may be voluntary, agent-liking.

For the same reason, there can be no sentiment of gratitude towards the liker in the usual sense of the term. However, there is often the noted kind of sentiment of gratitude, addressed to nobody, for the existence of the liker's liking sentiment, and hence of the liker as she is, and this sentiment of gratitude has some importance (the importance of the object one is grateful for "compensates," in some sense, for the absence of someone to be grateful to).

Finally, the liking person may inform the other of her sentiment in order to please her, by communication or by giving – or giving more than otherwise – as a signal. Even if her objective is to be liked in return, this often reveals her liking since she most often wants to be liked when she likes, and all the more, the more she likes.

The reciprocal liking can be of various intensities, as is the case for each of its factors. Its absence in unreturned love is one of the most common topics of fiction.

7.10.2 *The complementarity of mutual liking*

Most of the benefits that you derive from being liked by someone are the greater the more you like this person. The sense of self and of social existence provided by being an object of attention, still more of appreciative attention, and more again of appreciative and kind attention, is enhanced the more you care about the other person. Your social status as you see it is correspondingly augmented. And you care about this person in particular when you like her, and more so the more you like her. Moreover, the warmth of the relation with someone who likes you is greater the more you like her.

This advantage of liking, or liking more, the person who likes you adds to other effects of liking or liking more, which, however, can affect your satisfaction both ways: if you like someone (more), you are (more) pleased by what is good for her, but you also suffer (more) from what is bad for her.

Nevertheless, the advantage of liking more someone who likes you can elicit your liking her more, by the process described in Section 7.8. Most of this effect is bound to come involuntarily, by a kind of mental process akin to cognitive dissonance in the case of cognition. Part of this adjustment can be more or less voluntary, though, by reasoning and by focusing attention. In this process, the voluntary and involuntary aspects, and the conscious and unconscious processes, are often closely interrelated.

The result is both a creation of affection or positive sentiments and a reallocation of existing ones. Indeed, liking uses capacities for emotional involvement and for attention which have a dimension of scarcity.[3] Now, from the foregoing you benefit from liking more people who like you more, *ceteris paribus*. Then, the described process of formation of your sentiment realizes this allocation. This process, and notably its voluntary part, can be helped particularly by a material allocation of your attention – you see particular friends, you generally marry only one of the persons you could love.

7.10.3 Reactions and interactions

A priori and apart from any other effect, if you like someone more, you benefit more from her liking you, she likes your increased liking and you like her resulting increased satisfaction; she also tends to like you more by the described processes of reciprocal liking, and you appreciate her liking you more. A similar reciprocal process is at work for both individuals. Both the involuntary and the – usually more indirect – voluntary effects are at work, notably in the complementarity of mutual liking and in causal likings.

---

[3] Both attention and emotional involvement rest on basic human capacities which have limits, and they are necessary to liking. The allocation of your liking capacities is a major aspect of your situation in the world, in particular with regard to people. Another old folksong puts it as "The heart of my sweetheart is so small that there is place for only one good friend." However, Victor Hugo suggests that motherly love is different and is a public good: "A mother's heart is like the bread a God partakes and multiplies: each has her share and all have the whole" (however, issues about one being more loved than another are common in families). Moreover, liking capacities can also be increased by training and practice and can present this kind of increasing return to scale.

Finally, both agents can have a similar set of reaction towards the other. Each liking tends to augment the other by reciprocal liking. A dynamic can develop and there are states of equilibria. However, there can be several equilibria, with both individuals' liking being higher or lower in one state of equilibrium compared to the other.[4] A priori, people prefer equilibria with higher liking, but many phenomena can intervene and possibly qualify this (e.g. suffering from the poor situation of people one likes, various effects of gifts induced by liking, and so on).

7.10.4 Information

Someone who likes someone else wants her to know it because this sentiment pleases the liked person and because this may induce reciprocal liking. Insofar as this information is provided by the liking person for the purpose of pleasing the other, this entails benefactor-liking in return. However, this is benefactor-liking for this action of informing rather than for the sentiment itself (for which, as we have seen, benefactor-liking is usually quite limited – since it implies liking both voluntarily and for the final purpose of pleasing the other person). Insofar as the person who likes informs the other of this fact for the purpose of being liked in return, this entails no benefactor-liking, and yet it generally reveals the initial liking since people benefit more from being liked by someone else, and hence want it more, the more they like her.

Providing this information can use any means of communication. Moreover, if a liking sentiment induces benevolent giving, this act a priori reveals the sentiment to the beneficiary. However, there can be liking without giving, and this sentiment can induce reciprocal liking. There can also be a gift or favour for the specific purpose of showing the liking

---

[4] Such liking dynamics and equilibria are discussed in Kolm 1984a, chap. 10.

sentiment, or of proving it thanks to the cost of the gift for the giver. More generally, the informational effect of giving can be an extra motive which, added to others, induces a gift that would not have taken place otherwise. A message of liking of any kind can prove this sentiment even if its aim is to induce being liked in return, for the reason just noted (one likes more to be liked, the more one likes). This information about one's sentiment tends to be mutual, with reinforcing effects ("I like you, I like you too"), thus favouring the transmutation of these individual sentiments into what is often better described as a kind of collective and joint mutual sentiment of the pair of individuals (our friendship, our love).

7.11 All liking effects

Giving in order to be liked, one of the most common interpersonal relations, necessarily results in frustration to a greater or lesser extent. It is, indeed, the paragon of self-defeating endeavour. The reason, of course, is that it cannot induce the strong benefactor-liking because the final objective is not to benefit the receiver. Such a gift can induce only the milder agent-liking type of causal liking. Nevertheless, the receiver benefits from the gift for all possible reasons. Moreover, this gift also generally informs her that the giver likes her, although indirectly, because this is generally a condition for desiring to be liked, as we have seen; the cost of the gift for the giver even proves this liking and reveals its intensity; and if this is news for the receiver, this may induce her reciprocal liking; but this possible effect of information is something else. The central issue is that being the object of benefactor-liking cannot be elicited purposefully by giving. It is necessarily a by-product of giving directly because of liking.

Indeed, directly giving to someone or favouring her because one likes her elicits benefactor-liking, and it *ipso facto* informs about this liking. More specifically, the cost of the gift for the giver provides a measure of the intensity of this sentiment. This information then induces directly some liking in return for the reasons described. The receiver's liking of the initial giver for any reasons, possibly supported by gratitude for the gift and for the sentiment, may induce the beneficiary to give in return. This is full liking reciprocity mobilizing all its ways of influence of all types.

7.12 Imitation, contagion, conforming

Among the most basic social facts are the imitation of acts, attitudes or sentiments, and "contagion" of these items when the duplication is not chosen if the term imitation is restricted to wilful acts.[5] This is supported by the sheer pleasure of being in tune with others in sentiments and action; the pleasure derived from this community – or, rather, communion – of sentiments is another important focus of Adam Smith's *Theory of Moral Sentiments*. Moreover, other people, or a shared social sentiment, may appreciate that you conform with prevalent acts, attitudes, or sentiments, or judge deviations unfavourably, and you may care about this opinion (possibly because of some kind of social pressure). At any rate, the behaviour, conduct and feeling of others provide available patterns the duplication of which straightforwardly solves the problem of the conscious or unconscious selection of sentiments, attitudes and acts. These facts tend to be stronger the more the imitator is aware of her models.

Now, being the beneficiary of giving and the object of liking sentiments makes you particularly aware of these acts, motives and sentiments. This awareness is reinforced by the affects carried in the process. Furthermore, we have seen that liking tends to induce showing this sentiment to the other person, in giving or otherwise. These are the conditions most

---

[5] Guillaume de Tarde, whose work is often considered the beginning of sociology, sees imitation as the basic social fact.

favourable to imitation or contagion, all the more so that these acts, attitudes and sentiments receive general social approval. Now, your benefactor or liker is directly available as the object of your giving and liking. And social judgments approve of such grateful conduct. This leads to mirror-image imitation, which directly constitutes reciprocity or can reinforce its other causes, in attitudes, sentiments, and actions. These reciprocal actions and attitudes can result both from direct imitation (wilful or from an effect of contagion) and from imitation or contagion of the sentiments that induce them. This can thus lead one to give in return, to like the liking giver, and also to emulate her in seeking her liking notably in giving for its direct and demonstration effects.

7.13 Interdependent and dynamic liking

All the described relations of reciprocal liking, the related givings for direct or informational reasons, reciprocal giving because of liking and gratitude, and imitation-contagion-conforming, constitute a network of relations which introduces, in situations of mutual liking, a positive feedback in liking (and giving) which produces dynamics and evolution, and also equilibria in liking (and giving).[6] There often are several such liking or giving equilibria, and, indeed, several stable equilibria, some with high degrees of liking and others with low degrees. People commonly prefer the former ones unanimously (although we have noted some reasons for the opposite preferences, in particular because liking someone more makes one more sensitive to her misfortune). Hence, one should try to avoid deteriorating dynamics and low stable liking equilibria, and to favour the dynamics of self-improving mutual liking and high stable liking equilibria. However, this meets two interrelated types of difficulties. One is due to the fact that sentiments are largely involuntary.

---

[6] This dynamic interaction is analysed in Kolm 1984a, chap. 10.

The other is that giving in the proper sense of the term cannot be an object of mutually conditional exchange or agreement, and cannot be imposed by force. Strategies for reaching high stable mutual likings rather than lower ones are essential both in small-group therapy and in choices that influence social structures, relations and attitudes at all levels of societies, through institutions, organizations, rules, and education.[7]

7.14 Asymmetry

In these respects, love is intense liking. It is noteworthy, however, that the symmetry of the noted relations with disliking, hating or hurting is very limited. As we have seen, being wilfully hurt by someone certainly tends to elicit disliking that person, but being disliked or hated does not a priori elicit disliking or hating in return, and disliking – short of hating – does not generally entail liking the other person's harm and hence harming her, or the desire to show one's aversion. Only peripheral phenomena have counterparts. Imitation and contagion can intervene in both types of relationship. Resentment is somewhat akin to gratitude. It favours disliking the person who is the object of the sentiment but this a priori does not tend to induce hurting. Moreover, resentment is not a norm as gratitude is, and giving to show gratitude has no counterpart. Revenge and retaliation, of course, correspond to the two other types of motives for reciprocity.

7.15 Conclusion

Even though we all live immersed in liking reciprocities of various types and intensities, understanding these phenomena turns out to require careful attention, distinction and analysis. They are not prime and basic mental and social facts but the result of interacting deeper psychological

[7] Ibid.

phenomena. Although various types of relations often work jointly, two of them should be distinguished in the first place, reciprocal liking and reciprocities in giving in which liking motivates the return giving. An important issue concerns the formation of sentiments, with the particular role and ways of action of the will, and, in the other causes, the involuntary processes that nevertheless tend more or less to adjust sentiments to particular situations of their holder (somehow as classical cognitive dissonance does for beliefs). In the end, these analyses, which are necessary for understanding and, when needed, forecasting, are also the basis of choices and actions aimed at fostering the quality of society at all levels and with regard to most values. These values supported by liking reciprocities, indeed, are not only the direct quality of social relations and of people when giving and liking others, but also, as we shall see, social and economic efficiency and welfare, and justice and liberty (giving redistributes wealth in respecting freedom and, indeed, thanks to it).

8

Other reciprocities: continuation, relational, imitation, extended

8.1 Presentation

The last two chapters have analysed the two basic types of genuine reciprocity, balance (matching, comparative) reciprocity and liking reciprocity. Their theories will be presented in chapters 18 and 19, respectively. The present chapter completes the general presentation of reciprocity by considering the other phenomena involved and can propose a more general synthesis. The presentation of continuation reciprocity completes that of the trio of types of reciprocity in a broad sense, but is only brief here because this process relates closely to sequential exchange discussed in chapter 3 (and applied in following chapters). The central and comparative triangular structure of the phenomenon of reciprocity can then be understood better. Other important phenomena are then considered: the appreciation, in reciprocities, of the relation or of the process in themselves, and the cases of status and symbolic reciprocities; the roles of imitation of acts and conforming; and the particular ways in which the reciprocitarian motives induce the various types of extended reciprocities.

8.2 Continuation reciprocity

Reacting in reciprocity to an act, an attitude or an expressed judgment in order to induce its repetition is common but requires a number of conditions. This act, attitude or judgment has to be desired by the reciprocator, and the reciprocation has to be desired by the initial actor. The repetition should be a possibility. Moreover, the initial actor should believe that this new act, attitude or judgment of hers will again be rewarded, for instance again by a reciprocation. This latter act should then be possible and the first actor should think it will be performed. If the reciprocator is still of the same mind, however, this new reciprocation will be motivated by the desire to induce again an act she likes from the initial giver. And so on. Hence, with steady motivations of this type, the foreseen process should be endless, which is not realistic.[1] This becomes, in fact, a sequential exchange discussed previously. The successive acts can occur without further conditions or be triggered by particular needs of the receiver or means of the giver. As we have recalled, a solution to this unrealistic endlessness can be found in uncertainty about the end of the process or the behaviour of the other agent. In fact, the protagonists do not usually foresee the whole future process consciously, and this limited rationality intervenes in a sense as such an uncertainty. A solution can also be found in an end by an act, attitude or expressed judgment with a different motivation. It cannot be a simple gift, since the problem would remain posed about the previous act. Therefore, it has to be induced by past acts, including the last but one (this is necessary for there being a last but one, and therefore a last one). This last act can thus be motivated by sentiments of balance reciprocity – notably egalitarian fairness –, liking resulting from the interaction (liking reciprocity and gratitude can intervene only when some liking and benevolent acts have been introduced otherwise), or sheer imitation. These other motives may be those of one participant only. In the case of balance reciprocity, the last

[1] The timing of the acts could accelerate in time in such a way that all their dates remain finite, but, then, the speed of reactions would have to become unrealistically high.

appreciated act, attitude or expression is, or plays the role of, a reward for previous benefits, bestowed out of a sense of balance or fairness and propriety or duty. In the case of liking reciprocity, the last act, attitude or expression is motivated by liking the other person. These motives are quite frequent. In particular, both the liking and the sense of fairness can develop in the course of the relationship, from the simple fact that the persons come to consider and know each other, in a relationship profitable to both. However, these sentiments would then be more or less present before the last move. Hence, this is a case of mixed motives, in particular of mixed and evolving motives. This is indeed common.

Of course, each agent may desire the other person's acts in question for any reason. Normally, this is, or includes, the act itself or its consequences, such as the gift received. There can also be, a priori, the fact of being the object of attention, the interaction in the process, a status brought about by the relationship, and so on. However, these latter benefits are limited, in the pure continuation case where liking is absent from the motives, by the fact that this absence limits the value of the attention, the warmth of the relation, or the status that can result from being liked. However, liking, continuation, and possibly fair balance, are commonly associated in reciprocities of a mixed nature, and continuation of the effects of being liked and of liking may be sought.

As has been noted, retaliation for deterrence begins like continuation reciprocity but does not develop like it since the aim is to prevent further harm rather than to induce repetition of the initial fact. It builds up a threat, and it makes verbal threats credible. However, continuous mutual restraint from harming because of a threat and a fear of retaliation can be seen as a repetition in time. A difference, however, is that if the retaliating act is not beneficial in itself to the actor (theft, not respecting some constraint, etc.) it is costly for her, whereas giving less in a sequential exchange is beneficial in itself.

We have also remarked that simple continuation reciprocity tends to present some property of balance in value within a certain range, since reciprocating more than is necessary for the inducement is a waste for this agent, while reciprocating too little will not suffice for the inducement. Long sequences of acts can elicit many strategies, but these reasons for the relevant kind of approximate balance will nevertheless also be at work (see chapter 3, section 3, in particular note 10). A similar reason tends to adjust deterrence to the costs and profits of the harm prevented.

8.3 Comparing the three polar motives of reciprocity

We have now seen the three polar motives of reciprocity: *seeking* **balance**, *induced* **liking**, and *inducing* **continuation**. They correspond to three basic fields of sentiments respectively. Balance reciprocity rests on duty, propriety and norm following. Liking reciprocity lies in the field of altruism. Continuation can be induced by interest although one may want the continuation of various aspects of the relationship. Figure 5.1 summarizes this structure and the three basic dichotomies it implies. **Self-interest** is opposed to both the altruism of liking other people and the duty of balance and fairness which are **social motives** (moral or not). The **duty** or propriety of balance is opposed to the **pleasure** of satisfying one's interests and benefiting people one likes. **Altruism** in liking others opposes the *ego* which requires both the satisfaction of its interest and the protection of its social place in balance reciprocity.

These are the essential structures. Other relations are adventitious. For instance, one may derive pleasure from doing one's duty (and some hedonist philosophers have said you ought to seek pleasure), find satisfaction for one's ego in altruistically liking others and still more in being liked by them, seek material interest for acquiring social status or for giving to people one likes, and so on.

8.4   Relational, process, status, or symbolic reciprocities

The foregoing analysis has focused on and emphasized the basic pure motives of the acts and facts of reciprocity or reciprocating. However, as we have also emphasized, reciprocity also denotes a relationship. In particular, it is often a more or less steady relationship, and this is an important feature of it. The relationship as such is often the relevant aspect. The reciprocity can then associate various motives in various ways and proportions, although not all such associations are possible (e.g., as we have seen, strong liking or love is generally inconsistent with counting or measuring gifts induced by a reason of balance, whereas balance is possible with milder liking, and its fairness can even be required for it). The relationship may be one aspect of the acts of giving that is appreciated, and the continuation of which is sought. Its steadiness is particularly important for the basic sentiment of liking. The appreciation of the relationship can itself have various quite different motives, such as appreciating the social intercourse in itself, or the attention or sentiments towards oneself. Particular reciprocities also result from different roles or statuses of the participants, and support and manifest these relationships. Such relational reciprocities can thus be process reciprocities, status reciprocities, and so on. The gifts of relational reciprocities may matter in themselves, but their intrinsic value often becomes secondary, or even vanishes, as they become mere pretexts for or symbols of the relationship. Recall again the cases in which people give to one another identical drinks or meals, or wedding rings. This place of reciprocity makes it a central issue in the conception of society that sees it neither as a Durkheimian whole nor as a heap of individuals related at most by self-interest, but as a complex of living relations.

8.5   Imitation and conforming

We have seen that the imitation – or, rather, contagion – of sentiments can lead to or reinforce liking reciprocity through a mirror-image duplication of liking the other person. There can be reciprocation of benefiting the other simply from the imitation of an act, or from acting in conformity with acts of others. The receiver is particularly aware of the act she benefits from, and the giver is straightforwardly available as beneficiary of her replication. Nevertheless, contagion or imitation of sentiments and of acts, or conforming to conduct, can also occur for agents not concerned with the initial sentiments or acts.

Finally, all the effects that can induce reciprocity, analysed in the two previous chapters and in this one, are gathered in a summary on the graph of figure 5.2. The theory of the working of these effects is the subject of part IV.

8.6   The motives for extended reciprocations

Extended reciprocities and, more generally, reciprocations – generalized, general, and reverse – are important phenomena. Their motives belong (or are akin) to those of ordinary (bilateral) reciprocities and reciprocations, but they cover only a part of these motives. There are reasons for this difference and limitation. One is the substitution of an agent for another in generalized and reverse reciprocities. The other is that, in general reciprocity, the other party is not seen as an individual but rather as a group – the group of other people –, or a social entity – "society." Chapter 4 has fully shown how each motive of the standard, direct reciprocities can, or cannot, constitute a motive of an extended reciprocity.

We have, indeed, seen that most of the explanation rests in the substitution of one person for another because of liking relations or because they belong to the same group. With the sign $\rightarrow$ denoting either "gives to" or "hurts," $A \rightarrow B$ entails $B \rightarrow C$ because A likes C or B acts towards the group (AC); or $A \rightarrow B$ entails $C \rightarrow A$ because C likes B or acts on behalf of the group (BC). The motives of the actions can a priori be liking, balance, gratitude, continuation, revenge or deterrence (and imitation can play a role).

More generally, someone who has been well treated often tends, as a consequence, to be favourable to other people in general, or to think that she owes something to others in general. Similarly, someone who has been hurt by some person sometimes tends, as a result, to be hostile and rough towards others, or to take revenge on society. Conversely, someone who is generous and helpful towards someone else is often seen as deserving a reward, notably to be helped when she needs it, which would maintain some balance; moreover, one is prone to like this generous character and this is favourable to helping her when she needs it. This effect remains when you happen to be the beneficiary of this person's generosity, and it adds to the specific reasons you have to appreciate being helped or given to. This reverse reciprocity has classically been emphasized by moralists and even by religions, as the source of worldly immanent reward for altruism. It is even often suggested that the return gifts overcompensate the cost of the initial benevolence (e.g. by René Descartes, Adam Smith, and Jeremy Bentham). When this is the case, the initial giver can come to give for a purely self-interested reason. Then, however, she is self-interested and no longer a generous person deserving a reward. She may then be given to in order to induce her to repeat her giving, in a reverse continuation reciprocity, and the benevolent agent is the agent who gives to her and thus, indirectly, favours the final beneficiary. This reward of merit or inducement of further actions may be provided by society represented by its institutions.

On the dark side of reciprocation, similar effects exist for such an "anonymous" extension of revenge and of retaliation for deterrence into the motives for punishment. However, the liking effect has no such parallel, since, although you are prone to dislike wrongdoers, you are probably much less to harm people simply because you dislike them (in the way that you tend to give to people you like). These "objective" motives for reciprocation can be present for anyone, in particular the victim in addition to her specific reason as victim, and the standard implementer is society at large represented by its *ad hoc* institutions of justice. Unlawful harm has indeed to be prevented as respect of law and hence by society at large. Punishment for the deterrence of such actions constitutes a part of this activity. However, the other motive for punishment, namely the notions of deserts and merit which induce seeking some sort of balance, raises a major issue about the progress of civilization. A first step is the socialization of revenge for violence into lawful justice. Nevertheless, this motive remains no less barbarian for being a "motive of society." It even is more so since revenge might in part be excused as a primitive reaction and sentiment whereas social rules should be based on reason. The next progress in this respect will therefore be the suppression of such motives from the reasons of law.

9

Reciprocity and social sentiments

9.1 Introduction

Reciprocities are closely related to a complex of sentiments about society and about one's place in it. The motives for reciprocations are not emotional or motivational atoms. Each is a compound of several such sentiments, and each of these constituent sentiments also applies in vast other domains. Balance reciprocity rests on senses of equality and impartiality, and, sometimes, fairness and equity, distributive or compensatory justice, and all the sentiments that can accompany the sense of moral indebtedness (sometimes questions of dignity, inferiority or dependency), and it is supported by senses of propriety or duty, social or moral norms, and sometimes sentiments of guilt or shame. Liking reciprocity mobilizes affection of various types and intensity, concepts of responsibility, and the sense of self and of social existence. Gratitude mixes balance and liking. Revenge and resentment can mobilize issues of responsibility, senses of imbalance and balance, propriety and impropriety, and sometimes injustice, and they can be motivated by anger or by social norms and shame.

Moreover, fairness and affection may be not only motives for reciprocity but also objects of the relation. Such a reciprocal fairness is an important ingredient in the realization of social justice and social peace. The essential social normative motive of "universalization" – such as Kant's categorical imperative – is a kind of putative reciprocity ("act as if it induced other people to act likewise"). Other sentiments also have some relevance.

This chapter focuses on the relations between reciprocity and these sentiments, and their consequences.

9.2   Fairness, equity, justice

Reciprocity and fairness are a priori very different things. However, there are, between them, a number of important relations or possible relations of different types.

9.2.1 Balance reciprocity and justice, equality, retribution, reward and compensation

To begin with, there is a *common structure of ideal equality in both fairness and balance reciprocity* in general. This fairness can *more particularly apply to the items of a balance reciprocity*: the mutual favours or gifts between agents.

Indeed, two types of equity are among the basic sentiments that induce balance reciprocity. They are not the only sentiments leading to this conduct, however. There are also desires of balance per se, as something proper or required.

These two types of fairness inducing balance reciprocity are applications, to the items of the reciprocity, of two of the types of justice, compensatory and retributive or rewarding. This sense of *compensatory justice* says that the gift (favour) should be compensated by a return gift establishing some sort of balance, that this is just or fair. The sense of *retributive or rewarding justice* says that the initial giver deserves or merits a reward for her sacrifice on behalf of the other.

These two sentiments of justice are different, although they may lead to the same or similar results. No idea of deserts, merit or reward is present in compensatory justice; only issues of balance or equality matter. Some idea of balance between the two gifts is also present in retributive-rewarding justice, but it is a derived concept, the way to reward the deserts or merit of the initial giver. In compensatory justice, by contrast, the notion of the appropriate balance or equality is primary, with reference to the initial state and to somehow compensating for deviations from it.

In retributive-rewarding justice, only the initial giver and her responsibility matter. This is why the reward can a priori be provided by a third party, in a typical reverse reciprocity (a "Descartes effect"). In particular, this third party can be a public authority acting on behalf of society as a whole. However, the reward of deserts or merit can also be provided by the initial beneficiary, in a standard return gift. Then, the notion of a duty to reward is sometimes supported by a sentiment of gratitude.

Compensatory justice can produce its effects in this respect in two ways. The issue is balance, or some sort of equality, between the two gifts. However, the compensation can refer either to the situation of both individuals or to that of the initial giver only. In the former case, the return gift is necessarily from the receiver to the initial giver, and hence it is decided by the receiver (who may, however, be influenced by social judgments, morals, norms or social pressure). In the latter case, by contrast, the initial giver may be compensated by another agent, in a reverse reciprocity. This agent may, for instance, be a public authority acting on behalf of society as a whole. It may also be the initial receiver concerned with the initial giver's situation.

Negative reciprocation following harm raises similar issues, although not with a symmetry. Retributive justice then is punishment for a reason of deserts or merit – in addition to its possible role of deterring similar actions in the future. This punishment may a priori be inflicted by any agent. If the punisher is not the initial victim, this is a case of reverse negative reciprocation. This is for instance a basic role of public authorities, notably because, in a "state of law", it has the monopoly of lawful coercion. The punisher may also, in particular, be the initial victim. Then, however, the motive is usually not to punish *per se* but, rather, to take revenge.

Compensatory justice for harm can be attached to various comparisons. The most important is probably compensation for harm done for the victim: the restitution of things stolen, other compensation, *praetium doloris*, and so on. Another aspect is that the compensation may be demanded from the offender. This is a (compensatory) balance of the two-way effects as valued by the victim. Indeed, from the point of view of the offender, and hence overall, compensation in case of harm is often something particular. Compensation for both agents and overall can be achieved in the case of theft without collateral damage, by restitution or payment of an equivalent value. In other cases, however, harm is generally a by-product of some other advantage sought by the harmer, and there is a priori no reason for the value of this advantage and of the harm done to be equal, although in many cases the harm tends to increase with the advantage. The converse of benevolent giving, harm motivated by pure malice, *schadenfreude* or sadism seems (fortunately) to be much rarer.

Both retributive punishment and compensation by the offender are according to the offender's responsibility, which depends on the situation, on the actor's possibilities, and on a priori assignments of rights and duties. Of course, all compensations required or punishment inflicted can be implemented by the judicial system and the public force (the monopoly of lawful coercion).

9.2.2 Reciprocal fairness

A thoroughly different relation between reciprocity and fairness is that the gift or favour of one agent towards another can consist of being fair in any respect towards this agent, in acts, judgments, or the corresponding attitudes, notably at some cost of any kind for the agent who behaves in this manner. Such a fair conduct may elicit a returned favour which may be of the same type, possibly about similar items. This is *reciprocal fairness.*

Reciprocal fairness is amenable to all the extensions of reciprocity: negative reciprocation (not being fair towards unfair people), and, for both positive and negative forms, all the cases of extended reciprocity, for the general reasons – generalized, general, reverse (the "Descartes effect"), or chain reciprocal fairness or unfairness.

Reciprocal fairness can be motivated by most of the usual and general motives for reciprocity. This may be any of the motives for balance reciprocity. In particular, the motive may be retributive-rewarding or compensatory fairness (it may be fair to be fair). Continuation can also play this role: people are fair so that others continue to be fair towards them. Liking someone can also induce being fair towards her, and you tend to like someone who treats you fairly – notably if she chooses to do so actually freely rather than doing it in order to comply with a strong moral obligation (or under strong social pressure). However, the liking induced by fairness or inducing it is milder than the stronger liking that induces, or may be induced by, favouring the other more than is required by simple fairness.

Fair behaviour towards another person can a priori be one of the gifts or some of the gifts in a reciprocity of any type, along with other gifts of different natures. However, the tendency to similitude in the gifts of a reciprocity can lead to both gifts (or a larger number in longer reciprocities) having this nature, and, moreover, to more or less similar issues of fairness in each.

9.2.3 From reciprocal fairness to distributive justice

In a particular but particularly important case, all the attitudes and behaviours of fairness in a situation of reciprocal fairness concern the very same issue, such as sharing something between the participants, or choosing a rule for their relations. Then, if both agents' conceptions of fairness lead to the same result, the outcome is chosen by both agents unanimously. This transforms a situation of conflict into a unanimous choice. The central point here is that fairness or justice implies impartiality by the very nature and definition of these concepts. That is, an agent's impartial view, when it considers this agent's own interest, is not influenced by the fact that this interest is specifically her own (and similarly for the interests of the people that this agent particularly likes or dislikes). Hence, these views can coincide with each other, while this is not possible for interests when they are opposed by the nature of the issue – a distribution or sharing for instance.

This type of situation can apply to several issues of sharing. One is sharing a given resource between the agents. Another is sharing a cost, such as the cost of a public good for these agents, or the payment of a given collective liability or contribution. Yet another case concerns the conclusion of an agreement, possibly the solution of some bargaining: the issue then is sharing the corresponding surplus. The category of justice at stake here is *distributive justice*. This can apply with more than two participants, each behaving fairly towards others, for all these cases of the distribution of a given resource, reaching a collective agreement, or contributing to a public good or a given liability.

However, the solution leads to a unanimous choice only if the participants have a congruent conception of the relevant principle of fairness. Now, there are a priori a variety of such possible conceptions. Essentially, the distribution can be equal in some good, according to need, according to merit or deserts,[1] or according to some right either acquired or ascribed by a social choice or social position. However, when this "substance" of justice is agreed upon with sufficient precision (which good, need, merit or right), the very

---

[1] The difference between merit and deserts is that in merit individuals are entitled to – or liable for – the effects of their given personal capacities, whereas this is not the case with deserts.

nature of the concept of justice, fairness or equity tends to provide a solution unanimously agreed upon. The key property of these concepts is indeed the noted one of impartiality, by which each sees herself on the same footing as others (Thomas Nagel's "view from nowhere"). This leads in particular to equality in the relevant items (such as goods, reward for given merit, the satisfaction of a given need, or compliance with a given right), from a requirement of pure rationality.[2] When this equality is impossible or too costly in other terms, the same sentiment entails a preference for a lower inequality in the relevant items. Such comparisons of inequalities, and the building of corresponding indexes of inequality, constitute one of the most intensively studied topics in social science. This analysis consists of the consideration of various sentiments about changes in inequality – and in the underlying unfairness – produced by various structural changes in the distribution, and of showing the relations among these properties.[3] The agreement about the relevant "substance" of justice (and about the relevant second-best structure of inequality if necessary), can result from reason applied to the issue in question, shared values, social norms, influences among agents in the reciprocal interactions, or influences, imitations (or "contagion") of judgments.

The question of distributive justice is a priori raised everywhere and permanently in society: why does this thing belong to this person rather than to any other, or why are not unequal situations compensated for by some other transfer? Distributive justice does not give rise to such a permanent universal dispute and debate because of a broad consensus about this topic in a given society. And this agreement has a reciprocal form: each person acknowledges the relevant property of others, and hers is similarly acknowledged. In particular, any encounter between people raises issues of fairness as

---

[2] See Kolm 1971 (1998), foreword, section 5, of which section 6.3 above has shown an application.

[3] See Kolm 1966 and the handbook edited by Jacques Silber (1999).

long as the other is seen as a person – with the respect that this implies – and any peaceful interaction that is not only a truce implies reciprocal acknowledgment of rights and rules. The issues of justice and fairness are thus pervasive. However, prior to all the cases of specific "microjustice" stand the general rules of society – a reciprocal respect of general rights – and the main distributions concerning the allocation of the product of the main resources, notably of given human capacities, which often lead to widespread redistributions. These redistributions follow, or should follow, principles of justice, some of which are closely related to issues of reciprocity, as will be pointed out shortly (chapter 14).

9.3 The principle of universalization: the categorical imperative

When asked why they bother to vote in large-scale elections in which their own voice makes no actual difference, most people answer: "What if nobody voted?" They are immune to the remark that their own voting will not induce other people to vote. In fact, such a popular version of Kant's categorical imperative is a main reason for people to participate in collective actions and freely contribute to public goods. The moral indictment is: "Act in a way such that, if everyone acted the same – or followed the same principle – you would want the result" (for Kant, if everyone acted according to the same "maxim", you "could want the result"). This conduct solves prisoner's dilemmas, "coordination dilemmas" in which one coordinated solution is preferred by everyone, and the corresponding dilemmas about free contributions to public goods (see chapter 12), because each action obeying this principle does not take into account the possible *actual* choices of the other players. This principle amounts to assuming that the others reciprocate (or duplicate) your act. It is putative reciprocity with each of the others. This could be a kind of actual reciprocity only if the others adopt this principle for themselves because you do; then, it would be a reciprocity in the principle of one's action rather than in the action itself, and it would have to have the particular logic of reciprocal contributions to public goods analysed in chapter 12.

9.4 Other social sentiments

Comparative, matching or balance reciprocities are motivated by various more basic sentiments. The noted sentiments of justice, fairness or equity are only some of them, and they are not always present – they seem to be more often present in revenge reciprocation than in (positive) reciprocities. Other sentiments motivating such reciprocities are a sense of duty, or of propriety and adequacy, in particular in following a norm of conduct. Moreover, such reciprocities are often motivated by the desire to avoid moral indebtedness. One often wants to avoid this indebtedness because it can mean dependency, subjection or inferiority, and this arouses the corresponding sentiments. These sentiments can go as far as undermining dignity and arousing shame or guilt. Symmetrically, this imbalance can put the initial giver in the position of a moral creditor, which can elicit sentiments of pride, or of superiority, domination and power.

Liking and love are also in themselves quite apart from reciprocity, and yet they tend to induce reciprocities in actions and sentiments, and they constitute the material and vector of liking reciprocities, in rather complex processes analysed in chapters 7 and 19. These reciprocities also involve the sense of self and of social existence, and notions of the responsibility of the other person. The sentiment of gratitude, also discussed, has aspects of both balance and liking.

10

Reciprocity in the modes of economic realization

Science – and simple understanding – begin with the distinction and classification of phenomena, in pointing out the critical discriminating properties. Approaching a social process from the point of view of economics means beginning with "transfers." In the strict sense, the term "transfer" denotes the ordinary transfer of a good from one agent to another, but, by extension and for convenience of vocabulary, it will also denote, here, a service provided by one agent to another, and, more generally, any change in the world that is both costly in some sense for an agent and favourable to another. This can be an act of the former agent. Hence, transferring can mean acting favourably; giving can refer to such an act; and taking can mean forcing the other person to perform such an act. The distinction and comparison of the various modalities and modes of transfer are particularly important for understanding society. With respect to types of social relation and motivations, four types of modes of transfer can be distinguished: *taking* by force (forcing); *gift giving*; *exchange*; and *reciprocity*. As before, exchange is understood here as standard exchange between self-interested agents (as with market exchange); that is, a set of transfers that are mutually conditional (implementation is by external obligation, or by promise keeping, or if it is by moral obligation alone, this is an obligation to abide by an agreement, and not, for instance, to give in return). Reciprocity means here reciprocity proper, or "positive" reciprocation, and the corresponding transfers have the nature of gifts. The simplest relations presently considered will be between two agents, but a larger number of agents can be directly involved, as with collective agreements among more than two persons (which are exchanges), contributing to or deteriorating collective concerns or public goods, and extended reciprocities (generalized, general, reverse, chain).

Of course, each transfer can be closely related to others belonging to different modes. For example, a person may take something or acquire it in exchange in order to give it to someone else; or she may buy, or acquire in reciprocity, the services of someone else for robbing or forcing a third person; "bands of brothers" can be bands of thieves or of killers; and so on. The fact that a person can behave selfishly towards some people, in particular in markets, with the aim of giving what she obtains to other people (or of using it for any other non-selfish purpose) was a main interest of the clergyman-economist Philip Wicksteed (1888, 1933). He called such a restrictively selfish conduct *nontuism*, in order to distinguish it from general egoism. Note that nontuism violates Kant's dictum of always treating others also as ends, just as purely egoistic relations do.

The most elementary property is the smallest *number of transfers* involved in the relations in each mode, which is the number of transfers in the most elementary relations in each mode. Forceful taking and giving need one transfer only, whereas exchange and reciprocity need at least two interrelated transfers, one in each direction.

The second property – a deeper one – concerns *freedom*. The use of force and taking by force violate the liberty of one agent, while the other three modes respect the freedom of all involved agents. There is, however, a major difference in this respect between the two two-way transfers, exchange and reciprocity. In both cases, the pair – or a larger set – of transfers is freely chosen or accepted by the participants.

In addition, however, in reciprocity each single transfer is free by itself. For example, the initial giving of a gift/return gift relationship is, obviously, decided by the giver alone, but the receiver is also free to hand out a return gift or not, and to choose this return gift. This latter agent may feel an internal obligation to return the favour, but she is free from external obligations in this respect (or their equivalents in promise keeping or abiding by the agreement). An internal obligation can also be felt for the initial giving, or, indeed, for a single isolated gift, and in all these cases the cost of non-giving may be increased by a requirement of norm following and by social opinion or pressure. Nonetheless, the act is, in the end, a free one, since otherwise it would just not be gift giving but force and constraint. In an exchange, in contrast, each transfer is conditional on the other by an external obligation − such a "transfer" can mean the set of transfers in one direction. When one transfer is performed, the other has to be completed too. Legal obligation can be used to enforce such a contract, but the enforcement can be any other threat either of the use of force (by the other party or yet other agents) or of denying further benefits or possibilities, notably of exchanges, for instance in the continuation of a sequential exchange (obeying a moral of promise keeping or of respecting an agreement is also included in this kind of constraint). Each single transfer is not free by itself. The expression "I give you this if you give me that" cannot refer to "gifts" in the proper sense of the term, but only to the terms of an exchange. On the other hand, "I give you this because you have given that to me" would refer to a return gift for a previous gift (although most often this sentence will not be uttered and the idea will remain implicit). The fact that the transfers of a reciprocity cannot be mutually conditional by external obligation, and, to a lesser degree, the fact that the acts occur successively (although return gifts for expected gifts may occur in particular cases) will be important features in the theory of reciprocity, both for the possibilities

Table 10.1 *The four dichotomies of the four modes of economic transfer*

Coercion	Exchange	Reciprocity	Pure gift-giving
Forced	Globally voluntary		
Individually coerced transfers		Independently voluntary transfers	
Independent one-way transfer	Interrelated two-way transfers		Independent one-way transfer
Self-centred motivation		Other oriented	

of realization, and for the nature and quality of the social relation (see chapter 22).

Finally, the third property – the deepest one – concerns *motivation*. Taking and exchange can be performed by selfish or nontuistic people. In contrast, the givings and reciprocities that differ most from the other modes and are the most interesting for the quality of society are based on positive other-regarding sentiments or reasons, notably altruism, aspects of justice and fairness for balance reciprocity, and gratitude.

Table 10.1 summarizes this discussion. Needless to say, this typology of modes of transfers bears a priori no relation to the types of goods (commodities, services) that are transferred. However, particular cultures establish as norms such correlations, some of which commonly are important aspects of the culture (for instance, particular services or goods must be transferred as gifts – perhaps in reciprocity – rather than sold and bought, etc.). These cultural traits can change, and these modifications are often important aspects of overall cultural changes (notably in "modernization" whereby, typically, more goods become amenable to exchange).

The relative positioning of these four modes is meaningful and interesting. In the modes with overall freedom, reciprocity is situated between exchange and pure gift giving. It consists of interrelated two-way transfers, as exchange does, but it shares with pure gift giving both the other-oriented motivation and the fact that each transfer is individually

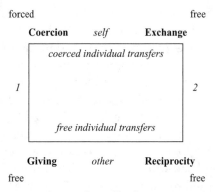

Figure 10.1 The quadrangle of economic transfers

free. Similarly, exchange is situated between coercion and reciprocity. As reciprocity, it consists of a set of several interrelated and globally voluntary transfers. As with coercion, however, these transfers are individually forced and the direct motivation is self-centred (although there can be Wicksteedian "nontuism").

This discussion can also be summarized with the quadrangle diagram of figure 10.1. The four corners of the square respectively represent the four modes of transfer: coercion, exchange, giving and reciprocity. The sides containing coercion and gift giving, and exchange and reciprocity, correspond to the smallest numbers of transfers of one and two, respectively. The sides containing coercion and exchange, and giving and reciprocity, correspond to selfish and other-oriented conducts respectively. They also correspond to transfers that are individually forced and free respectively. On the other hand, only coercion corresponds to force when all transfers are taken jointly since exchange is free in this respect.

A society of any kind (a nation, a region, an organization of any type) can use several of these modes in proportions that constitute a basic characteristic and can be measured as the proportion of economic values transferred in these modes.

The comparison of these proportions across societies is a major aspect of the comparison of these societies, and the evolution of these proportions over time reveals an essential aspect of the transformation of these societies. This has been used, in particular, for providing a general taxonomy and analysis of economies, and for studying the evolution of economies in the processes of modernization and "development" and their various types. Several technical devices have been used for such studies, depending on the issue one wants to emphasize. In all cases, the term exchange refers to self-interested free exchanges of the market type. One can consider the four modes, or three modes by lumping two of them together.

In important studies, the three modes are exchange (market), the public and command economy with coercion, and (private) reciprocity.[1] Private gifts are included in reciprocity (reciprocity is a set of gift givings and a pure gift can be seen as a limiting case of a reciprocity in which the return gift vanishes). Transfers by the public sector lead to its assimilation to the system of "redistribution" by a central power, as considered by some scholars such as Karl Polanyi (1944). The economy of an actual society is a regime which is a mix of these three systems in various possible proportions. The comparison and evolution of economies are fruitfully illustrated by the representation of the three corresponding proportions in a triangular diagram in which each proportion is the distance of a point representing the economy to each side of an isosceles triangle including the point. The summits of the triangle represent each of the pure systems, and one system is absent for the points situated on a side of the triangle.[2]

The proportions of the four modes in a society can also be represented by a point in the quadrangle of figure 10.1:

---

[1] The reciprocities or exchanges that may be at work in the political and public processes are not considered as reciprocity or exchange.

[2] See the analyses using such a device in Kolm 1984a.

the distance of this point to a side is proportional to the volume or proportion of transfers in the two modes indicated at the corners on the opposite side (the sum of these two volumes or proportions). Hence, points on a side correspond to the case in which only the two modes of the corners on this side are present. The corners correspond to the pure modes. The sides correspond, respectively, to selfishness (the upper side) which opposes concern for others (the lower side), and to a single agent's decision (the left-hand side) which opposes interactive choices (the right-hand side). A higher or lower point corresponds to more selfishness and more concern for others respectively. And a point more to the left or to the right corresponds to more individualistic decisions and more collective choices respectively. This also corresponds to various classical emphases in the conception of society: Hobbes was obsessed by the top left (coercion, plus a social contract), many economists are by the top right (exchange), whereas many anthropologists first see the bottom right (reciprocity), and utopians favour the bottom left (pure giving).

Part III

Values and reasons

11

The values of reciprocity

11.1 The issues

Relations of reciprocity have a number of good consequences – some of which are very important – and also sometimes bad ones. Very briefly, they will be shown to permit a generally peaceful and free society and to correct "failures" of markets and organizations in various ways, liking reciprocities are appreciated for liking and balance reciprocities for social balance or fairness, and yet reciprocities may also take the place of an efficient price system and balance reciprocity is sometimes imposed by oppressive norms. Understanding these effects is important for two reasons, acting and explaining. Indeed, reciprocity can be more or less favoured or promoted, often indirectly, by collective choices regarding institutions, rules and education, and by individual choices in choosing a type of relationship with other people in specific circumstances. These choices then have to evaluate reciprocities and try to foresee and understand their various effects. However, such wilful and conscious decisions are usually only a small part of the causes of reciprocities or of their absence. Indeed, these modes of social relation result essentially from a social and psychological process of evolution involving the joint formation of sentiments, culture, traditions, habits, social structures, institutions, and moral and educational views. This process includes conscious choices about many issues, unconscious or partially conscious influences on more or less distant consequences, the formation of views, opinions, sentiments and personalities, and many mechanisms of selection of psychological, cultural or other social traits (with, in a very distant and general background, genetic selection of the basic human material). These selections of all types, including direct and indirect choices interwoven with other effects, tend to create social forms that favour the thriving of society. In particular, they can establish reciprocities because of such effects. Hence, understanding the favourable effects of reciprocity is part of the explanation of this mode of social relation.

Both explaining and evaluating in order to choose are common questions. Even people who discard explaining for the sake of it may require explanations in order to make the appropriate choices. As for evaluation, its question is posed by the very fact that we have to choose. Let us point out that for economics, notably, this has always been a central concern. Economics has always been a normative science, and it is largely the only normative social science (setting aside law and political philosophy). This is so because it aims at guiding action in evaluating the reasons for it and its consequences (it is a praxeology). The standard question addressed to authors of economic studies is: "What are the conclusions for policy?" The best-known economist – although a special one – has proposed that "The aim is not to know the world but to transform it." Of course, the proper and useful evaluations generally involve more than concern with economic goods in the strict sense. This is the case, in particular, concerning the modes of economic interaction.

Thus, we have to consider the values – including the shortcomings – of reciprocities. The overview is as follows. The reciprocity of respect permits the existence and performance of other peaceful social interactions, in particular of otherwise self-interested exchanges and markets.

Reciprocity also constitutes a main corrector of "market fail-ures" in taking the place of missing or imperfect markets, ending sequential exchanges, inducing free contributions to non-excludable public goods through various mechanisms, voluntarily internalizing externalities, or sustaining mutual trust. These "failures" are cases in which self-interest is self-defeating as a consequence of social interactions. Then, the relevant reciprocities are important instances of conducts that, in not pursuing self-interest, promote it in the end. How-ever, reciprocity can also take the place of some allocatively efficient markets and exchanges. This may lead to losses in allocative efficiency. Indeed, although a single gift is Pareto efficient because it maximizes one individual utility (the giver's), the pair of gifts of a reciprocity does not have this property prima facie. However, relationships of reciprocity are also often appreciated in themselves, for the intrinsic quality of interpersonal relations based on mutual appreci-ation and equity. Moreover, reciprocities are also important, and in part necessary, for the efficient working of organi-zations of all types, for the same reason as with markets: they permit a better use of information and can replace coer-cion, notably in reciprocal trust and trustworthiness, promise keeping, goodwill, assistance and cooperation.

In addition to reciprocity's effects on the distribution and allocation of goods and on the efficiency of social systems, a very important aspect of this interaction concerns the style of social relations it introduces. These relations are bound to be positive and appreciated with liking reciprocities (with the drawback that liking someone more makes one more sensi-tive to her misfortune), and more ambivalent with balance reciprocities, in which one may like the aspects of social balance and justice, but possibly dislike the moral or social obligation of a norm if there is one. At any rate, the very exis-tence of direct and final concern for other people implied by reciprocities is often important and valued. A priori, in liking and balance reciprocities people consider the other person also as an end in itself;[1] they do not consider her only as a means to their own satisfaction (as with standard exchange or self-interested continuation reciprocity, for instance). In fact, the various types of behaviour and conduct in society are evaluated differently from a normative or moral point of view, both by the actors and by other people: taking by force, self-interested exchange, benevolent giving, norm-abiding, and so on, are judged very differently in this respect.

Finally – and, arguably, most importantly – these actions and relations are related to different types of personality of individuals. Personality determines acts, but, conversely, an individual's behaviour can also influence her sentiments, outlook and preferences through the avoidance or reduction of dissonance between acts and sentiments (behaving as if one had some motive, for any reason, makes one feel a "motivational dissonance" which tends to make one ill at ease, and this uneasiness is soothed by more or less adopting this motive, through a process which can mix spontaneity and wilfulness – in a clear similarity with Leon Festinger's "cognitive dissonance"). Moreover, the actions, reactions, opinions and sentiments of other people, and the examples and arguments they provide, generally strongly influence the individual's judgments, feelings, world views, attitudes and conducts. There are societies of benevolent, helpful and hospitable people, societies in which a price is demanded for every service, and societies in which you are happy to lose a cow, or an eye, if your neighbour loses two. Most people think it makes a difference. The good society is made up of good people, not just of well-fed, or even happy, individuals. Most ethical views judge that there is a progress from feeling good, to doing good, and to being good – indeed, being good

---

[1] Except in cases of balance reciprocity in which the aim becomes only the norm and the comparison of acts rather than concern for the actors as persons as well.

induces doing good, which provides a feeling of high quality as by-product and immanent reward.

11.2 General respect and sociability from reciprocity

A society is not a permanent war of all against all. However, purely self-interested individuals have no reason to respect others, be polite towards them, or abstain from taking the property of people weaker than them, or enslaving them. Why do most people not behave this way?

The simple sociability of general respect and helpfulness cannot be explained with purely self-interested individuals. There are other motives, be they benevolence, the duty to behave properly, or sheer imitation, obtained with the aid of education and the judgment of others. However, people at large do not behave in this way when they themselves commonly face tougher behaviour towards themselves. This is proven by all experiences in which this is the case; praiseworthy or saintly characters who are consistently helpful but not helped, nice when other people are nasty towards them, and respectful when they are shown little respect, happen to be rather rare, and they matter little statistically for the characterization of the general ethos of social interactions in society. Now, the general motive and situation of this general respect and sociability cannot be a case of sequential exchange when this behaviour is between people who a priori will not meet again with reversed roles, the common case in a sufficiently large society. It cannot even be the desire not to disrupt such a beneficial social order when the individual actor is small among many others. Moreover, the attitude and helpful behaviour of the general sociability in question are not obtained and obtainable by force (private or public). Hence, this is a case of generalized and general reciprocity, from and towards anonymous others even though they are specific in each encounter. All the corresponding sentiments and behaviour can intervene: imitation, sense of balance, a priori favourable sentiments towards others, norms of conduct, and the judgment of other people.

This extends to the respect of more important items, such as the property and freedom of other people. Purely self-interested individuals should take the property of others when they can, and even enslave them. The reason why this is not the common situation in steady societies is threefold: self-defence and protection, fear of the police, and voluntary restraint. These three means exist in various proportions. Self-restraint from harming and robbing others suffices in particular societies. It is never absent in the whole of society, and it is generally quite important (individuals who lack it *fully* are pathological types). It comes about as general morality resulting from education, imitation, social norms of "proper" behaviour and probably some "innate" propensity, and it works in close association with the other means using force or the threat of it. However, a person would doubtless be less prone to manifest this respect if the others did not also do so, notably towards herself. Hence, generalized and general reciprocity are at work here, in the family of the noted "helping behaviour" but applied to the more straightforward restraint from harming. Again, this conduct cannot result from a purely self-interested sequential exchange since being respected by some sustains or induces respecting others (and a single individual's behaviour has little effect on most others). The outcomes are very important, notably including general social peace (relative scarcity of direct violence), and the possibility of property rights and hence of exchanges. This general reciprocity permits society to be something other than a war of all against all or a police state or some mixture of both, to escape these two horns of the Hobbesian dilemma, which waste resources, jeopardize peace and freedom, and make for particularly distasteful social relations.

Similarly, and for the same reason, people do not maximally use fraud, lying and deception in social relations and notably exchanges. This often simply makes these relations and exchanges possible. And, generally, it tends to make these exchanges more efficient.

12

Reciprocal corrections of market failures

12.1 Reciprocal solutions for correcting market failures

The situations of general sociability, respect, peace, and honesty could not be obtained by contracts of mutual agreement and exchange alone because of impossibilities and costs of constraining people and concerning information in a broad sense (plus the very basic fact that sentiments are important per se and cannot be bought).[1] In the case of honesty limiting deceit and fraud, this impossibility of a correct contract is due to asymmetrical information. For general respect of people and property, this agreement would be an overall contract involving everyone (akin to the kind envisioned by Thomas Hobbes). However, such a sufficient *actual* contract is not possible because of costs and impossibilities in information, communication, contact, discussion, transaction, and writing the contract in sufficient detail. Such limitations to exchanges or agreements have many other occurrences. They include what is called "market failures" and extend more generally to agreement failures. Their causes are impossibilities or costs in the domains of information, imagining possible events, writing sufficiently detailed contracts, and, for implementing the contract, checking, monitoring, constraining as required,

---

[1] The consequences of this latter market failure are analysed in chapter 15.

and in particular specifically excluding a person from a benefit that comes along with other advantages or that occurs jointly for several people. These "failures" are faced in a number of ways. This is one of the functions of the public sectors which, however, have their own difficulties, costs and impossibilities with respect to information and constraining (as well as limitations concerning the motives of their members as persons or as subjected to the political process). Other solutions rely on conduct of the people involved that depart from pure individualistic self-interest. Among the types of conduct leading to this result, reciprocations have important roles. This applies particularly to sequential actions and to collective action and the provisions of public goods.

12.2 Sequential relation

Person A may give something to person B, or abstain from hurting her, for purely self-interested reasons, because she expects person B to reciprocate correspondingly. There can thus be mutual transfers or respect without binding agreement, hence, in particular, when the corresponding binding agreement is not possible or is too costly in any way (a "market failure"). The result may be beneficial to both parties, and in particular to person B, from the point of view of their pure self-interest. If person A may reiterate her gift or respect later, person B's motivation to reciprocate may simply be that of continuation reciprocity for the sake of her self-interest. This possible reiteration is often not the case, however. At any rate, when this mechanism is at work, it rests on the assumption of a continuing sequence, which has a last move raising the same problem. Without the consideration of further reiteration, person B's answer has to have a non-self-interested motivation. This cannot be full liking reciprocity, or gratitude, aroused by the previous gift, since this giving's final intention was not to benefit person B. Person B's motives should thus be in the family of balance reciprocity, such as maintaining a balance, justice or fairness, or rewarding deserts or merit, sustained by conducts of behaving properly, doing one's duty, or even acting according to honour. They are not strict, direct and intrinsic self-interest. Nevertheless, they serve this person's self-interest in permitting this "exchange" or mutual respect (as if by an immanent reward of duty-bound conduct), since self-interested person A would not give in the first place if she knows that person B will not return a gift or do her part because she is purely self-interested.

Both parties benefit from this moral or balance reciprocitarian conduct of this person, and this explains the various processes that lead to the existence of such motives and conduct. Indeed, the benefit for others (such as person A) leads society to praise this conduct and its motives, and to consider them as moral (in addition to the intrinsic morality of balance reciprocity due to its properties of impartial equality and rewarding merit). This induces this conduct and motivates it by seeking approval and praise, including in one's own judgment; in particular, moral education is a notable means of this influence. Moreover, the own benefit of the person (B) tends to induce her to adopt these moral or reciprocitarian motivations, which are both profitable and morally valued, by a psychological process which associates effects that are conscious and unconscious, and voluntary and involuntary. These two types of forces for adopting such conduct and motive reinforce one another, and they can finally overcome narrowly self-interested impulses. One could, in addition, imagine that genetic selection has paved the way in laying down broad tendencies. They can come both from benefit to others and from benefit to the agent herself. This makes for two very different types of theories, however. The influence of benefits to others can play through group selection only, whereas that of benefit to oneself rests neither on group selection nor on kin selection which sociobiologists see as the cause of "altruism" (quite simply, moral or reciprocitarian individuals would tend to survive more because of the benefit they derive from relations of the type in question).[2] If the term "rational" is used – as it sometimes is – for serving one's self-interest in a narrow sense, these effects show that it may be rational to be irrational, and they can provide a basis for explaining such irrationalities.

The general logic of sequential exchange was considered earlier. The case in which there are more than two moves introduces important facts. One is the possibility of punishment and threat of punishment for maintaining the sequence of transfers, services or contributions. Moreover, a frequent case is that, in a steady relation of mutually favourable acts, some sentiments in the family of liking develop progressively, even if there is no benefactor-liking at the onset, and this sentiment can motivate the last action (this may not be foreseen from the start, however, but we have pointed out that backward induction or other detrimental consideration of the last act does not actually occur beyond a few moves). Finally, we have also recalled the possible role of uncertainty about the end of the process or the other agent's behaviour for sustaining the relation.

12.3 Reciprocities and public goods or collective actions

12.3.1 Outline

It often happens that each of a number of individuals can perform some act, prefers everyone to act in this way rather than that no one does, but prefers not to do this herself when she takes what the others do as given, whatever it is. This is a typical simple case for contributions to a public good. However, the act can also be any kind of collective action, or respect for other people's property and integrity previously

---

[2] Another mechanism for the natural selection of pro-social traits, based on sexual selection, will be presented shortly.

discussed – then, general respect and peace can be seen as a public good. A collective binding agreement may solve the problem. However, in important and common situations, such an agreement may not be reachable because of the large number of people concerned or of costs of transaction, and access to the good cannot be sold to each person because of difficulties, costs or impossibilities of exclusion. In these cases, if everybody has a purely individualistic and self-interested reasoning, no one will perform her act, and nothing of the public good is produced (the Cournot-Nash solution of "free-riding"). This is, indeed, the outcome in a number of cases, but it is not in many others which are conspicuous in life.[3] Then, other reasonings or sentiments by the participants lead to different outcomes. One type refers to the shortcomings of the purely individualistic reasoning and reactive behaviour that take the actions of others as mere parameters and lead to the Cournot-Nash solution. The common knowledge (in the technical sense) that other solutions are preferred by everyone can lead to such other solutions. Psychologically, this tends to induce reasons for conduct – generally implicit ones – akin to the very common "folk categorical imperative" that says: "I do this because what if nobody did?" (This

---

[3] Taking the trouble to vote in large-scale elections, for people who do not consider the probability that they may be the pivotal, decisive voter (others being in a tie), is a case in point, and there are innumerable other cases in voluntary participation, abstaining from polluting, and so on. Many laboratory experiments on voluntary contributions to public goods have refined the fact in their special context (see notably Orbell and Wilson (1978), Ames and Marwell (1979), Schneider and Pommerehne (1981), Güth, Schmitterberger and Schwarze (1982), van de Kragt, Orbell and Dawes (1983), Isaac, Walker and Thomas (1984), Kim and Walker (1984), Isaac, McCue and Plott (1985), Dawes, de Kragt and Orbell (1988), Andreoni (1988a, 1988b), Isaac and Walker (1988a, 1988b), a general discussion by Dawes and Thaler (1988), and a general review in Ledyard (1995)). Only motives and reasons for voluntary contribution that belong to the realm of reciprocity are noted here. There are a number of others, however. For instance, mutual approval or status seeking, in the person's reference group, is beyond the present scope (see, e.g., Holländer 1990), as well as many other social or moral causes of contributing (the specific effects of all possible motives are presented in Kolm 2008).

is the main reason given by people when asked why they vote in large-scale elections in which their own vote makes no relevant difference). Other reasonings, motives and sentiments leading to the required action – such as voluntary contribution to a public good or a collective action – belong to various types of reciprocity, based on continuation and sequential exchange, balance or matching and equity, liking and reciprocal liking, or gratitude.

These different motives are considered successively: strict self-interest, the categorical imperative which is a type of putative reciprocity, matching reciprocity, and liking reciprocity. A notable property will be the role of constraint in matching reciprocity: a constraint is required, and yet it does not actually bind people. Of course, the various individuals can have different motives, and each individual can have mixed motives. Moreover, there are a variety of structures through which individual actions can jointly have the relevant effect, depending on the technology and the number of people. For instance, the contribution of each individual may be favourable to each other – although perhaps only very little when the participants are numerous; or there may have to be several contributions to make a difference – possibly all of them. To analyse the effects of these motives and emphasizing the aspects most germane to them, we will often consider the simplest situations in which all the individuals have the same motives, and the simplest technical structure (which can be presented as individual contributions to a pure public good, and even sometimes with only two alternatives for each individual, cooperating or contributing or not).

12.3.2 Strict self-interest: a cumulative sequential exchange

People may be strictly self-interested. If they reason individualistically in taking others' behaviour as given parameters, the outcome is a Cournot-Nash equilibrium of free-riding: usually, too little action is undertaken or the good is under-produced (except for exceptional indirect or income effects), and nothing is done or produced when the participants are sufficiently numerous and "small." A general agreement can solve the problem, but it may be prevented by the noted impediments, notably the impossibility to exclude from the benefit of the good, which prevents obtaining a payment in exchange for this benefit. Contributions can then be made compulsory, notably by a public sector.

However, there is often yet another possible solution, relying on free contributions and self-interest alone: the transformation of the contributions into a sequential exchange and a "continuation reciprocity" if the contributions (the good) are divisible. In this case, people first contribute a fraction of their overall contribution, possibly a small one. Then, other small contributions are provided, each in the hope that other people continue contributing further, and so on in a recurrent or continuing process. Each contributes under the threat that others will stop, lower or delay their own contribution if she does not continue (or contributes less or more slowly). The common house is thus built stone after stone. This is a *cumulative sequential exchange*. The question of the end of the process, already discussed for the standard sequential exchange, is present here. However, the process can theoretically be endless if the successive contributions are decreasing but with a sum converging to a finite amount. However, if the good benefits the contributors only when it is fully completed (in finite time), the contributions have to be provided faster and faster on average (if the contributors also benefit before, the process is a kind of collective sequential exchange that creates a durable public good). Morever, the necessary divisibility of the good and the general visibility of the contributions may not be the case.

12.3.3 Universalization or "Categorical imperative": a general putative matching reciprocity

We have noted that a common answer given by people to explain their contribution or participation is "I do it because what would happen if nobody did?" This is for instance the main answer received when people are asked why they vote in large-scale elections in which their vote makes no relevant difference and they don't imagine being a "pivotal voter" in a tie. People cling to their view and their slogan when it is pointed out to them that this is nonsense from the point of view of their individual action – which does not influence that of others.

This motivating reasoning is a rough kind of Kantian "categorical imperative": the person acts according to what the consequences would be if all others acted the same. The imaginary condition ("as if") amounts to matching contributions from others – that the agent's own contribution matches in turn. This is a kind of matching reciprocity, only the other people's contributions need not be actual. This motive can be called a putative general matching reciprocity. The other people's contributions become actual if the others hold the same reasoning and act in consequence. This "imperative" is in the realm of duty (Kant's favourite motive). Although this reasoning and the corresponding conduct are widespread, they are a priori also quite demanding in terms of risk to self-interest. This is why they are particularly present when the individual costs of contributing are small (such as voting or individual abstention from polluting public places). They also exist in other cases, however. Of course, everybody's interests are best served when this conduct is widespread.[4]

However, other, less demanding, motives in the field of balance reciprocity also exist.

---

[4] A full analysis of this "universalization" principle of conduct is provided in Kolm 2008.

12.3.4 Matching reciprocity and the necessary non-binding constraint

A very common position is: "I'll do my share if the other people do theirs." This differs from the categorical imperative by the requirement that others' contributions should be actual. Nonetheless, this goes beyond individualistic self-interest in individual action, which advises defecting in the situation under consideration. This is a typical matching reciprocity based on a sense of fairness in contribution and in sharing the burden of a public good (a type of balance reciprocity). It also is a moral conduct (or a half-moral one if one takes full morality to be to contribute without condition).

This matching reciprocity transforms a game of the prisoner's dilemma type into a coordination game in the sense that all individuals want to act some way if the others act this way. As with typical coordination games, there are several such Cournot-Nash equilibria. There is, however, a major difference. In the standard coordination game, the players are indifferent about these solutions (for instance, they prefer that all drivers drive on the same side of the road, but they are indifferent between it being the right side or the left one). In contrast, in the present "contribution or participation coordination game," all players prefer all to contribute sufficiently rather than that no one contributes. Hence, the moral willingness to do like others associates with a preference between the alternative (coordinated) solutions. In addition, the willingness to do like others results from self-interest with standard coordination, whereas participating or contributing if the others do is a moral stance in the participation or contribution coordination (although the preference for one coordinated solution over the other results from self-interest). In fact, there can often be various levels of contribution of each and various attitudes in the population, but, in order to focus on the essential phenomena and for simplicity in presentation, the expression will be as if there were only two alternatives, cooperate (participate, contribute) or not, and if all individuals had the same attitude. In spite of the fact that individuals all prefer one Cournot-Nash solution to the other, the choice is not easier than in the standard coordination game but more difficult. Indeed, in the standard coordination game, a simple sign may rally all actions, since people are indifferent among the coordinated solutions and know the others are as well. In contrast, in the present situation, the fact that all the participants have the noted ethics and unanimous preferences for one coordinated solution does not suffice to secure the solution. Even if each knows these characteristics of the others, this does not induce her to believe that the others will contribute, and hence to contribute herself, since each follows her interest in defecting if she has not sufficiently ascertained that the others contribute. Hence the solution might not be reached short of a binding agreement or mutual credible promises with mutual trust.

One way of making an individual sure that the others contribute (cooperate, do not defect) is that they be forced to contribute. Since others also make the same reasoning, all individuals should be forced to contribute. This coercion seems to make this situation not a case of reciprocity in the retained sense (which implies that the acts in question are free). However, this may not be the case and this situation is in fact deeply paradoxical. Indeed, each individual is forced to contribute, and yet she contributes voluntarily because she knows the others contribute and she is sure of it. Hence, she is not actually forced. That is, she voluntarily and freely does what the constraint requires her to do. She is forced to do what she wants to do. The constraint is not actually binding. Nevertheless, it is reached by the act and there is no slack, no extra margin of freedom. Since the constraint is not binding, it is redundant in this sense. It is not useless, however: it is, for the others, the guarantee that the individual contributes. All the same, given this person's mentality, this guarantee is not necessary so long as the others contribute. And the others in fact know that this person would freely contribute if they themselves contribute, if they know her motives. In the case in which there are two people only and the acts are visible, no constraint is needed, since each knows that if she shows she contributes, the other will contribute too. The paradox of the necessary non-binding constraint is only for larger societies (for the same reason as in a pair, no constraint is needed in the variant of the game in which each contributes if at least one other contributes). Practically, since the constraints are not actually enforced, they may require only light coercive means. The policeman may in the end become practically a mere symbol or signpost indicating that the cooperative solution is at work (rather than "enforced"). This is the result of the half-moral matching reciprocitarian conduct (full morality would be unconditional contribution, whatever the motive for it – it can be backed by a categorical imperative argument or not).

This matching reciprocitarian motive has variants. In one of them, the individuals want to contribute if the others want to contribute. The focus is on others' intention. The condition is their "goodwill" (in the sense of *bonne volonté*). Someone motivated in this way acts if she can and if the others would have acted if they could have. She excuses an individual for not contributing if this person is not responsible for her abstention. There can, indeed, be reciprocity of intentions. In a third case, the condition may be that the other people both want to contribute and do contribute, that is, they freely contribute. In this case, an obligation to contribute a priori does not suffice to induce others to contribute freely. Nonetheless, it may suffice if the individuals foresee that this constraint will not actually be binding. Of course, the free contribution is trivially guaranteed if individuals' conduct is that they contribute when others are in the same state of mind as they are (since this homogeneity is a priori assumed here). Moreover, an individual may require that only a subset or a fraction of the others act as required or intend to, or that they have this property to some extent, while her own action is also sometimes amenable to various forms or degrees. All these interesting and often important cases will not be discussed here.[5]

Moreover, the ethics in question can be seen as a set of relations in pairs of individuals. Indeed, each individual contribution to the public good benefits each other consumer of it, and hence it is a gift to her if it is voluntary. The balance reciprocity between these two gifts between two individuals amounts to the noted ethics – with the added structure that each such individual contribution benefits both individuals.

Finally, in a number of situations the beneficiaries of the public good or the participants to the collective action constitute a priori a community of some sort (or, possibly, become one as a result of this collective action). This is favourable to relationships of reciprocity among them. In particular, fairness among them can induce the noted matching or balance reciprocity. Moreover, a sense of community can lead these people to more or less like one another. This introduces, first, a concern of people for the interest of others in the public good and the contributions, and second, the possibility of motivations for reciprocity based on liking.

12.3.5 Sequential collective reciprocities

The provision of public goods may also involve sequential actions. In particular, contribution may be rewarded or its absence or insufficiency punished at a later period. Then,

---

[5] A full analysis of all these cases is proposed in Kolm 1984a. The basic case of individuals willing to contribute if the others do is also presented by Sugden (1984) under the term reciprocity. It is applied by Swaney (1990) in a model of a case of depletion of a common resource, that is, of a "tragedy of the commons" (Hardin, 1968). Laboratory experiments displaying such behaviour have been performed by Croson (1999) and Fishbacher, Gächter and Fehr (2000), with notable results showing the proportions of people behaving this way or not, or doing this to some extent, in the population of the experiment.

this is no longer a case of a pure non-excludable public good in the sense that punishing (or rewarding less) is to be taken as a form of exclusion – a more or less partial one, but sufficiently strong punishment has the effect of complete exclusion. Sequential provision of public goods permits forms of punishing (the benefits from the good can have various structures, with goods which can be more or less fungible or durable). This situation can be associated with various possible motivations, including pure self-interest and various types of reciprocitarian motives. The intricate logic of punishing found in a sequential exchange between two people occurs with a sequential provision of public goods with a larger number of people, with possibilities multiplied by a few specific features. (1) *Non-specific punishing*: contributing less because a contributor has provided less affects not just this person but also all other consumers of the public good, including those who contributed correctly; it is thus interesting to introduce possibilities of specific punishing, affecting one agent only, when this is possible. (2) *The public good of punishing*: punishing a defector also serves other parties; this punishing is in fact another public good in itself; this raises the issue of punishing agents who fail to punish defectors, with the same problem for this new collective action, and, indeed, a theoretically endless regression of situations of this kind. (3) *Partial contribution*: a contributor of only a part of the public good (or of its cost) sees the effects of her withholding contribution correspondingly diminished; in particular, a contributor "small in a large number" has practically no actual effect by herself; this reinforces the two previous problems. (4) As for all sequential contributions, punishing others by contributing less constitutes a *direct benefit* rather than a cost.

The possibilities of self-interested sequential exchanges are strongly diminished when passing from a two-people case to the case of a public good with a larger number of participants, because the punishment aspect of not contributing is jeopardized by the two facts that a single contribution is a smaller part of the whole, and an abstention punishes all consumers and not just a former non-contributor. Other motivations and possibilities are, therefore, particularly interesting. The reciprocitarian motive of contributing if others do (or if sufficiently many others sufficiently contribute) can apply, dynamically, to the observed others' contributions in the previous period (a tit for tat behaviour) or more generally in the past. This can lead to an equilibrium with overall contribution. The sequentiality permits bypassing the paradox of the non-binding constraint.

Another case overcomes the failures of punishment by non-contribution for public goods by possibilities for individuals to specifically punish others who fail to contribute. This is sometimes possible by direct action or by reporting the failure to an authority in charge of punishing (or to public opinion that condemns the failure). This may be costly for the punisher, possibly more than the personal benefit she expects to obtain by this threat (notably in the case of a 'small' agent in a large number) – this punishing cost is then incurred (also) for the sake of others, society or morality. Interestingly, there are two standard and opposed types of values, conducts, cultures and even societies in this respect. One type favours this individual law enforcement, whereas the other finds such individual punishment in the name of morals or society rather repulsive. When associated with a tendency to contribute, at least if others contribute, the former type consists of two manifestations of desire for the right order, whereas the later type is basically motivated by benevolence applied both in contribution and in forgivingness (although inducing others' contribution is favourable to all other consumers of the good). These are two very different polar types of socially minded characters. This also corresponds to two classical stereotypes of national cultures (there are cultures of punishment).[6]

---

[6] The behaviour of contributing if others contribute plus individually punishing evaders at a net cost for oneself is the object of interesting experiments by Falk, Fehr and Gächter (2000) and Fehr and Gächter (2000b).

12.4 Reciprocities as correcting or superficially creating economic or social inefficiencies

"Market failures" in general, and any such "failures" of exchanges and agreements, are the classical economic reasons for productive inefficiency in a broad sense, which in the end entails Pareto inefficiency (it is possible to satisfy some people better while no one is less satisfied). A classical conclusion is that the public sector should take care of these domains. However, public sectors have their own "failures." Indeed, they have the same two basic causes of failures as markets, exchanges and agreements, namely difficulties, costs and impossibilities in information and in constraining. Moreover, the various motivations of members of the political process and the public sector do not a priori guarantee optimality or efficiency – "benevolent dictators" hardly ever exist, and the "political market" among competing politicians is hardly a perfect one. Now, the various possible individual motivations that are not purely self-interested in intent and not purely individualistic in reasoning provide spontaneous, decentralized and free solutions and remedies for these failures and inefficiencies in a number of cases. For instance, they are responsible for the fact that observed voluntary contribution to public goods is often much better – and free-riding lower – than predicted for purely individualistic and self-interested participants (this is observed, for instance, in various voluntary participations, in voting – the public good being the maintenance of electoral democracy – and in laboratory experiments which are by now numerous).[7] In this role, reciprocities are less demanding in terms of motivation than pure altruism, since the self-sacrifices of individuals are lower because they are accompanied by benefits from the self-sacrifices of others. It is noteworthy that these motivations, whereby people are directly concerned with others' benefits or conduct (for reasons of balance, fairness, justice, respect,

---

[7] See note 3.

liking, and so on), constitute economic "externalities," and externalities are another classical source of market failures. In this case, these particular externalities correct other "failures."

On the other hand, externalities of the altruistic kind can also impair the functioning of the exchange system and its productive efficiency. A transfer by giving, hence at a null price, does not play the game by which the price system efficiently transmits information about possibilities and desires and can secure productive efficiency.[8] The distortion is also direct in any benevolent price rebate. This result also a priori holds for the set of givings that constitute a reciprocity (of the balance or liking kind), unless the return gifts happen to have the same market value as the gift, which sometimes is the case, notably in balance reciprocities.

However, gift-giving and reciprocities are, on the contrary, most often Pareto efficient if individual preferences are taken exhaustively, including the effects of the interpersonal sentiments characteristic of these relations. The simplest property is that since a giver freely chooses her gift, she is less happy with different levels of it and, therefore, the result is Pareto efficient. Reciprocities also often give rise to apparently inefficient allocations whereas the overall relation is Pareto efficient when full account is taken of the relevant sentiments of fairness, proper balance, liking and altruism, and interests in being considered or in the quality of the interaction. Satisfaction elicited by such preferences often compensates for possible strictly economic losses. This will be analysed fully in chapter 22, by introducing both the economic effects and the intrinsic values of the various types of relation and interaction, in particular self-interested exchange and various types of reciprocity. A number of applications will be shown. As an example, George Akerlof's (1982) "efficiency wages,"

---

[8] See the general discussion in Kolm (1984a), and the model presented by Laurence Kranich (1998).

chosen by an employer in order to benefit from the reciprocitarian labour supply of the employees, seem to induce a wasteful involuntary unemployment, but employees' preferences include their preference for this kind of conduct. We have also noted that such issues particularly interested the economist and clergyman Philip Wicksteed, whose concept of *nontuism* can reconcile market efficiency and altruism. Nontuism, indeed, means that when you operate in a classical market, you do not need to disregard the interest of everybody except yours – that is, to be selfish –, but only that of your vis-à-vis in the deal, while you can be altruistic towards everybody else. You can in particular give your profit, and seek profit to give it.

13

Reciprocity in trust, and intrinsic values

13.1 Reciprocity in trust, relational capital, and efficiency

Conducts and relations of reciprocity are also frequent in the working of most organizations, including firms.[1] They commonly improve this working and are often necessary for it, particularly because of the impossibilities and costs of specific information and checking. They take the form of mutual aid, including in questions of information and advising. This happens between members of the organization, or between the organization as such and its hired employees, in which case it is a particular case of reciprocity within an exchange or market relationship. These reciprocities within organizations can also have all the extended forms: generalized, general and reverse.

These effects of reciprocities as correcting microeconomic deficiencies of markets and improving or making possible the working of organizations are important causes of economic and social efficiency. In particular, impossibilities or

---

[1] Julio Rotemberg (1994) analyses the issue of altruism at the workplace and its effects on productivity. More precisely, he considers mutual altruism. However, these liking sentiments have causes, among which the fact that others like and help oneself, which lead to the two types of liking reciprocity. Moreover, balance reciprocity and continuation reciprocity are also important in this situation, with roles for the various types of extended reciprocities.

costs of contracting or enforcing contracts, and of imposing hierarchical command, and resulting uncertainties about the behaviour of others, are corrected by a family of conducts that are largely supported by their being – in these cases – reciprocal, notably keeping one's promises, hence being trustworthy, and also trusting, along with voluntarily paying one's due and doing one's part. These conducts and attitudes can be at work between individuals, within organizations (including firms) between members or bureaus and between the management and other parts, between organizations or organizations and individuals, for social relations of various types and importance. They are essential factors of economic efficiency and social cohesion.

Trust, in particular, can replace impossible or costly contracts, and permit the working of incomplete contracts, and it has a particular importance. It can elicit, and rest on, all the mechanisms of reciprocity, and in addition it has a number of very specific characteristics in this respect. The basis of the particular characteristics of the relation of trust is that an individual can have, in this relation, not two positions – as with giving and being given to – but three positions: trusting, being trusted, and being trustworthy. Therefore, first of all, the favourable attitude, the "gift," can be both to be trustworthy and to trust – to be trustful. Hence, the "return gift" to someone who trusts you, in the same field, can be to trust her, but also to be trustworthy, to deserve her trust. In fact, we will see that there is another reason for trusting the "truster." However, the "return gift" to someone whom you can trust should be that she can trust you, since the other alternative, trusting her, is implied by her trustworthy character.

Second, trust, being made up of two personal situations, trusting and being trusted, and of the two corresponding attitudes and conducts, trusting and deserving trust – being trustful and trustworthy –, entails a particular structure, raised by the psychological relation between the propensities to these two attitudes and the corresponding actions. This relation comprises two possible effects. The first one is that, other things being equal, an individual tends to attribute to others the properties of mankind she observes in the sample of it she has the most intimate knowledge of, namely herself. For this reason, if she is trustworthy she tends to think others are and hence to trust them. And if she tends to trust them, this tends to reveal that she herself is prone to be trustworthy. Similarly, if she is not very trustworthy, she tends to think that others are not either and hence to distrust them. Conversely, if she is prone to distrust others, this may reveal that she is not very trustworthy herself. However, in the case of distrust and diffidence, another effect can lead to the opposite relation. Indeed, someone who has high standards of morality can tend, for this reason, both to be trustworthy because she applies these standards to her own conduct, and to demand much from others in order to trust them and, therefore, to be frequently diffident and untrustful. If trusting is the "gift," by trusting someone because you think she is trustworthy because she easily trusts others, you practice a "reverse reciprocity" (a "Descartes effect"). Correspondingly, you may distrust someone who tends to be diffident about others because you think this to reveal a general disbelief in trustworthiness that reveals her own character in this respect. Nevertheless, you may also trust someone who tends to distrust others because you think that this reveals, in this respect, very high standards that she presumably also applies to herself. The first effect (trustfulness suggests trustworthiness) can be a particular cause of direct reciprocity (trusting people who trust you, and distrusting those who distrust you), among the other, ordinary causes.

Indeed, the general reciprocitarian structures fully work for trust, with again a number of specific particularities in addition. If someone trusts you, balance reciprocity commonly induces you to trust her – and in addition she is probably trustworthy at any rate as we have seen; but this also often induces you to be trustworthy towards her in order to "deserve" her trust, which also comes into the general family of balance reciprocity. If you can trust someone, this implies *ipso facto* that you trust her if you are in the appropriate relationship; and balance reciprocity induces you to be trustworthy towards her, when the occasion arises; moreover, being trustworthy, she is probably trustful as well, and you may not want to disappoint her in this respect. By the standard "helping behaviour," you tend to trust if you have been or are trusted, and to be trustworthy if others have deserved your trust, even if they are not the same people, thus leading to generalized and general reciprocities in trust and in trustworthiness.

The standard reciprocities present here are of the balance type. In addition, however, you tend to like someone who trusts you and someone you can trust. This only reinforces the relationship, and it may also induce side gifts which also reinforce and symbolize the relationship and express both sympathy and satisfaction. It also emotionalizes the relationship and thus reinforces it, and opposite characteristic emotions arise when trust is denied – a possible offence – and especially when it is betrayed. Finally, of course, sequential exchange for the continuation of trustworthy conduct is very important, and both sides of trust are of course also heavily influenced by imitation, conforming, previous or a priori knowledge of the other person, hence social proximity and a common culture and education, and the practices, norms and morality of the society.

The effects of the bundle of conducts constituted by reciprocity, trust, promise keeping or doing one's part, on the efficient working of various social systems have been studied for various organizations and in particular for firms. The positive effects of this relational capital on productivity at an overall level and on growth have been the object of a number of important recent empirical studies, notably by Putnam (1993), Berg, Dickhaut and McCabe (1995), Knack and Keefer (1997), Helliwell and Putnam (1999), Glaeser *et al.* (2000), Alesina and La Ferrara (2000b), and Zak and Knack (2001).[2]

13.2 The intrinsic values of reciprocity

Last but not least, reciprocities have direct and intrinsic social values which are often very important. These values are judged both by the preferences of individuals, notably participants, and from higher standpoints of a moral or more "social" nature (which are also taken by individuals).

In particular, liking reciprocities, or the liking dimension of reciprocities, support and promote sentiments of liking other persons, more specifically mutual and reciprocal liking, which are the basis of the most highly valued complex of social sentiments. You generally like being liked, especially by people you like; liking others is a source of major satisfactions (with, of course, opposite effects sometimes); and you probably approve of people liking each other, both for their sake and on moral grounds. The social intercourse of the realization of the givings or favours is also commonly valued. It often is the best of times. Gifts are the standard symbols of liking of all types and intensities, from simple esteem to love.

All kinds of givings, favours and reciprocities the final aim of which is to benefit the recipient, or to show and prove that she is liked, promote the social recognition and existence of the beneficiary, in a way that is absent in purely self-interested exchange, and still more in taking by force. This effect is all the stronger when the giver's attention and concern are more respectful, benevolent, or kind.

[2] For an individual, the set of positive and favourable attitudes towards her, and propensities to help or support her, for the various possible reasons (status, family, reciprocity, etc.) constitute her "social capital" (Kolm 1966).

Balance reciprocities, or the balance aspect of reciprocities, are quite different from liking reciprocities or the liking aspect of reciprocities in this respect. Such relationships can either be liked or disliked. They often constitute and entail balanced social relations, in a framework of fairness and justice in which dues are paid and merit is rewarded, with dignity and the satisfaction of accomplished duty. However, they are also sometimes a domain for oppressive norms, guilt, shame, and heavy social pressure through opinion or otherwise. When reciprocities are considered in social design, the point is that, although not all reciprocities are valued, there exist types of reciprocities that are highly valued and, indeed, considered to be among the best of social relations.

Finally the moral praise of being "good" is applied to types of actions, conducts, attitudes, intentions, motives, thoughts, and sentiments of persons addressed to other persons, such as respect, aid, gift giving, forgiveness, benevolence, compassion, pity, solidarity, kindness, helpfulness, liking, friendliness, amicability, generosity, consideration, gratitude, fairness, and the like. People who act in this way and hold such thoughts, sentiments and motives are also praised as being "good" in this sense. Now, the good society is not only a collection of well-fed individuals, satisfied persons, or free agents. It is not only structured by institutional justice. It also comprises good acts, actions, attitudes and intentions (this is clear for various kinds of altruism, but the concept of "justice" has for long referred to an individual virtue in behaviour towards other people). Ultimately, the good society is made up of good people. This aspect of society cannot be separated from the others. In particular, services and goods cannot be separated from the way they are transferred, acquired and produced. Such conducts, attitudes, motives, and sentiments can also remedy a number of other vices of societies such as miseries, social disregard and discrimination, various injustices, oppositions between distributive justice and individual freedom (giving redistributes in respecting liberty and thanks to it), and many productive inefficiencies for the reasons discussed above. Normative judgments, social and institutional design – and, of course, education – cannot leave out this most basic dimension.

14

Normative uses of reciprocity

14.1 The values of reciprocity

Properly reciprocal and, in particular, reciprocitarian conducts result from the appropriate sentiments, and sentiments are more given than chosen. However, there are a number of ways in which relying more or less on reciprocity can be chosen. Such a choice should rest on the values and possibilities of reciprocities, qualified for their possible shortcomings. These choices and instruments include various types of social and institutional design. They rely on the existing or potential relevant social sentiments. Hence, they are also closely associated with ways of shaping and modifying such sentiments, in education both in childhood and in the general culture, including the effect of imitation and psychological and emotional "contagion." At an overall level, social structures and these formations of social sentiments are closely interdependent (Jean-Jacques Rousseau published simultaneously his work on moral education, *Emile*, and his work on political theory, *The Social Contract*, and he considered the second to be an appendix to the first).

The values and shortcomings of reciprocities to be considered have been pointed out. They relate to efficiency, justice, and social relations. Reciprocity permits general sociability and social peace (through reciprocal respect), in particular the general possibility of a market system, and it corrects a number of market failures, although it can also somewhat impair strict economic efficiency in not making the best use of the information role of the price system. Balance reciprocity manifests local justice, and we will see that it can have a basic role in overall distributive justice. Liking reciprocities have a basic function in the quality of social relations. Balance reciprocity also has such a function through securing fairness, equity, equality, and sometimes dignity or social status; however, its possible demand by more or less constraining norms or social pressure can have unfavourable effects in restricting both freedom from the interference of society and other people, and mental freedom, by constraints which are either internalized or the effect of social opinion, and which can thus be seen as having a particularly vicious nature. Finally, extended reciprocities, and notably generalized and general reciprocities, have an essential role in maintaining social cohesion and a functioning community with individual freedom.

We will first recall the central role of reciprocity in the movement of cooperatives, and its basic function in sustaining the general rules of a free and peaceful society. The particular but notable reason for helping called putative reciprocity will then be pointed out. We will also remark that the basic structure of rational overall distributive justice can be seen as a reciprocal form, which favours its being supported by reciprocitarian sentiments. Moreover, the social system called the "welfare state" rests on a variety of sentiments and ethics of reciprocity. Finally, we will recall that reciprocity has been the most common "directing utopia" of social thinkers.

14.2 Cooperatives

The most direct institutional impact of an ethic based on reciprocity is in the movement of cooperatives. A cooperative is sometimes a name given to an association of purely self-interested members. Most of the time, however, a cooperative rests more or less on an intrinsic ethic of mutual help and is essentially based on relationships of reciprocity. Liking reciprocity is then presumed to be present to some extent among the members, and balance reciprocity and the accompanying conception of fairness are also often deemed important. Historically, a number of reciprocitarian cooperatives have failed and disappeared. Others have thrived but have lost most of their initial specific motivations and have become ordinary firms or associations – although they often keep their founding ideal as ideological decorum. Yet other reciprocitarian cooperatives continue and keep their initial ideal or some of it, but, when they are immersed in an economy with a different basic rationale, this is often in relation with particular social or political situations.[1]

14.3 General rules of society

The general rules of society, including its overall distributive system, are demanded and maintained by sentiments that include crucial aspects of reciprocity. General rights, including basic rights and relevant property rights, are generally accepted or desired, which implies that each accepts to respect those of others and to abide by the rule, given that her own rights are similarly respected. This is not the object of an explicit exchange in the strict sense. The logic of this situation has been discussed previously, and the essential role of reciprocity in it has been pointed out. Moreover, present-day societies engage in large-scale redistribution implementing other ideas and sentiments, notably benevolence and solidarity, and some egalitarian justice. Reciprocity is also very

---

[1] Reciprocity was the foremost value in the historical movement of cooperatives. The historical, factual, and theoretical relations between reciprocity and cooperatives are presented in Kolm 1984a.

present in the reasonings, sentiments and situations concerning this distributive justice. Two instances are shown in the next two sections.[2]

14.4 Putative reciprocities

Particular needs of people can be faced by savings or insurance when they can be envisioned *ex ante*, by others' help in single gifts or in reciprocities, or, when the individual need is repeated without a strong correlation in time among individuals in a population, by alternative mutual aid sustained as a self-interested sequential exchange or by motives of fair balance or of liking and very often by a mix of these motives.

Helping as a single gift – individually, collectively or institutionally – can be motivated by mere sentiments of compassion, equality or affection. However, among the various motives people have to help others who have a particular need, an important and frequent one is expressed as: "I help her because she would have helped me if our situations were reversed." This reasoning and motive is a putative, imaginary or hypothetical reciprocity. If the situation has actually been the reverse one with the reverse help, or if one expects that it could become the reverse one with the reverse help, this would be ordinary reciprocity, sustained by the possible reasons of interested continuation, liking, balance or fairness, with a possible role for gratitude; but the reasoning in question is held in cases in which an actual reverse situation is not possible. The primary motive of putative reciprocity is a notion of balance possibly accompanied by fairness between the two agents. Other, different sentiments can accompany cases of putative reciprocity, such as compassion or general fairness. There are also putative extended reciprocities, either generalized ("I help her because I would have been helped myself if I needed it, possibly by someone else") or reverse

---

[2] An extensive review is presented in Kolm 2004.

("I help her because she would have helped others if needed and if she could").

The reasoning, sentiment and motive of putative reciprocity are the source of a number of cases of helping, aimed, for instance, at victims of disasters, people suffering from personal or social handicaps, and so on. This motive is important in the support of free public education which compensates for disadvantages in the family environment. It is also the basic reason for the general support of public health insurance in large regions, for instance in Europe. Standard public health insurance demands the same premia from everyone, whereas profit-making private insurance adjusts the premia demanded to the actual risks presented by various people. These risks differ because of people's a priori, given propensities to be sick, that is, their a priori, given health status. That is, public health insurance provides, in addition to private insurance, some compensation for the inequalities in a priori, given health. The preference for this solution is expressed by the standard remark about private insurance: "it is already too bad that these people are more, or more often, sick, and in addition they would have to pay higher premia." Even people who do not have particularly poor a priori health accept and generally approve of this reason, notably with the further reason that they would themselves be so helped if they had the a priori bad luck of having such poor a priori given health. This is an argument of putative reciprocity.[3]

14.5 Macrojustice

Overall distributive justice follows a general principle which leads to a distribution which happens to have a structure of reciprocity. If, as it is the case in our societies, the basic

---

[3] Applications of the concept of putative reciprocity can be found for distributive justice in Kolm 2004 (pages 360 and 447) and for the question of joint giving in Kolm 2008.

rule is social freedom, or the classical basic rights or freedoms, that is, people are free to act and fully benefit from the consequences of their acts, in particular to work, earn, and exchange without forceful interference, as long as they do not use force against others, then distributive justice can only distribute the items given to society, that is, the "natural resources." The largest part of these resources in terms of economic value, by very far, consists of the given productive capacities of individuals. These capacities are incorporated in persons, however, and the distribution takes the form of a redistribution of incomes. Then, it can be shown that this redistribution should amount to an equal sharing of the incomes that the individuals can earn with the same given labour different from their actual labour (but with their different capacities).[4] This distribution also amounts to each individual yielding to each other the proceeds of the same labour. This has a structure of reciprocity, more precisely of balance reciprocity in which the balance is the equality in labour. This equality in sacrifice entails that this redistribution is amenable to support by sentiments of reciprocity.

14.6 Welfare states

Moreover, a series of services such as health and health insurance, education, retirement pensions, unemployment income and insurance, or low-cost housing are more or less provided publicly or by the concerned individuals themselves, according to the particular society. When they are largely provided publicly or collectively, the regime is a "welfare state." The justification of services and protections in the welfare state relies importantly on concepts of reciprocity.

Pensions and education can be provided in a framework of intergenerational reciprocity, which logically parallels the

---

[4] This is the theory of "macrojustice" (see Kolm 1996a, 1996b, and particularly 2004).

intergenerational reciprocities in the family. This leads to the chain reciprocities of pay-as-you-go pension systems, and of free public education, and to the conception of a direct (but delayed) reciprocity between educating the young and their later financing older people's retirement pensions.

In the chain reciprocities, economically active people pay the pensions of the retired ones, given that their retirement will be financed by the next generation (this is an anterior generalized reciprocity), and that the pensioners have paid the pensions of the previous generation (a delayed or posterior reverse reciprocity). Similarly, active people finance the education of the young given that their own education has been financed by the previous generation (a delayed or posterior generalized reciprocity), and that the young will finance the education of the still younger (an anterior reverse reciprocity). We thus have the four cases of chain reciprocities combining the two cases for the extension of reciprocity – generalized and reverse –, and the two cases for the non-simultaneous timing – posterior (delayed) and anterior.

Moreover, the relations can extend beyond successive generations. This is trivial for the lengthening of life duration leading active people to finance pensions of the generation of their grandparents. The most interesting, however, is that deficit and borrowing financing amount to augmenting the spread between the related generations. For instance, active people can finance the redeeming of a debt incurred for financing the pensions of their grandparents. In fact, social systems are rather often indebted and in deficit. The deficit may be of the specific sector, or in the general deficit of public finance. The financing of education can lead to similar remarks.

Another very important relation between the "welfare state" and reciprocity is that a moral of putative reciprocity seems to be the main reason for the strong attachment to a system of public health insurance by vast populations (in Europe, for instance), as we have seen.

14.7 The Good Society: the classical scientific directing utopia

Members of genuine cooperatives often pride themselves on social relations that avoid the selfishness of the market and the hierarchy of firms and administrations. This is related to a long line of normative social thinkers who saw in cooperatives and associations of mutual aid of various types, relying on relations of reciprocity, the way of avoiding both the inequality, domination and unfreedom of hierarchical organizations and the selfishness, hypocritical hostility and alienation of market exchange relations. Indeed, since relying on pure altruism on a large scale and for a long time would doubtlessly constitute an unrealistic and utopian demand on motivations, reciprocity remains the only more or less possible alternative to selfish exchange and hierarchical command. In it, indeed, people give, but given that they are given to. By joining freedom and an orientation towards others, liking and fairness, and often a sense of community, reciprocity can provide the needed ingredients of the "good society." It goes without saying that the freedom-reducing aspects of weighty norms and social pressure – present in a number of reciprocities as we know them – are to be avoided. These are by no means all there is to reciprocity, however, and they are absent in many cases of reciprocity. In fact, extensions of reciprocities tend to suppress conditions of some of their drawbacks. For instance, exploiting the return gift (i.e. giving in order to receive a return gift) does not work for a generalized reciprocity in which the beneficiary of the return gift is not the initial giver. Or again, the possibilities of social pressures of all kinds that are present in small-group relations are much diminished at the more extended social levels relevant for general reciprocities.

Moreover, the various types of systems of economic and social relations coexist. The question concerns the scope of each. In particular, their relative importance has a determinant influence on the general *ethos* of the society in question, that is, on the general style and type of sentiments, attitudes, relations and personalities in it. A society's ethos is a major feature of its quality. There are societies of merchants, societies of bureaucrats or of company men, and societies of brothers. Hence, a main issue of social improvement consists in the consideration of the possibilities of qualifying an ethos produced by the association of a pervasive market with a hierarchical organization of production and of government. This can be an important function of a larger scope for reciprocities.

Finally, the noted social thinkers were all keen on using the scientific knowledge available in their time (see, for instance, Piotr Kropotkin's use of Darwin, Marcel Mauss's ethnographic inspiration of his social remarks, the relation between Saint-Simonians and industry – and their later role in it –,[5] or the general "scienticism" of nineteenth-century socialist thinkers). We should certainly do the same by using all available and obtainable knowledge. Action, being intentional, implies imagining possible worlds. This holds true for social and political action. The scope of possibility is uncertain, however. One possible mistake is to see as possible something that is not; but a worse one consists in failing to imagine the possible and better situations. Indeed, you may achieve the best possible alternative by trying to reach an impossible one, but never by implementing an inferior possibility. Hence, lack of imagination may be more dangerous than utopia, especially if the latter is taken as directing utopia, showing a direction for heuristic progress – while how far one can go along this way appears clearly only in practice.

These exercises require using all the relevant information in an integrated synthesis. For motives and possible social

---

[5] Saint-Simonians cared so much about reciprocity that they used to wear coats buttoned at the back so that each of them needed another to dress and undress.

relations and structure, the basis is a phenomenology of social sentiments, notably those at work in reciprocities, which tells one what one is really talking about. Besides these basic considerations, all the facets of social science are bound to contribute. Reflective psychology shows relations and interactions. Anthropology displays a variety of existing social forms which, at one and the same time, are instances in the domain of the possible and suggest constants that may be characteristic of "human nature" – insofar as such a thing exists. Sociology presents other examples and proposals of explanation. Psychological theories propose still other explanations of various types. Social psychology suggests generally more local explanatory concepts and a wealth of systematic observations, either *in situ* or in laboratory experiments, which can falsify some proposed psychological explanations, or at least cast doubt on them, and show the proportions of behaviours of various types in specific sub-populations and conditions. Economics can contribute with its description and analysis of various economic systems, its knowledge of the requirements of successful production, its specific concepts for modelling the conducts of individuals in isolation and in interaction, and its analysis of the logic of notions of equity, fairness, equality and inequality. Of course, the disciplinary assignment of these various types of information is thoroughly irrelevant. When considering a question, all the relevant information is to be considered. There is no valid reason to restrict oneself to one aspect only (as the Chinese dictum puts it, "Do not care whether the cat is black or white as long as it catches the mouse").

15

The logic of good social relations

15.1 Introduction

15.1.1 The nature of good social relations

"Hell is the others," a character of Jean-Paul Sartre says. Paradise may be the others too. The quality of social relations is an essential part of the quality of a society, a basic factor of the happiness, blooming or misery of its members, a widespread cause of the success or failure of its workings, and, indeed, a main consequence of the quality and virtue of the people themselves. The quality of social relations differs widely from one society to the other, and among various segments of a society – a fact that begs for explanation. This quality may also be improved as a result of social organization, or progress in social consciousness or education, and these possibilities of improvement should be understood.

However, the explanation of the quality of social relations raises major puzzles. People often complain about the poor quality or deterioration of social relations, and yet they are their own doing. They would often all benefit from better relations, and yet they fail to improve them. Can the required relations be obtained by exchanges and markets, or are they impaired by such selfish interactions, or, again, does the working of exchanges and markets require some of these good relations in the form of honesty? Do other-regarding conducts require out-and-out altruism, which could explain some insufficiencies, or are some more moderate and balanced social conducts sufficient? For instance, varieties of reciprocities may be relevant, or needed. In these cases, there would commonly be multiple equilibria with good and poor relations: which of them is reached, and how can one induce the best solution? Furthermore, when several alternative types of conducts are relevantly considered, how can one compare the value of the various cases from the point of view of people whose preferences depend on this type? These questions, and others, raise a number of social-logical problems considered here.

Good social relations consist of the aspects of people's acts and attitudes towards others the final motives of which are to be favourable to these others, and the corresponding sentiments. A simple exchange is not warfare, but it aims at serving oneself, by obtaining as much as one can from the other and handing out to her as little as one can. Force and threat are also a priori excluded from this type of relations. Favouring others should be, at least to some extent, according to their judgment. The corresponding motive can be some sentiment favourable to the other, but it can also be some norm (social, moral, or both), a sense of duty or of propriety, or habit. From this definition, these aspects have the nature of benevolent gift giving (hence, their analysis will often use the vocabulary of gift giving for convenience in presentation, although this will cover a variety of types of relations). Aspects of acts and attitudes, and sentiments, of good social relations sometimes associate with others of different natures in actions or in more complex relationships. They can thus be associated with exchange in the strict sense or with command and hierarchy, and give the corresponding benevolent dimension or aspect to these relations; but, then, the various aspects of such more or less mixed relationships should not be confused.[1]

---

[1] Since genuine good social relations, like gifts, cannot, by nature, be bought and sold, they have no price. Hence, according to Kant's (1797) classification, they have a "dignity."

This simple concept of good social relations is manifested in a large variety of actual conducts, with many types and all degrees of intensity. This includes, for instance, voluntary non-aggression and refraining from doing harm of any kind; spontaneous respect and consideration for others; politeness and civility; gift giving and generosity; help, aid, assistance and charity; being honest, trustworthy, reliable, faithful and trustful; love and friendship; and so on.

Good social relations are valued by people who benefit from them. They manifest the virtue of the people who have the sentiments and attitudes and perform the acts. They are approved and valued by other people. They are also praised by most morals (this excludes Nietzscheanism, Spencerism, and the like). Indeed the function of morals is to induce actions, attitudes and sentiments among which those favourable to other people are particularly important.[2]

Their basic nature of benevolent gift giving implies that acts and attitudes of good social relations cannot be obtained by standard exchange, they cannot be bought and sold, and they cannot be imposed by force and threat. These methods are inconsistent with giving, because of the very nature and definition of a gift. This may vindicate the rather frequent complaint about the insufficient quality of social relations. Indeed, a gift, in particular, cannot be bought (one can sometimes buy the item that is given, but not the fact that it is given for free as a result of the corresponding motivation). Gift giving, therefore, constitutes a "market failure" for the intrinsic reason that it transfers a good or a service while not being a market act by nature and definition. More precisely, it implies two externalities: the receiver's situation or the gift she receives in itself for the giver, and the gift for the receiver or any other person who approves of it (or has any opinion

---

[2] Acts favourable to others constitute the whole domain of morals for a widespread liberal and humanistic modern view that abstains from moral judgments about acts that concern the actor alone, and judges all facts according to their final effects on humans.

about it). The gift has no market price, but if this is seen as it having a market price of zero, the gift naturally appears to be in short supply from the benchmark of exchange and of the market. Public enforcement cannot do better for the same reason: a gift cannot be imposed either. However, if, more appropriately, the absence of a market price for a gift is included in the constraints of the society, then the gift is Pareto efficient. Indeed, being chosen by the giver alone, it gives her utility its highest value, and the giver is worse off with any other level of the transfer or service (this does not imply that the set of gifts of a relation of reciprocity is efficient, an issue that will be studied in chapter 22). Then, any complaint about insufficiency of the gift is in fact about the giver's benevolence. This is about this person's psychology.

Indeed, complaints or regrets concerning disregard for other people, insufficient helping or charity, and unsatisfactory social relations are about selfishness in various forms, that is, about people's motives and psychology. This seems natural since proposing a gift is the decision of a single person, the giver. There are, however, various ways of influencing more or less people's propensities to give (or be honest, etc.), such as providing reasons for such acts, suasion, education, showing examples, and various possible influences on the culture of society. Changes in preferences (including norms, habits, etc.) that underlie actions raises a problem for comparing efficiency (Pareto-wise), but there may be sufficient comparability to ensure improvement in this respect: this issue will be discussed further shortly. However, skepticism is often expressed about the possibility of people becoming much more altruistic than they are. Christianity has been trying to make them so for two millennia now, with no evidence of progress.

Note that one cannot even buy gifts with gifts, in the proper sense of the term "buying": each act or transfer would not have the independent freedom which is implied by the nature and definition of gift giving (and, correspondingly, each motivation would not be that of providing a gift but that of receiving one). One can, of course, more or less induce gift giving by various means; in particular, one can attract or induce gift giving with gifts if the other person is prone to return gifts or to imitate. However, this differs from exchange in the strict sense, and this behaviour will turn out to be very important.

Indeed, people's pro-social acts generally also depend on various conditions and not solely on motives or preferences. They depend, in particular, on such acts by others. Actually, when people who complain about general selfishness are asked if they themselves give sufficiently, a common answer is: "I would if the others did." This can mean: "I would give them if they gave me" (under similar circumstances). This is reciprocity proper. However, this answer may also mean: "I would give if they also gave to the people to whom I give, or if they gave in general." This reason may refer to efficiency: "My own giving can solely be a small part of the needed giving, so it is ineffective unless the others also contribute." However, this may also be a demand for fairness meaning: "I would do my share of giving if the others did theirs." These reasonings may concern others' giving either to the same persons to whom the giver in question gives or in general, because it augments the general level of giving in society. The answer may also just be a question of merit and reward: "I would give to others if they themselves gave, because then they would deserve it." In a diad (two persons), the reason is essentially reduced to reciprocity proper, plus – possibly – some place for a general reward for the other's giving conduct.

The foregoing applies to the various types of social relations, and reciprocity proper is the main reason for conduct of the type "giving if others give" in relations in which the bilateral aspect dominates. Giving if others give, or acting morally if others do, and only in these cases, and the corresponding propensities or preferences, can be called *conditional altruism*, or *conditional morality*. These cases contrast with the unconditional cases in which the behaviour or preference holds whatever the others do. A conditional altruist also is, formally, a conditional egoist, but the benchmark retained here is pure egoism and hence altruism is the attitude under scrutiny.

The existence and scope of these particular relational goods thus require a particular analysis, with a special concern for the possibilities of improvement within a realistic account of the capacities of human beings, who probably are "neither angels nor beasts" (as Blaise Pascal puts it). The purpose of this chapter is to point out the crucial phenomenon underlying this question. This consists of an interaction between the structure of people's preferences concerning society and their own actions, on the one hand, and social interdependences, on the other.

The central logical problems raised are summarized in the next sub-section and analysed more in depth in the following sections. Section 15.2 presents the polar types of individual preferences about combinations of social conducts of oneself and of other people, and the resulting social states. People's comparison of social situations in which they have different preferences about social situations is considered in section 15.3. The consequence shows that giving and pro-social conducts tend to be favourable in the end, in spite of the self-sacrifice they seem to entail from the narrowest point of view, and reciprocitarian preferences – rather than only full altruism – suffice for this result. The evaluation of the possible scope of good social relations is completed by a synthesis of the various social effects and psychological relevance of relations of reciprocity.

15.1.2 Outline of the basic logic of the quality of social relations

In a common situation, all people prefer that everyone's attitudes and actions towards others be better, but they fail to correct or improve their own, with the result that the whole set of the social relations in question is wanting. However, this may basically result from two standard types of preferences. Either people prefer to fail whatever the others do (a classical prisoner's dilemma type of relation), or they would manifest attitudes and actions favourable to the others if the others had such attitudes and performed such actions, in a typically reciprocitarian conduct, but the others don't behave this way. Symmetrically, when good social relations prevail, this may be because people are unconditional altruists, or because they react positively to others' positive attitudes and actions towards others, in a reciprocity that may mobilize motives of social balance, fairness, liking and gratitude in direct, generalized, general and reverse reciprocities, and the usual effects of imitation and norms of conduct.

Helping others when others do not help oneself (and one another) is probably more demanding, from the point of view of motivation, than helping others when others are helpful. This may lead to a materially inferior situation for the person, and this conduct is not supported by all the sentiments and conducts that favour the other case (reciprocities of all kinds, gratitude, imitation, etc.) – it even resists tendencies to take revenge. However, a society of unconditional altruists ends up with everyone helping others, and, therefore, the propensity to help others when others are unhelpful is not used. It is a priori superfluous. Deleting it leads us to the less demanding reciprocitarian motivation, with the same final outcome.

However, the equivalence between these two kinds of preferences of the population at large is only for staying in a social state with good, helpful social relations. Indeed, this is the only stable state with an unconditionally altruistic population, whereas the general absence of good, helpful relations is also a stable state with a globally reciprocitarian – and, possibly, vengeful – population (these are Cournot-Nash solutions).

However, the idea that people can become out-and-out altruists, substantially more than they are now, seems utopian and unrealistic. Fortunately, a thinner specification of motivations and preferences and the consideration of the dynamics of the social situation show that preferences that remain essentially reciprocitarian can also lead to the favourable and superior social state. An individual may initiate giving (in the form of any behaviour favourable to others) if she believes that this will sufficiently induce sufficiently many others to also behave this way – this can be, for instance, people with whom they are particularly in relation, and this behaviour may then spread to larger circles and be reinforced by the effects of other similar initiatives.

The required motivations can then be based on all the tendencies to reciprocate or replicate (reciprocities of all kinds, imitation, gratitude, norms, etc.). Their existence and formation are to be considered. Their spreading can be favoured by education, the various types of selection discussed in chapter 16, and other progress of the general social and moral ethos of the society. This dynamics is more likely to be successful the more people prefer the resulting situation to that which results from overall selfish preferences. This effect can play a part in the overall dynamics of the question, through various processes of trial and error, and a general understanding of the effects (people may also influence their own preferences to a limited extent, by the noted processes of focusing attention and reasoning, but in the present case people also benefit or suffer from other people's preferences, and such attempts meet the problem of collective action again, at a deeper level).

This question meets another problem, however, that of specifying people's preferences between situations in which they do not have the same preferences. However, this question may have a solution in the present case. Let us compare again the cases in which the population is essentially selfish or reciprocitarian (or unconditionally altruistic), and always prefers overall good social relations to overall poor ones. Selfish preferences lead to overall poor social relations, whereas reciprocitarian (or fully altruistic) preferences lead to overall good social relations. Now, it seems that the situation of overall good social relations is bound to be more appreciated by altruistic or reciprocitarian people than by purely selfish ones. The former probably know better how to appreciate good social relations. Then, since, when globally selfish, the population ends up with poor social relations, which its members find worse than good ones; since, when good relations prevail, the population is better off when it is globally altruistic or reciprocitarian; and since these preferences tend to induce good social relations; then, taking all effects into account, people are better off when they are globally altruistic or reciprocitarian than when they are selfish. Hence, this comparison does not impair the formation or transformation or preferences towards more reciprocitarian (or altruistic) ones through whatever process. It may even induce such processes, for instance by choices of general public education, or by mechanisms of selection of any of the kinds analysed in chapter 16.

15.2 Preferences and their consequences

The logic of the issue can be presented in the simplest way by considering individuals who can make two choices in acting toward others, described as "giving" (as a gift), denoted as g, and on the contrary "keeping," denoted as k, and who see others as globally either giving (G) or keeping (K). The latter alternatives will notably occur if all (or most) others respectively give (g) or keep (k). An individual's situation will be described by a pair of letters, the first denoting the individual's behaviour (g or k) and the second her perception of others' behaviour (G or K). There are four possible situations: gG, gK, kG, and kK. An individual will have preferences among her four possible situations, described by the (transitive antisymmetrical) binary relation "$\succ$" ("is preferred to"). As usual, an individual's choice of an act (g or k) given her perception of others' acts (G or K) is assumed to be consistent with her preferences.

Let us then add two other assumptions. First, given the individual's act (g or k), she prefers the others to give (G) rather than to keep (K), so: $gG \succ gK$ and $kG \succ kK$. This can be both for the material advantage of receiving and for the intrinsic appreciation of being offered something or of living in a society with positive interpersonal relations.

Second, the individual prefers a society in which everyone gives to a society in which everyone keeps (oneself too), or: $gG \succ kK$. The reason can be a preference for good social relations – involving oneself or between others (with respect to material advantage, note that each individual both receives and gives in the giving case, that there can be reasons for either behaviour to be more productively efficient than the other – this is discussed soon –, and that the relations discussed here will refer solely to a fraction of the whole of social relations). It will also be assumed that all (or most) individuals have the same preferences in question which correspond to the general culture or ethos of society. Moreover, the relation $gG \succ kK$ will in fact be a consequence of the assumption $kG \succ kK$ when the condition of either pure or conditional altruism $gG \succ kG$ is introduced.

Given the above assumptions, only four preference orderings are admissible.

The first ordering obtains when individuals prefer to keep whatever the (given) behaviour of others:

$$kG \succ gG \succ kK \succ gK. \tag{1}$$

If agents act individually (non-cooperatively), each chooses k, which she prefers to g whatever the others' acts are (a dominant strategy). Then kK prevails, a situation that each individual finds worse than the possible situation gG (a classical "prisoner's dilemma"). Individuals cannot strike an agreement that all give to others given that others give back – which would achieve gG –, even if they have the means to make such an agreement and to enforce it, because this would be opposed to g meaning gift giving, from the nature and the definition of a gift. Similarly, this "exchange failure" cannot be corrected by the classical means of imposing the solution (gG), because gift giving cannot be imposed by force either, by nature and definition. This constitutes the inherent inefficiency of egoism, and more generally of "insufficiently moral" behaviour, sentiments and preferences, intrinsically entailed by the nature of gift giving and of good social relations.

In contrast, if people are unconditional altruists and prefer to give whatever others' (given) behaviour is, their preferences are

$$gG \succ kG \succ gK \succ kK \tag{2}$$

or

$$gG \succ gK \succ kG \succ kK. \tag{3}$$

In either case, each agent individually prefers to choose g, whatever others' acts are. Hence, they all choose g, and therefore they achieve the situation gG that they all prefer to all others, as if by immanent justice. These preferences, however, imply not only giving if others give, but also giving if they keep, and hence, with respect to others' behaviour towards oneself, not only returning good for good, but also returning good for evil.[3] This is rather saintly behaviour, and one should probably expect that, in standard societies, it will be neither widespread nor easy to elicit on a sufficient scale by the means of influencing preferences and voluntary behaviour. Note, however, that since situation gG obtains,

---

[3] The difference between preferences (2) and (3) is not relevant. The preference $kG \succ gK$ may be due to the resulting material situations for the individual (if G does not lead to a much less efficient economy than K with which market exchange can thrive). Hence, $gK \succ kG$ may describe a strong preference for one's giving behaviour – or especially in comparison with others' behaviour – a preference that seems very "altruistic." However, a preference may be altruistic at a higher level, in the sense that the agent prefers others to behave altruistically, rather than herself (this provides another reason for $kG \succ gK$).

the problematic "saintly" section of the preference structure, $gK \succ kK$, is in fact virtual.

If this problematic part of the preferences disappears, it is replaced by $kK \succ gK$, which is "an eye for an eye" with respect to reaction to others' behaviour towards oneself. The preference ordering then becomes

$$gG \succ kG \succ kK \succ gK. \tag{4}$$

This leads the individuals to give (g) if the others give (G) and to keep (k) if the others keep (K). This case is conditional altruism.

Doing as the others do because they do it, whatever the specific reason, can be called replicating behaviour, or *replication*. If the act of an agent affects another individual who reacts by an act that bears similar effects on the original actor, this is reciprocal behaviour or *reciprocation* (this "similarity" implies at least that the acts are both either favourable or unfavourable to the other person). Reciprocation can be conceived of as a particular case of replication (the acts are defined as concerning the other person). Reciprocation of acts favourable to the other is *reciprocity* (this corresponds to the classical concept of reciprocity in social science, in which this term denotes a set of gifts related by this kind of reaction). The reciprocation of unfavourable acts is basically revenge.[4]

These conducts and their variants and specifications can rest on a number of reasons, motives or basic reactions. All types of balance and liking reciprocity can play a role. Beneficiaries of benevolence tend both to like others and to feel indebted towards them, and hence to help them for these reasons. Reciprocity can be motivated by gratitude. Giving to givers (who give to oneself or to others) can be motivated by the desire to reward their merit for a reason of rewarding-retributive justice. The replication of giving to specific others

---

[4] In all these cases, in their proper form, the motivation for the reaction should not solely be to induce future similar acts (e.g. retaliation solely for deterring future harm, or giving solely for receiving future gifts).

or of giving in general can be elicited by the sense of fairness from doing one's share if the others do theirs. But it can also result from direct and basic imitation. Gifts also elicit gifts in "generalized reciprocity" such as the classical "helping behaviour," in which someone who has been given to tends to give (even to persons other than the initial giver). This can result from reciprocity between an individual and the group of others ("general reciprocity").

With preferences of type (4), however, if people act individually, there are two possible stable (Cournot-Nash) equilibria, gG and kK. The former is unanimously preferred, and, indeed, it is unanimously preferred to all other situations. However, it seems that society might be trapped into the inferior and inefficient situation kK. Indeed, if society is in kK, it cannot move to gG by collective agreement, even if people could make an agreement and implement it, because this would be contrary to the nature and to the definition of gift-giving, as noted earlier. With such an agreement, there can be, in particular, no motivations of bilateral gift-giving reciprocity, gratitude, rewarding gift-giving behaviour, being influenced by receiving gifts, and imitation of giving. However, two new phenomena have to be pointed out here.

First, the hypothesis of a simultaneous or timeless game is not realistic. It is, in particular, ill-suited for describing conducts of replication, reciprocation, or reciprocity. When an agent individually decides to give rather than keep, this may induce others to do the same, at least in proportion to the agent's act and importance in society. In particular, others may so behave towards this person in direct reciprocity to her choice. But the noted wider effects such as "helping behaviour," helping helpers, reward, doing one's share if others do, and so on, also lead to giving inducing further giving. All these are the reactions of conditional altruism. If they are sufficiently strong, the agent may in the end benefit from individually switching from k to g. Solution gG can thus be reached, and it is stable in the strong sense that each individual loses from deviating from it, whatever others' behaviour when she does so.[5]

Moreover, giving (as a gift) is one way of yielding the corresponding item: this transfer can also result from coercion or from agreement or exchange in the strict sense.[6] A law cannot decide that people should give (freely), but it can decide that they should yield the corresponding item. If the preference structure (4) means that people choose to give (yield freely) if others yield (and not solely give) then such a law induces them to give (freely) because it guarantees that the others yield. But, then, this yielding behaviour is de facto voluntary, that is, the constraint is respected but it is not effective, and everyone gives (freely). This solution fails, however, if preference structure (4) means that the individual gives (freely) solely if the others also give (freely) and do not solely yield (even though, in the previous case, all people end up giving freely).

The main point is that, under normal assumptions, the preference structure (4) can achieve the unanimously preferred – and probably morally most commendable – situation gG through individual choices. Now, these preferences are certainly more frequent than unconditional altruism (preferences of type (2) or (3)), and easier to elicit through influences on preferences. The aspects of balance in replication and, notably, in reciprocity and other reciprocation – doing as the others do and possibly also incurring what they incur – can

[5] A detailed analysis and modelling of this dynamics can be the object of a long study. One parameter that can be of importance is the size of the population involved in an interrelated series of gifts (or other "good" social relations). Large numbers of "small" agents may hamper the diffusion of information about others' behaviour, but this occurs both when they give and when they fail to give.

[6] This "transfer" can be an actual transfer for a gift in the strictest sense. It can also be any act favourable to the "receiver" and more or less costly in some way and to some degree for the actor. It can also sometimes be the external manifestations (in speech, gestures, and so on) of respect, compassion, pity, friendship, love, approval, praise, esteem, admiration, and so on, insofar as the manifestation without the sentiment helps or pleases the "beneficiary."

be justified by the particular rationality of equality.[7] Norms of reciprocity, balance or fairness, can crystallize these reasons and motives into guidelines for behaviour.

In fact, (Pareto-)efficiency, first best optimality, and, certainly, morality, require preference structures (2), (3) or (4) to prevail. That is, the partial preference $gG \succ kG$ only is required in addition to the basic assumption that agents always prefer others to give rather than to keep. This is not an innocuous demand, but nor does it justify deep pessimism.

The conclusion reached above as to the inefficiency of egoism (preference structure (1)) and the efficiency of either unconditional or conditional altruism (preference structures (2), (3) and (4)) strongly contrasts with the opposite famous message from Adam Smith's *Wealth of Nations* (if you need meat from your butcher, do not rely on his altruism, but on his selfish interest in an exchange relation).[8] However, Smith's previous *Theory of Moral Sentiments* emphasized sympathy, and this contradiction – German scholars' "Das Adam Smith Problem" – may find an answer in the foregoing results: pure altruism may be too scant, but reciprocity – discussed in *Moral Sentiments* – suffices and is more possible and frequent.

15.3 Inter-preference comparisons

However, the noted intrinsic inefficiency of egoism and efficiency of unconditional or conditional altruism do not imply that people are better off in the latter cases than in the former,

---

[7] See Kolm 1998 (translation of 1971), foreword, section 5 (also in Kolm 1996, 2004).

[8] This argument was, in fact, commonplace in Smith's time and place – the eve and locus of the Industrial Revolution, with merchants and capitalists seeking moral respectability. Smith read it in Mandeville and, more specifically, in the *Essays on Morals* of the Jansenist Pierre Nicole (1675), translated into English by John Locke. The argument was indeed used as early as the fourth century by the fathers of the Church for justifying not excommunicating merchants whose business, selfish and uncharitable as it was, nevertheless served others in the end (intentions would be judged later and by one more competent).

because preferences are not the same in the various cases. Reaching conclusions of this type requires a hypothesis of "inter-preference comparability," which is described by a second level of preference. These preferences have to be understood as meaning some ordinal level of enjoyment rather than directly and solely preference. That is to say, they do not directly describe the fact that someone prefers to be an altruist rather than an egoist, say. Such preferences would raise problems of meaning, logic, and consistency. Rather, they admit only the possibility of saying that, in given circumstances, someone would be happier (or more satisfied) if she were an altruist than if she were an egoist (the discussion of this issue has an analogue for interpersonal comparisons).[9]

The objects ranked by these new preferences will include a third parameter that denotes which type of ordinary preference ordering the individual has. They will be triples xyz, where y is either g or k, z is either G or K, and x can alternatively be e for *egoism* if the individual has type (1) preferences, u for *unconditional altruism* if she has preferences of type (2) or (3), or c for *conditional altruism* if she has type (4) preferences (there are twelve such alternative triples). For each given x, preferences about pairs yz are those implied by type x preferences.

One possible property is $ugG \succ egG$ or $cgG \succ egG$. This means that the individual enjoys more a society in which everyone gives freely if she is an altruist than if she is an egoist. This can be explained by the fact that the egoist is insensitive to the social and moral intrinsic value of the act of gift giving, whereas the altruist has such a sensitivity and positively values such acts. It is again assumed that these preferences are shared by all individuals in society. Since $egG \succ ekK$ from relation (1), these assumptions respectively entail $ugG \succ ekK$ and $cgG \succ ekK$. However, we have seen that kK is the outcome with type (1) preferences, and gG is the

---

[9] See the theory of "fundamental preferences" in Kolm 1998 (translation of 1971), foreword.

outcome in the other cases. Consequently, all individuals end up better off if they are altruists of some sort (u or c) than if they are purely selfish (e).

Morals judge actions and choices, including conditional ones, and the corresponding individual preferences. That is, they judge, here, the preference structures (1), (2), (3) and (4). In particular, they rank them – this ranking can be called the moral or ethical preference (an expression not to be confused with the description of the morally best of these structures as being the moral ones). Very commonly, the selfish preferences (type (1)) are found to be the worst. Moreover, a number of morals praise returning good for evil, and hence they value unconditional altruism (preferences of types (2) or (3)) higher than conditional altruism (type (4) preferences). This is, for instance, the case with Christianity and with Buddhism. Christianity, in particular, sees unconditional altruism as Christian preferences; it could label conditional altruism as "biblical" preferences; and it would probably describe the selfish case as "pagan" preferences.[10] The foregoing results thus imply that the members of a more moral society end up being happier (with reasonable assumptions). Although this cannot be the direct aim of moral "conversion" or *metanoia*, at least these people would not be indirectly "discouraged" by the fact that it would lead to a situation considered to be worse. Moreover, an important result is that conditional altruism suffices, and this is less demanding on the grounds of motivation.

15.4 Reciprocal and replicative behaviour, and efficiency

Since this logical core of the existence of good social relations relies heavily on relations of reciprocity, practically all

---

[10] However, Luke's "give and you will be given to" may solely be the advice to exploit other people's propensity to return gifts.

the issues of effects and possibilities of reciprocity intervene here. They are only briefly noted in the rest of this chapter, and are analysed more completely in other chapters of this volume.

As we have noted, the foregoing considerations hold for all types of pro-social behaviour, and not solely for giving in the strict sense. This holds, in particular, for all types of reciprocal, replicating and conditional behaviour (corresponding to "conditional altruism"). This is, for instance, the case with people who contribute freely if the others contribute fairly, who respect norms if the others do, in particular who keep promises if the others do, or who "act as if the others acted similarly or according to the same principle" (that is, folk Kantianism) if the others follow the same notional condition (which makes this condition become actual if they choose the same act or principle).

All such behaviours can have positive effects on economic and social efficiency, in addition to the noted intrinsic inefficiency of egoism and efficiency of altruisms or equivalent behaviour. These effects can also be indirectly favourable to the establishment of pro-social behaviour, with the sufficiency of conditional and reciprocal relations. The following list provides but a sample of these effects on efficiency.

The most classical type of inefficient interaction is that of the prisoner's dilemma. The structure is the one described above with preferences of type (1), in which the available choices may represent very different things, such as helping or not, cooperating or not, being honest or not, contributing to a public good or not, and so on. The standard conclusion is that the inefficiency described above will be obtained. However, if one player behaves reciprocally or replicatively and the other knows it, the latter's choice leads to the outcome that both players prefer to the inefficient equilibrium, without agreement between them. The game, of course, is transformed, since it becomes a sequence of non-simultaneous moves, with information about the first move for the reciprocating or replicating player (although all this can also be notional and simultaneous), and a new principle of conduct for this player. This can describe many actual situations.

Similarly, if I need something from someone but can pay only later, and for some reason no binding agreement is possible, the self-interested other will not help me if she thinks I will not pay later, but she may if she knows that I reciprocate favours. More generally, a common pattern is sequential exchange, a sequence of alternate or simultaneous transfers (or other aid) between two agents, in which each is motivated by the desire that the relation continues. If this is the sole motivation, however, the last transfer – if known as such – will not take place, and so the whole relation may fail to materialize (notably by "backward induction").[11] Then, an additional reciprocal motivation can secure the last transfer and, ipso facto, the whole relation.

All kinds of reciprocal and replicating conduct can secure efficient relations through such effects. They can, more generally, replace contractual agreements and save corresponding costs of transacting, contracting, monitoring, reporting, enforcing, collecting information, etc. They can also replace public coercion for respecting rights, financing public goods, implementing transfers, and so on, and, hence, again save costs of information or lack of it, coercing, administration, and so on. These behaviours can thus remedy standard "market failures" and "government failures". In any social relation, they are bound to favour trust and loyalty, and to lower uncertainty about others' behaviour. It is classical to note that the most efficient organizations (firms, bureaus, etc.) use fair amounts of voluntary, non-contractual, but reciprocal support between members and between them and the organization, in the form of goodwill, mutual help, loyalty, voluntary transmission of information, reciprocal relations

---

[11] See Hammond (1975), and Kurz (1978a, 1978b, 1979). As we have seen, uncertainty or bounded rationality that prevents backward induction can permit this process with purely self-centred motivations.

between effort and productivity on the one hand and bonuses on the other, and so on.[12]

15.5 Psychological possibilities

Reciprocal and replicative conduct thus suffices for avoiding the inefficiency of self-centredness in terms of the quality of social relations and of various other consequences of social interactions. It has been emphasized that one of the remarkable aspects of this result is that this conduct seems to be less demanding on the grounds of motivation than pure and unconditional altruism or goodness. This proposition can be tested by introspection, casual observation, and systematic investigation. Experimentation has been amply used by psychosociology to show the wide scope of reciprocitarian behaviour.[13] In particular, the propensity to act favourably towards others when one has benefited from different others' favours, or generalized reciprocity, is one of the most documented results of the literature under the name of "helping behaviour."[14] Imitation can also play a role in this regard; in particular, being helped provides a close observation of helping and a telling experience. Moreover, reverse reciprocity also matters: one tends to give to people who give (and not necessarily to oneself). "Helping behaviour" induces people to reciprocate towards others in general (or towards the "generalised other," as G. E. Mead puts it). Indeed, people tend to hypostasize these "others" into "society as a whole," and to

---

[12] There is a vast literature on this topic in industrial sociology, the sociology of organization, and experimental sociopsychology (classical pioneering empirical work is found in: Adams, 1963, 1965 and Adams and Rosenbaum, 1964). A noted recent sociological, historical, and econometric study which strongly emphasizes the productivity of reciprocity is that by Putnam (1993).

[13] Economists have recently taken up this trend: see Güth, Ockenfels and Wendel (1997), Fehr, Gächter and Kirchsteiger (1997) and chapter 23.

[14] A sample is provided by the papers of the collective book edited by Macaulay and Berkovitz (1970) (this literature is fully referenced and analysed, and is used, in Kolm 1984a).

give when they have been given to "by society." This is the very important social phenomenon of general reciprocity. All this notably applies to the crucial giving dimension of good social relations in general. Of course, education and the making of the general cultural ethos of society play major roles in the establishment of these patterns of conduct.

15.6 Reciprocity and the economy

A number of famous scholarly analyses of society claim that the paradigm of the market and of its type of exchange can or should be applied to all social relations, or have applied it beyond its field, for instance to the study of family life or politics. They have sometimes found a normative value in the free exchange that underlies this view. However, we have seen the paramount importance of social conducts (or of aspects of social conducts) that belong to the realms of gift giving and reciprocity, and which therefore cannot be bought, sold, and marketed, and are opposed to both market exchange and coercion. Family life and family economics, in particular, consist primarily of relations of this type. From the normative point of view, good social relations, which are so important for the quality of society and a good life, are based on behavioural traits that belong to this category (although the converse may not hold because of the possible role of strong norms and social pressure in gift-giving and in reciprocating). It has been stressed that reciprocity and replication constitute basic ways of overcoming a number of "failures" of exchange and other relations, and therefore of improving efficiency and economic productivity. The normative aspect of the economy is also concerned with the intrinsic quality of social relations, however, since people spend so much of their lifetime in economic activities, notably at the workplace. The crucial giving aspect of these relations, which cannot be secured by exchange or command, can be induced and sustained by the interdependence between conducts in reciprocities and replications with the corresponding plausible motivations.

Textbooks about economic systems used to be surprisingly different according to whether they lay on the economics or on the anthropology bookshelf. The former typically used to begin with "There are two kinds of economic systems, market and planning," whereas the latter's usual opening is: "There are three kinds of economic systems, exchange, redistribution, and reciprocity." Exchange corresponds to market here, while redistribution is taking and giving by a central power, a process in the family of "command" and "planning" in the modern world. Hence, if one is not blind to the various possible shortcomings and "failures" of hierarchies and markets on the grounds of the nature of human relations, morals, and also efficiency, one has to be curious about the third alternative, reciprocity. The various relational shortcomings referred to include reinforcing selfishness, rewarding cheating, nurturing hostile relations, alienation, exploitation, domination, and considering others solely as means, as instruments – a violation of Kant's "imperative." And although giving and reciprocity – understood here as a set of gifts and return gifts – have their share of oppressive norms and social pressures for giving, and of gifts with poor motivations and effects, it happens that the pro-social conducts that are almost universally praised and appreciated also belong to this category. Of course, reciprocity is the only mode of conducting economic transfers solely in a number of groups of limited size, but its relative extent, along with other modes in a variety of possible ways, is bound to be a crucial variable for society, its performances, and its intrinsic quality.

16

How and why? Understanding and explaining reciprocity

16.1 Understanding

The main focus, so far, has been on understanding reciprocity. The term understanding is to be understood here in two senses. The first is the common sense of knowing the whereabouts, the various elements and types, the workings, the influences, and the reasons for actions. For reciprocity and its various types, clear and explicit awareness and knowledge of all these elements, workings and possibilities are by no means a priori obvious. They should be a posteriori, though, once the descriptive analysis is presented, apart from the specific analysis of the effects of strategic interactions (this is the object of chapter 20). The reason is the reliance on understanding in the second sense, which is the technical sense in which this term is used in social science (Max Weber's *verstehen*). This refers to the fact that we speak of things about humans, and we ourselves belong to this category. To begin with, the crucial items are sentiments, which cannot be given a definition – they can only be specified. When we mention a sentiment, each of us understands what the term means from her own subjective experience. This refers to our feelings, but this information is supported by our experience of life in society, with watching others, hearing from them, interacting meaningfully with them, experiencing some empathy or compassion towards them, understanding their words, situations, and feelings, and being so understood by them. We can use our memory of these facts. We similarly understand the effects and causes of sentiments, and the reasons for actions, conducts and, in the end, behaviours. The large and presumably unique capacity for "compassion" and empathy that characterizes humans is at work here. The most important fact, however, is that each of us is a rather exhaustive sample of mankind.[1] Refusing to use this source of information is not possible concerning the meanings of terms denoting sentiments, feelings or emotions. For the rest, this rejection is inflicting on oneself the handicap of attempting to understand behaviour with only a chimpanzee's capacity for that. This may be suitable for understanding chimpanzees.[2]

In fact, we do not only constitute, for ourselves, an impressionistic dictionary of the meanings of sentiments and feelings, a showcase exhibiting their existence and possibilities, and a cellar stocked with previous experiences and information. Each of us also has in this way, at her disposal, a portable and flexible laboratory, and an extremely powerful one if one's methodological religion does not cripple its use. Any experiment in an "outside" laboratory is set up after coarse and fleeting observations in this "internal" laboratory and seems to provide only frequencies in populations at the cost of dealing only with quite simplified and primitive aspects of the actual phenomena. The method pointed out here is not only introspection; it is rational, thoughtful,

---

[1] It is extraordinary how far we can understand the sentiments, reasons and motives of people of cultures thoroughly different from ours, such as in tribal life, or very distant in time; it is, for instance, extraordinary that the Bible, ancient Greek tragedies, classical Indian epics or Buddhist scriptures can still serve as relevant reservoirs of meaningful and powerful examples of such sentiments and conducts.

[2] Chimpanzees pass by food and pretend that it is not there, so that others do not know it is. That is, they lie. Hence, they seem concerned with the knowledge and state of mind of others. However, experiments – for which chimpanzees are the right subjects – seem to have shown that they do this only because it works. They do not seem to have an image of the others' state of mind. That is, they are behaviourists. They are also pragmatist philosophers ("it works").

reflective, experimental, duplicable, shared, and in part verbally communicable introspection. Introspection may be "going to the window to watch oneself pass by." However, as far as feelings and sentiments are concerned, the opposite alternative, behaviourism, entails the following exchange when two behaviourists meet: "Hi, you feel great, how do I feel myself?"[3]

Besides understanding, the next epistemological exercise is explaining, that is, giving reasons or answering the question "why?" The preceding analytical description of reciprocities has explained behaviour by motives induced by sentiments (or interest), and it has sometimes explained sentiments by other sentiments, or by feelings, acts, situations and rationality. These explanations are obvious and clear, once one has become aware of them. One may want to go further, however, and also explain the propensities to experience these sentiments and their very existence. Indeed, the specific instances of existence of these sentiments have been explained, but their general possibility and the factors that can influence them have not: why can people like, why can there be pleasure, gratitude, and senses of balance or imbalance, fairness, moral indebtedness, duty, and so on, why are these sentiments influenced and determined as they are? A first and obvious remark is that explanation is never full; after each explanation, one can still address the question "why?" to each of its elements. If we decide to stop at some point in the regress, why there? An obvious and natural answer consists of asking why we want or need an explanation. The apex of Buddhist wisdom consists in refusing to answer useless "whys." "When you have been hit by an arrow, take care of the arrow and don't ask who threw it" is its most famous

---

[3] Only plain, superficial introspection accessible to anyone without training and specific education is considered here. The trained and taught introspection that is the basis of the psychological knowledge of advanced Buddhist studies is something completely different and the only way to know what "mind" means and is (see Kolm 1982).

aphorism.[4] Is curiosity a naughty vice, or is pure research "the honour of the human mind" (as the mathematician Kantor puts it)? Following Buddhist therapeutic epistemology, we should want to explain only insofar as we need it for improving things. This seems indeed to be a honourable objective and a rational – or reasonable – answer. One of the most famous economists has even asserted: "The problem is not to explain the world but to transform it." We could be more modestly satisfied with trying to contribute to alleviate its miseries. The normative aspects of reciprocity intervene here. A very ancient tradition has seen in the appropriate reciprocity the only potential for avoiding altogether the selfishness of market exchange, the domination of command, the disasters of fighting, and the utopia of a priori general unconditional altruism. Moreover, reciprocity favours social productivity by securing trust, by ascertaining mutual respect that permits benefiting from one's acts and exchanging, and by remedying a number of market and exchange failures (see chapter 12). However, a policy trying to promote the favourable aspects and effects of reciprocity needs to know which causes of reciprocity it can influence, if any.

Explanations of reciprocity have first of all to face two facts. First, there are several quite different types of reciprocity and of psycho-social processes that lead to it, based, respectively, on a sense of social balance or fairness with sentiments of social propriety and moral duty, on liking including a direct reciprocity in sentiments, and on interest. Second, each reciprocity is constituted of elementary mental facts which also exist without it (affection, sympathy, empathy, emotional contagion, understanding of causality, imitation, a sense of impartiality, elementary rationality, a sense of social balance and of fairness, a sense of duty or propriety, gratitude,

---

[4] The ultimate reference, for Buddhism, is the decrease of suffering. Hence it advises against seeking any explanation that does not contribute to this end. Especially since, being necessarily incomplete, it will create dissatisfaction in any "rational" mind.

a sense of moral indebtedness, the capacity to foresee and reason, the capacity to understand other people, satisfaction, a sense of self and of social existence, and so on). A full explanation should also explain these elementary facts (this can apply, for instance, to explanations by selection). However, one can also explain specific forms given the more basic and general facts. Several interacting influences then generally have to be considered. The causes of the specific sentiments and conducts intervening in reciprocity can be found in social influence in all its various forms and ways including education, in psychological structures and processes, in sociological evolution, and in the supporting biological material.

Simple psychology sometimes suffices. For instance, people have found that sequential exchange can be beneficial, and their giving in return may have turned into routine and habit, while they forgot about the strategic reasoning that justified it (the more easily so that the complete rational reasoning about the full future sequence is beyond direct and immediate intuitive grasp). This return giving could thus become simply something to do, an instinctual propriety, and hence de facto a balance reciprocity. The balancing of the return thus results from the initial benefit of giving in return sufficiently for inducing continuation, while giving too much would be a waste. This habit then could be admitted and transmitted. It crystallizes into a social norm, which could in turn be hypostasized into a moral norm – entailing a sense of duty. This possible origin and explanation of balance reciprocity is an alternative to its explanation as an application of the rationality of equality noted in chapter 6 (note that the relations between duty and propriety, the moral and the social norm, are reversed in these two explanations, although in both one entails the other – the moral is of the kind that derives from rationality in the explanation by equality). However, these two explanations of balance reciprocity can very well be both present and cooperate. The benefit turned propriety can select the items about which the rationality of equality will apply, thus introducing the sentiment of duty and the nature of a moral norm. At any rate, the last transfer can be explained by the normative aspects (social or moral, propriety or duty) and not by self-interest if it is certainly the last. Moreover, we have seen that balance reciprocity can be favourable to the interest of the parties in a number of cases (notably for remedying the various "failures" of markets and exchanges) and hence it can result from the cultural (or even the biological) selection of groups or of social processes discussed shortly.

16.2 Biology?

A number of scholars have found an interest in relating altruistic conduct and gift giving to biology and more specifically to genetic selection. A basic problem is that this approach does not seem to have a possible place for concepts as specific and discriminating as those provided by the analytical and reflective consideration of reciprocities, and hence for the corresponding results. Only very rough and coarse behavioural properties are considered. They can a priori mean many things and have many causes and reasons. This will undoubtedly characterize this approach for a long time to come, and hence it seriously limits the meaningful facts that can be learnt from it. Of course, it is a simple truism that mental facts "come from" chemical reactions and electrical circuits in the brain. In fact, individual experience, culture, including education, "are" even the anatomy of the brain, and not only its physiology, because they create interconnections of neurons. In any event, the relevant biological material, the neurons and the overall structure of their network, simply exist and are built under genetic information. However, even the biological and genetic evolution is not independent of culture which influences sexual selection in mating, differential probabilities of death and life duration, and reproduction rates in the various sub-populations. And human culture is as old as the hominization process of which it is an aspect.

From a practical point of view, however, biological influence has only a negative interest, by suggesting what cannot be influenced, since we envisage, as policy tools, neither neurosurgery, nor a eugenist policy of human selection or mating, nor cloning. And yet, there might be at least a speculative interest in considering reciprocal conduct in neurobiology and in selectional sociobiology. Reciprocity belongs to mechanisms of treatment of emotional information that play a regulating role in life in groups. In humans, as in many animals, this happens in a set of neuronic circuits part of the limbic system and joining the amygdala to the temporal, the cingulate, and the orbito-frontal cortexes.[5] It would be informative to find out how these zones differ in the various types of reciprocity and reciprocation, how they relate to zones corresponding to other sentiments such as greed, fear, liking, love, justice and injustice, and so on. As concerns explanation, natural biological selection, which made us, unfortunately but clearly cannot enlighten us much about the conducts in question.

There exist, of course, several possible genetic selective mechanisms that can favour and lead to the sentiments and conducts of reciprocity. Returning favours is a kind of altruistic behaviour. It is to be noted, first, that the sociobiological literature generally suggests explanations of behaviour, not of sentiments and feelings, whereas our evidence of human conduct is that behaviour is chosen because of sentiments and feelings (even reflex acts often result from habits of conduct driven by feelings or sentiments). Sociobiology has in fact been made for ants (whose sentiments are hard to guess). Human sociobiology thus needs to explain sentiments, or, rather, patterns of sentiments, that lead to conduct and in the end to behaviour (that is, it will explain all these elements jointly).

Mating selection can easily propose an a priori explanation for altruism in general. Indeed, other things being equal,

[5] See Adolphs (2000).

individuals should prefer to mate with altruists who will support and defend them and possibly their common offspring – if pairing has some duration, a trait which can be similarly selected –, and hence altruists would reproduce more (even if they survive less – with a genetic equilibrium between all effects). It might be suggested that this is why courtship usually implies giving. The offspring also inherit this altruism. Moreover, this preference for altruistic mates can itself be selected for, since it favours the possible survival of people who make such a choice (and of their offspring). This can a priori explain much more than the "selfish gene" alone, and not only altruism towards individuals bearing the same genes and in proportion to the size of the common genetic material (a degree of kinship which animals do not know beyond the closest relations).

This process, however, selects for altruism in general rather than reciprocity. The selection of revengeful people might be that they survive more because they hit back irrespective of cost, and hence their threats are credible. Selection for balance reciprocity could result from the fact that it can induce help or giving from other people expecting a return gift; the balance would be explained by this genetic selection along lines noted for the individual choice in sequential exchange: giving back too little does not suffice and giving back too much entails a disadvantage; yet, the individual would benefit from these mutual transfers. In fact, we know from Axelrod (1981, 1984) that, in a repeated relation, the strategy of reward and punishment which is the most prone to elicit cooperation is tit for tat (answer good with good and harm with harm) – plus an initial positive move. Tit-for-tat is reciprocation. These reciprocating behaviours thus favour people who practise them and can foster their survival and therefore be selected. All these mechanisms rest on the direct interest of the individual and do not need the standard devices of the sociobiological explanation of altruism, the selfish gene for nepotistic altruism towards kin and group selection for altruism beyond kin (Darwin's own theory of competing tribes).

However, the various contributions of reciprocity to social efficiency and to desired qualities of society (see chapters 11 to 15) could also promote it by group selection. In any event, reciprocity, giving when one is given to, implies much less self-sacrifice than pure altruistic giving, and hence will be more easily selected (reciprocitarians survive more, live longer, become a larger part of the population, reproduce more – even, possibly, in a given duration because they are more fit, and hence their proportion increases for this reason too).

In fact, reciprocal conducts of various types are observed in all human societies, although with various emphases and frequencies. Behaviours of these types also exist in a number of animal societies. However, a general problem noted above applies here. Close consideration of such human conducts has shown that they mobilize sets of sentiments, emotions, reasons and relations, each of which also appears in the motives of other conducts. This is, for instance, the case with liking other individuals, its reasons or causes and its effects, causal liking, responsibility, the situation of the ego, balance which also appears in other forms of fairness and justice,[6] rationality, anger, the role of others and of culture, duty, propriety, norms, gratitude, moral indebtedness, imitation, and so on. The full explanation should explain both each of these elements and their organization in reciprocal conducts. At any rate, any effect of biology on human conduct is heavily mediated by mental processes, effects of society, culture, education, and so on. Children raised by animals (*wolf-children*) cannot even walk, they cannot speak, of course, and they cannot be said to be able to think. Theories using biological selection can suggest only tentative explanations of very

---

[6] There are two reasons for equality in conceptions of justice. In rewarding-retributive justice, the reason is that one act or fact more or less restores a state of affairs disturbed by another. In distributive justice, the relevant equality is a requirement of rationality in the most general sense of providing a reason (the most developed explanation is in *Justice and Equity*, Kolm 1971 [1998], foreword, section 5).

rough, general and vague potentialities, which may propose, for instance, why ants support some other ants, but can hardly explain actual forms of human experience as we know them. Their possible mathematical refinement should not hide that they only deal with very crude variables and concepts. These lines of reasoning need not be totally rejected, but they should be considered for what they show, that is, they should be expressed more or less tongue in cheek. On the whole, the thrust of Marshall Sahlin's classic pamphlet *The Use and Abuse of Biology* is relevant here. The social use and moulding of the biological material is bound to teach us much more.

16.3 Social and cultural evolution

16.3.1 *Motives and behaviour*

In particular, cultural and social evolutions determine (and explain) more, and much more specifically, than biology alone. They involve individual choices, collective choices, and competitive selection of social forms and processes. Since reciprocal behaviour is obviously explained as deriving from motivational sentiments (plus, possibly, interest), these sentiments should be explained. These sentiments are liking people and its properties (see chapter 7), and the senses of balance or imbalance, fairness, and propriety and duty. However, it turns out that behaviour, actions and patterns of actions, and the sentiments that induce them are largely determined jointly, and should therefore be explained jointly. This relation between behaviour and sentiments is based on several mechanisms, in addition to the fact that sentiments motivate behaviour. One mechanism is competitive selection among social structures and processes each based on a style of conduct encompassing the corresponding behaviour and sentiments. Another effect is that not only do sentiments elicit behaviour, but also, conversely, behaviour tends to induce the corresponding sentiments, through a psychological process of avoidance of dissonance. This adjustment is in part spontaneous, but it also uses affecting one's sentiments through reasoning, focusing attention, or habit (see chapter 7).

16.3.2 Choice and influence

Direct individual choices play a role in the emergence of reciprocities in various ways. A most straightforward case is the elementary interest in giving so as to elicit a return gift, which can induce continuation reciprocity and sequential exchange. The effects of being liked and liking and their relations and properties (see chapter 7) are also quite primitive. Moreover, impartiality and basic properties of rationality lead to valuing equality, which leads to balance reciprocation (see chapter 6). Individual choices also associate into collective choices. Finally, one mechanism for the competitive selection of social forms and processes rests on individual choices to join one group rather than another (such as one type of firm, of other group, or of general way of behaving). These relevant social forms and processes imply in general different motives and conducts. Hence these individual choices generally imply the more or less wilful influence on one's own sentiments discussed above. This influence is often limited, especially in the short run. However, these psychological adjustments are fostered by imitation, contagion of sentiments, norm following, other people's judgments, social pressure, evidence of dissonance of one's thinking both with one's conforming acts and with the social environment, and so on. Moreover, these influences are particularly favoured when these sentiments are those of reciprocity, since they imply, then, both the presence of a partner providing a conspicuous example, and judgments, sentiments and acts addressed to the person, in a mutual structure with positive feedbacks. A person even sometimes welcomes these influences of other people on her own view, sentiments and motives, and even uses them by her choice of joining the group, because they achieve changes that she welcomes but cannot realize by herself, that is, for overcoming a weakness of her will.

16.3.3 Efficiency and values of modes

What is to be explained is the scope of the relations of reciprocity in interpersonal social relations. This is a part of the explanation of the scope of the various modes of relations: reciprocity, pure gift giving, exchange in the strict sense, or the use of force, and their various forms. The explanation uses a number of elements. Some are the specific circumstances (for instance, one of the agents in presence is much stronger than the others – and hence can impose her force – or this is not the case). Other factors are the possible performances of the various modes. Indeed, by various more or less direct or indirect mechanisms, the existence of a social process is fostered by the interests favoured by its productive efficiency and by the direct preferences of individuals about them. For instance, exchange and reciprocity can use decentralized local information that may not be available to a central planner; exchange permits the informational and motivational advantages of the price system; conversely, gift giving can disrupt the price system and its efficiency; however, exchange and markets have well-known inefficient "failures" which can be remedied by reciprocities or by centralized intervention if information and motivations (and the possibility of coercion for the centralized solution) permit it – these market failures can be, for instance, limits and costs of contracting (writing, checking, monitoring, implementing) and of constraining or excluding from benefits, the noted problem of sequential exchanges, situations of the type of the prisoner's dilemma and of free-riding nonexcludable public goods, etc.; more basically, mutual respect of the rights of others permits peace and property rights and can save the damages and costs of conflicts and the costs of protection, self-defence and police; in addition, giving and liking reciprocities entail valued social relations which are missing with relations of self-interested exchange or force; and so on. In fact, individuals have also often direct and intrinsic preferences about various types of social relations that characterize modes of realization. For instance, they often prefer reciprocal trust to general diffidence, convivial reciprocity to contractual obligations, and contractual obligation to hierarchical command or to intrusive social pressure by opinion or otherwise. In particular, all the values of reciprocity presented in chapters 11 to 15 can favour the existence of reciprocity, although mostly not by a direct choice but by more or less indirect − although important − social processes such as the following ones.

16.3.4 Processes of social selection of modes of relation

Indeed, the relative performance and interest of a mode of realization, and individual preferences about it for other reasons, do not explain in themselves the adoption of this mode (since this generally does not result from a single individual's choice). The social mechanism that translates these interests and preferences into this realization has to be pointed out. It can be of many types. Individual choices sometimes suffice. This is for instance the case with continuation reciprocity. There can also be an explicit collective choice. Public actions, or setting up the conditions of a market physically or by regulation, can be decided and realized in this way. This is rather less possible for reciprocity, although rules and laws that are favourable, or not unfavourable, to it can be important (e.g., in taxation). A frequent process for the establishment of such social forms is by social selection resulting from trial and error, with maintenance of the successful form by awareness of common interest, agreement which is often tacit, or the social inertia of habit and tradition. This can sustain a competitive social and cultural selection process of modes of realization. Such a selection can operate by economic competition among firms differently managed (for instance using more or less trust and decentralization); by political competition among alternatives that grant a different importance to the public, private and cooperative sectors and to various types and rationales of redistribution; or by other interactions of social forms and structures.

In this process, the roles of individuals consist in supporting or joining structures or processes that satisfy them more on material grounds or with respect to their preferences about social relations and freedom, for instance by joining one type of firm or a cooperative, or by supporting a type of change in any organization they belong to, or a type of public policy. In this social evolution, individuals who make such choices, and those who are more passively submitted to the change, both generally undergo a transformation in their behaviour and its direct motives, which is an adaptation to their new environment. This adaptation uses various modes. When joining a group, an individual can adopt the type and style of social relations that are standard in it – when in Rome ... She may, for instance, decide to trust others, as they do in this group, rather than demand detailed contracts. In the adaptation, existing reciprocal conducts often play an important role: people tend to face selfishly selfish people, to give when they are given to, to respect when they are respected, to trust when they are trusted, and to like others when they are themselves appreciated. Imitation and following norms or rules – possibly with social pressure of various possible types and intensity – also play important roles.

This adaptation concerns both behaviour and the sentiments that induce it, in a congruent way if excessive dissonance is avoided. Sentiments are then essentially influenced by the social environment and what it expects from the individual. The contagion of emotion and the imitation of world views and judgments play important roles. Required or favoured behaviour tends to induce sentiments in line with it (cooperation, hostility, and more specific forms) by a kind of psychological dissonance-avoidance. Conscious and wilful influence on one's own sentiments is generally restricted for "slaves of their passions," but it is in fact not absent, by reasoning, getting used to, or focusing attention. In the longer run, of course, education plays a major role in this respect.

However, other processes are at work in society, and a number of them influence and shape behaviours, motivations, and sentiments. In particular, culture and the formation of personality also have an important autonomous dynamics. In this process, there is no proof of overall optimality in any respect, no "invisible hand" theorem. Wars and mass slaughters would suffice to prove it. Even barring these extreme phenomena, the simple analysis of social processes shows reasons for their normative "social failure" according to any criterion (the possibility of correcting these failures is a further issue). In particular, this is the case for reciprocities, which inherently imply two related reasons that can induce them to be socially "inefficient," both resulting from the very nature of these processes (with given motives).

First, a relation of reciprocity cannot be an exchange in the strict sense (a mutually conditional exchange by external obligation – or promise keeping). In particular, as it will be made precise in chapter 22, the outcomes of interactions of reciprocity tend to have structures of the classical Cournot-Nash or Stackelberg types (although for a reason different from the one proposed classically in the former case). Hence, there seem, classically, to be allocations obtainable by exchange that are preferred by all participants. However, explicit, formal and binding agreements for mutual transfers or services are incompatible with a relation of reciprocity: the type of relation would differ, the transfers or services would not be gifts. As a consequence, individuals' preferences about the outcomes can be different, and there are also in general preferences about the type of relation in itself. For instance, the intrinsic value of a reciprocitarian relation may overcompensate for the losses of an otherwise inefficient allocation in the eyes of all participants. Therefore, the existence of a possible result unanimously preferred to the one obtained is ambiguous. This is a possibility, however. Although reciprocities commonly correct market failures, they also constitute one of them, in a sense.

The second risk of inefficiency inherent in reciprocity is that the reciprocal relation produces a feedback with the possibility of several equilibria and notably several stable equilibria in a recurrent process (such as those described in appendix A of chapter 22). The interaction may well lead to an equilibrium dominated by others that are clearly better (in particular that are preferred by all participants) and remain stuck in it.

For these two issues, the problem comes from the fact that people engaged in such a reciprocity are both too altruistic and not altruistic enough. They are too altruistic to perform an exchange in the strict sense, and yet their conditional altruism traps them into equilibria of particular types. The solution cannot be an intervention by force since this also violates the reciprocitarian relation. Short of particular dynamic processes of the type described in chapter 15, it can only be to induce people to take a broader outlook.[7]

This conclusion in fact holds true for most "failures" of social processes. This should be a main concern of institutional design and of general social information and education.

16.3.5 Education and development

In all societies, indeed, the values that underlie social relations constitute a foremost issue in education. Children are, jointly, strongly taught these values, shown, by the example

[7] Chapters 15 and 22 provide examples of these two inherent possible inefficiencies of reciprocity. These possibilities, their likelihood, and the ways of overcoming them, are amply discussed in Kolm 1984a.

of adults, how to accommodate them in real life, and provided with ready-made explanations that permit one to avoid the schizophrenia that should result from the frequent tension between both. Children are taught the value and duty of gratitude (this may be the parents' reward and interest), of respect, and of politeness. They are taught the value of giving, but also the excuse that "Charity begins at home" – as the proverb says. They are taught the goodness of generosity, and also shown how to keep it as a utopian ideal (in Europe), or for Sundays or tax-deductible contributions (in the United States). In many societies, the same ethos both values generosity highly and sees honour in relentless revenge. More generally, social influence in education and otherwise, and the various types of social experiences, are prime factors in people's attitudes and conduct towards others. This is confirmed and specified by many systematic observations and experiments noted earlier. They include the studies of "helping behaviour," a number of studies about personality, analyses of the role of imitation, analyses of child development along the lines of Piaget and Kohlberg, other studies on the formation of norms of pro-social behaviour, and so on.[8]

In particular, the line of studies about "the birth of the moral sentiment in the child," initiated by Piaget's book with this title, is rather encouraging. There seems to be evidence of a spontaneous individual development from obedience to authority to abiding by a rule, and then to a sense of impartiality among peers and the internalization of their views, which leads to a sense of equality and reciprocity. This later stage is to be explained by the fact that, in the course of interacting with peers, empathy leads to a sense of impartiality which, with minimal rationality, leads to a sense of equality and of balance-reciprocity (see chapters 6 and 18). Empathy

[8] The volume on *General Reciprocity* (Kolm 1984a) includes a full referencing of the relevant studies to its date of publication, and a corresponding discussion of these studies and of the conclusions that can be derived from them.

in interaction can also create the basis of liking reciprocity. In the end, however, this stage of moral development appears to be limited by education in the name of realism about life in society (or, rather, to be oriented towards charity or ideology and largely confined there). This should be a main field of study and action.

Part IV

The economics of reciprocity

17

General methodology of reciprocity analysis

The previous analysis of reciprocity should be continued by a formal analysis. This permits making the relations in question more precise and finding out the consequences of sets of relations, in particular the consequences of the interdependence among the acts, sentiments and attitudes of agents that concern others.

In the end, we will arrive at the discussion of the form most classic in economic analysis. In this form, there are two individuals indexed by i and j, who, respectively, chose items x_i and x_j and seek the highest value of *ordinal* utility functions $u^i(x_i, x_j, z_i)$ and $u^j(x_j, x_i, z_j)$, where z_i and z_j denote sets of relevant parameters (they can in particular include a description of the type of relationship between these two individuals when they make these choices). These utility functions can be generalized into preference orderings, which is practically relevant when some aspects of the choices have priority. The resulting interaction also depends on other items, besides domains of choice, such as the information of agents, the order of actions in time, and possibilities of communication and agreement.

In such a formulation, x_i or x_j can, for instance, be a gift of any kind, and the other the return gift (or a harm and the corresponding response). However, such functions u^i and u^j are, as such, mere "black boxes." Their specific structures and properties should be derived in a meaningful and legitimate way from the phenomena one wants to study. This entails a couple of remarks. In particular, the noted structure with u^i and u^j is the basis of game theory. However, our concern is not game theory. It is not, for instance, to "introduce reciprocity, or any other social sentiment, in game theory." The objective is the converse one. It is the analysis of reciprocity (or the consequences of other social sentiments). The only point is that some concepts of game theory may apply to this relation, and if any of them is useful for its analysis, this concept can be used. However, such "games of reciprocity" have two noteworthy types of relation with usual game theory. First, a number of structures that are crucial in such games are absent from usual game theory, such as the importance of the type of social relation which is an object of preferences and influences the preferences about the other items, or the question of fairness about the order of the moves in time. Second, games of reciprocity will also, as an aside, produce a number of contributions to game theory. For instance, the famous Cournot-Nash solutions are well known to have no actual justification (for one- or two-shot games). Now we will see that one concept of reciprocitarian conduct leads to this solution. This is the only justification provided to date for such solutions.

Our concern here is reciprocity. Reciprocity can a priori be about acts (which are parts of actions), attitudes, sentiments, or judgments (giving is an act, a favour can refer to favourable acts, attitudes or expressed judgments, etc.). Determination through the highest u^i or u^j (or the same for more general orderings) classically refers to items that are chosen by the corresponding agent. Gifts are chosen. Sentiments are largely unchosen. However, they are often more or less influenced by their holders by reasoning – for instance in the name of morals or of hedonism (pleasure seeking) –, by efforts to "get used to" something, or by focusing or diverting attention. Attitudes are determined by sentiments and are also more or less chosen. Acts are determined by sentiments – and by attitudes if they are meant to imply propensities to act.[1] Hence, if the chosen variables x_i are acts, the corresponding utility functions depend on the relevant sentiments (or attitudes) – and, at a deeper level of analysis, they may not be thoroughly given to the agent.[2]

An essential methodological point is that each relevant type of social sentiment should be analysed separately to begin with. They are very different from one another. Mixing them a priori and from the start can only produce confusion. The logic and the structural implications of each sentiment are then analysed by themselves, possibly with a maximizing conduct and utility functions u^i (or orderings), along with self-interested motives about the result for comparison. In a situation in which several such sentiments are present, it is then most often straightforward to consider them jointly, notably with the relevant utility function. Nevertheless, some associations of sentiments require a careful study. For instance, sentiments and hence attitudes and behaviour of fairness and balance associate well with moderate liking but much less so with stronger liking, as we have seen. Other cases demand careful distinction, for instance in the balance and fair reciprocity of fairness (important notably for agreeing about just distributions) with its two issues of fairness which should be adequately represented.

Consider, for example, that a utility function $u^i(x_i, x_j)$ can a priori encompass or represent various types of social sentiments, a number of which lead *qualitatively* to similar results in choices. For instance, these sentiments induce making x_i and x_j more similar or more equal in some sense (or the opposite); this is described by a preference for this similarity or lower inequality in these variables, that is, by the fact that

---

[1] Attitudes and acts are, of course, also determined by reason, custom, norms, prejudice, and so on.

[2] The fact that acts are determined by given sentiments does not mean that they are not chosen but that the principles of the choice are these sentiments which, for instance, determine the structure of utility functions or preference orderings.

function u^i increases when these variables are more similar or less unequal in the appropriate sense. These sentiments can be the following, some of which are comparative:

— equity, fairness, justice,
— a preference for equality or inequality aversion,
— comparative or balance reciprocity,
— liking reciprocity in giving,
— gifts induced by reciprocal liking,
— gratitude,
— continuation reciprocity (two steps of it or comparison of the sequences),
— imitation (or, on the contrary, distinction),
— conforming,
— a sentiment of inferiority (or on the contrary of superiority),
— envy,
— jealousy (jealousy adds to envy an aspect of self-debasement; moreover, while envy has no opposite – as with the sentiment of superiority for the sentiment of inferiority –, one particular meaning of the term "jealous" constitutes such an opposite – as with "being jealous of one's prerogatives").

Mixing all these possible sentiments, or several of them, from the onset simply constitutes confused thinking and can only induce faulty analysis. It prevents seeing and understanding some of the essential properties of the corresponding conducts. The logic of some of these sentiments has been extensively analysed, notably for justice, equity and fairness, for inequalities, for envy, and for reciprocity.[3]

A second essential methodological point is that the utility functions u^i should not be arbitrarily specified. The same

---

[3] The logic of fairness, justice and inequality has been extensively analysed (see, for instance, Kolm 1966, 1971, 1977, 1996a, 1996b, 2000c, 2004). That of envy is developed in Kolm 1995.

requirement holds for any other concept or relation considered or used in the analysis (such as liking, kindness, fairness, and so on). Arbitrariness, lack of justification, is the exact opposite of scientific analysis. Any specification of any concept used should be fully justified by facts. Moreover, it turns out that, for the phenomena under study, the arbitrary specification of concepts does not make the analysis formally simpler. All the properties can be derived with the properly general concepts with more simplicity than with such specifications. More importantly, this is the only way to obtain results in knowing the proper scope of their validity. Results obtained with arbitrarily specified concepts are a priori ascertained only for the case of this specification, which has no actual meaning. With respect to other cases, they can, at most, provide dim suggestions, with an unknown scope of validity, and which are, in fact, thoroughly unnecessary since the analysis with the properly general concepts shows exactly the proper results with their scope – and in a simpler way.[4]

The initial endowment of individual i can be described by a vector of quantities of goods X_i (goods of different qualities can be described as different goods). Similarly, gifts x_i and x_j, of any kind of nature, can also be considered as vectors of quantities of goods. Thus, $X_i, x_j, x_i \in X \subseteq \Re_+^m$ where m is the number of goods, and the restriction to set X can notably represent possible indivisibilities. Then, with a sufficiently large space of goods, individual i, initially endowed with X_i, receiving x_j, and giving x_i, has $X_i + x_j - x_i$ as final

---

[4] More basically, taking a number, calling it utility, kindness, fairness, liking, or whatever, and treating it as if it were the measure of a quantity, by adding it to, or multiplying it by, other numbers, possibly of the same type, or using it in ratios or differences, is a priori meaningless (that is, absurd), if not offensive (you can have expressions such as "my kindness multiplied by your kindness plus one," and so on), and this should therefore be either justified or avoided.

endowment. Then, individual i's utility function can be written, more explicitly, as

$$u^i(x_i, x_j) = U^i(X_i + x_j - x_i, x_i, x_j),$$

where the effect of the first argument denotes the purely self-interested and self-centred preferences of individual i about her allocation of goods. The considered social sentiments determine the effects of the last two arguments.[5]

The two following chapters analyse respectively the logic of the two genuine reciprocities, comparative, matching or balance reciprocity on the on hand and liking reciprocities on the other hand – sequential self-interested exchange is a type of standard exchange rather than genuine reciprocity with respect to the nature of the underlying sentiments and desires, which are the main criteria of distinction here. The formal analyses are preceded by considerations of the relevant basic properties which rest on the presentations of the reciprocities in chapters 6 and 7 and of the motives for giving in chapter 3, completing them in particular concerning properties that appear to be critical in the logical analysis.

[5] Other social sentiments such as comparative fairness, envy, jealousy, sentiments of superiority and inferiority, and possibly conforming or distinction, can make U^i depend on individual j's final allocation $X_j + x_i - x_j$, in addition to individual j's own $X_i + x_j - x_i$.

18

The theory of comparative, matching, or balance reciprocity

18.1 Reciprocitarian comparative sentiments

Reciprocity is motivated by comparison when the return-gift is elicited by sentiments based on a comparison between the gift and the return-gift. Such comparative reciprocity contrasts with liking reciprocity (although both are joined in a particular case, when the return giver wishes to show that she likes the other as much as she is liked by her).

Comparative reciprocities can involve various kinds of sentiments that elicit giving in return. The essential sentiment is the *propriety of balancing* the gift with some appropriate return gift. It has various different basic motives. Some of them focus on the overall situations, and others on the transfers (gifts). Some focus on one of the two agents, and others on both of them. Some refer to concepts or sentiments in the family of justice or fairness, whereas this is not the case for others. The sentiments or senses that can be involved are very varied: propriety, adequacy, fairness, justice, equity, equality, deserts, merit, moral indebtedness, shame, guilt, duty, or the requirement of a norm. These sentiments can be on the part of the initial receiver who gives in return, or of other people (including the initial giver). The initial receiver may care about these opinions and judgments of other people. Her decision to give in return can depend jointly on her own intrinsic judgment and on her view of other people's or society's judgments and opinions.

To begin with, a most basic concept is that the initial gift has disrupted the initial state, that some balance that existed in this state should be restored, and that this can be done by a transfer from the receiver to the giver that in some sense compensates for the initial gift. The notion of restoring balance can also focus on the giver – who has lost – or on the receiver – who has gained. The focus can also be directly on the transfers (gifts) and on their equality in value in some sense. The second transfer then appears as a compensation for the first.

Sentiments of fairness can focus on the situations or transfers only, or also on the fact that the initial gift is a free and voluntary act. Fairness can thus refer to *compensatory justice*, and require a transfer that compensates for the loss or cost incurred by the initial giver, or the benefit received by the initial receiver, or both jointly – which can be realized by a transfer from the initial receiver to the initial giver. This latter transfer is also simply a compensation for all the effects of the initial gift. This can also be seen as the requirement of the particular distributive justice that takes the initial state as reference (with an idea of maintaining a kind of status quo). Moreover, the initial transfer is free and voluntary (since it is a gift) and it benefits the receiver at some cost or loss for the giver. This tends to elicit the notion that *rewarding-retributive justice* justifies or requires rewarding the initial giver who deserves or merits it. Conversely, if the receiver has thus just received a windfall benefit without particular corresponding merit, need, or right, she may be the right payer of this reward.

These reasons induce the return gift when they sufficiently motivate the receiver directly or through other people's opinions and judgments about which she cares. These sentiments may indicate what is proper behaviour, duty, or a norm of conduct. Failing to provide the return gift, or a sufficient return gift, may elicit shame or guilt. It may also elicit sentiments induced by the unequal relation created by the initial gift alone, or by an insufficient return gift, between the two persons: moral indebtedness and, sometimes, a sentiment of inferiority or a lower status with respect to the initial giver or in general, or even a feeling of humiliation. By the same token, the absence or insufficiency of the return gift can make the initial giver a moral creditor – which may imply the power to ask later for a compensation chosen by her –, and it may give her a higher social status and a sense of superiority with respect to the receiver or in general (from which she may derive some pride).

Similarly, if, in giving sufficiently in return, the initial receiver can avoid impropriety, shame, guilt, moral indebtedness and sentiments of inferiority, she can also, in giving more, reverse the situation, become a moral creditor and – possibly – acquire the corresponding power of demanding something in return for the excess, and derive pride, a higher status and a sentiment or position of superiority.

This provides a remarkable structure and contrast in the various motives. The sentiment of proper balance tends to elicit a return gift neither lower nor higher in value than the initial gift. In contrast, sentiments of moral indebtedness, inferiority, guilt or shame tend only to elicit not giving too little in return. However, they have opposite sentiments in the same family, the sentiments of being a moral creditor with the corresponding power or status, of superiority, and of pride. These sentiments may be sought after, which can elicit giving in return more than required for balance. Therefore, for an insufficient (or absent) return gift, all the sentiments in question have an effect in the same direction of giving more and reducing the imbalance. In contrast, for a return gift higher than required for balance, the sentiment of proper balance favours its reduction whereas the other sentiments that this situation can elicit, when they are present, have the opposite effect of favouring a higher return gift and imbalance.

18.2 Basic concepts of comparative reciprocity

Formally, let X denote the set of possible gifts. Such a gift can be described as a set (vector) of quantities of goods. But there can be indivisibilities. Hence $X \subseteq \Re_+^n$ where n is the number of goods (any). Individual i receives gift $x_j \in X$ from individual j. She may answer with the return-gift $x_i \in X$. Denote as $x = (x_i, x_j) \in X^2$ the ordered pair of the two gifts x_i and x_j, and as $y = x_j - x_i \in \Re^n$ the vector excess of the gift over the return-gift. The views in question concerning the pair of gifts x will be those of the receiver i because we seek to explain her return-gift x_i, but they are generally shared by a wider society.

For each initial gift x_j, the return gifts x_i that are considered as matching gift x_j in an appropriate balance constitute a set that defines the subset B such that $x = (x_i, x_j) \in B \subseteq X^2$. For $x \notin B$, there is an *imbalance* between the two gifts. If the return gift x_i is deemed insufficient for matching the gift x_j, this imbalance is a *deficit*, and the corresponding pairs $x = (x_i, x_j)$ constitute the set $D \subseteq X^2$. If, on the contrary, the return gift x_i is deemed excessive for matching the gift x_j, this imbalance is a *surplus* and the corresponding pairs $x = (x_i, x_j)$ constitute the set $S \subseteq X^2$. The three sets B, D and S are separate, and can be considered as constituting a partition of X^2.

Moreover, imbalance, deficit and surplus are generally considered as being amenable to comparison by relations of more and less, which generally implies that they are representable by numerical functions $m(x)$, $d(x)$, and $s(x)$, respectively, a priori ordinal (i.e. defined up to any arbitrary increasing function).[1] In addition, one can say that the imbalance, deficit or

---

[1] A priori, the relations of more and less normally imply their transitivity, which only implies the existence of orderings of the x for imbalance, deficit or surplus. These orderings will most often be representable by functions m, s or d. This may not be the case, however, notably when some criteria for so comparing the x have priority over others that, nevertheless, have a domain of relevance.

surplus is zero when there is no imbalance, deficit or surplus respectively, and positive otherwise. This leads to taking $m(x) > 0$ if $x \notin B$ and $m(x) = 0$ if $x \in B$, $d(x) > 0$ if $x \in D$ and $d(x) = 0$ if $x \notin D$, and $s(x) > 0$ if $x \in S$ and $s(x) = 0$ if $x \notin S$. These functions are now defined up to any increasing, zero-invariant and otherwise arbitrary function. Since the present concepts of deficit and surplus specify that of imbalance in their respective case, one can take $d(x) = m(x)$ for $x \in D$, and $s(x) = m(x)$ for $x \in S$. Finally, one has $m(x) > 0$ for $x \notin B$ and $m(x) = 0$ for $x \in B$; $d(x) = m(x) > 0$ for $x \in D$ and $d(x) = 0$ for $x \notin D$; and $s(x) = m(x) > 0$ for $x \in S$ and $s(x) = 0$ for $x \notin S$.

The sentiment of imbalance and propriety of balance is concerned with index m and tends to favour and elicit its reduction. The sentiments of shame, guilt, inferiority and moral indebtedness are concerned with index d and favour, and tend to elicit, its reduction. The sentiments of pride, superiority and moral credit are concerned with index s and may tend to favour and elicit its augmentation. When a sentiment has a converse, one can associate both into one single generalized or extended sentiment. One thus has sentiments of shame/pride, inferiority/superiority, and moral indebtedness/credit. This leads to considering the extended or *generalized deficit* $\delta(x)$ defined as $\delta(x) = d(x) = m(x)$ for $x \in D \cup B$, and $\delta(x) = -s(x) = -m(x)$ for $x \in S \cup B$. Indeed, these extended sentiments tend to favour and elicit a reduction of the generalized deficit in the entire domain. However, it is common that an individual, for a given question, can have sentiments of shame, guilt, inferiority and moral indebtedness about a deficit, without having the opposite sentiments in the case of a surplus.

The variations of indexes m, d, s and δ with x can be expressed by the fact that δ is increasing in x_j and decreasing in x_i in the sense that it increases when x_j is replaced by $x'_j > x_j$ and decreases when x_i is replaced by $x'_i > x_i$ with the relation ">" between vectors denoting this relation between each of their coordinates (quantities of each good). Actual cases are often more specific in that social norms hold that only particular goods matter.

18.3 Neutrality

The property of balance or imbalance is said to be *neutral* when the gifts x_i and x_j are the only characteristics of individuals i and j that influence the indexes m, s and d. Then, the meaning of terms implies

$$s(\xi, \xi') = d(\xi', \xi),$$

for all $\xi \in X$ and $\xi' \in X$.

This implies that, for $\xi \in X$ and $\xi' \in X$,

$$s(\xi, \xi') > 0 \Leftrightarrow d(\xi', \xi) > 0$$

and hence

$$(\xi, \xi') \in S \Leftrightarrow (\xi', \xi) \in D,$$

and

$$m(\xi, \xi') = 0 \Leftrightarrow s(\xi, \xi') = d(\xi, \xi') = 0$$
$$\Leftrightarrow d(\xi', \xi) = s(\xi', \xi) = 0 \Leftrightarrow m(\xi', \xi) = 0$$

and hence

$$(\xi, \xi') \in B \Leftrightarrow (\xi', \xi) \in B.$$

It also implies that, for all $\xi \in X$,

$$s(\xi, \xi) = d(\xi, \xi),$$

hence $(\xi, \xi) \in B$ and

$$d(\xi, \xi) = s(\xi, \xi) = m(\xi, \xi) = \delta(\xi, \xi) = 0.$$

In particular, in the absence of gifts, $(0, 0) \in B$, $m(0, 0) = 0$, $\delta(0, 0) = 0$, and there is no imbalance.

Hence, neutrality also implies that, for all $\xi \in X$ and $\xi' \in X$,

$$m(\xi, \xi') = m(\xi', \xi)$$

and

$$\delta(\xi, \xi') = -\delta(\xi', \xi),$$

that is, functions m and δ are respectively symmetrical and antisymmetrical in this sense.

Neutrality is not the case when the concepts of balance or imbalance under consideration find that what should be compared are the gifts relative to specific characteristics of the giver or of the receiver, such as their capacities, their needs, their merit or deservingness (apart from those that can result from the gift in question in itself), their social status or position, the various possible specifications of these notions, or who is the first or the second giver. When there is no neutrality for any such reason, it is generally possible to define gifts relative to the considered characteristics such that neutrality holds for these new items. Such transformations are classical and much discussed and studied in the field of the theories of justice and equality and of measures of inequality.

18.4 Structures of imbalance

If both gifts include quantities of the same good, only the net amount transferred of this good may be relevant. That is, functions m, d, s, and δ depend on x_i and x_j only through $y = x_j - x_i \in \Re^n$: $m(x_i, x_j) = \tilde{m}(y)$, $\delta = \tilde{\delta}(y)$, $d = \tilde{d}(y)$ and $s = \tilde{s}(y)$. In vector y, each dimension is the *net* quantity of one good transferred from one individual to the other, with the proper sign.

If, moreover, there is neutrality, $\tilde{m}(y) = \tilde{m}(-y)$, $\tilde{\delta}(y) = -\tilde{\delta}(-y)$, $\tilde{s}(y) = \tilde{d}(-y)$.

It sometimes also happens that the money value of the gifts is their relevant measure, $v(x_j)$ and $v(x_i)$, with $\delta(x)$ which can be taken as $\delta(x) = v(x_j) - v(x_i)$, and $m(x) = |\delta(x)|$, $d(x) = \max[\delta(x), 0]$, and $s(x) = \max[-\delta(x), 0]$. This implies neutrality. If, moreover, the case of the foregoing paragraphs holds, $\delta(x) = v(y)$, for instance $\delta(x) = \sum p_k y_k$ if y_k is the dimension of y for good k and p_k is the price of good k. These reductions to money value are not the case in many instances, precisely because reciprocity is not in the sphere of exchange in the strict sense.

18.5 Choice

Let us now denote as $\mu(x)$ a function that can be $m(x)$, $d(x)$ or $\delta(x)$. Function μ can also represent a concern for comparing x_i and x_j that mixes the sentiments in question in any proportions.

Let us also consider a further motive, the simple, direct, self-interest for one's own endowment. Individual i's initial endowment is X_i, and her final endowment after receiving the gift x_j and giving the return gift x_i is $X_i + x_j - x_i = X_i + y$. Assume that individual i has a preference ordering representable by an ordinal utility function U^i. With the sentiments under consideration, U^i depends on $X_i + y$ and on $\mu(x)$:

$$U^i = U^i[X_i + y, \mu(x)].$$

The sentiments concerning $\mu(x)$ are such that U^i is a decreasing function of μ. If, given the choice of function $\mu(x)$, its specification changes as it is allowed to, for instance by an increasing sign-preserving function for functions m, d, or δ, function U^i incurs the corresponding contravariant transformation. Moreover, it often happens that these preferences of individual i are lexical (lexicographic), and hence cannot be represented by a unique utility function such as U^i, because individual i achieves balance or absence of deficit with priority, at least in some domain. Then, the maximand writes $U^i(X_i + y)$ given that $x \in B$ (or $x \in B \cup S$).

Consider the three cases of imbalance aversion with $\mu = m$, deficit-aversion with $\mu = d$, and deficit aversion plus surplus seeking with $\mu = \delta$ (the case of surplus seeking only, with $\mu = s$ and U^i increasing in it, can also be considered but seems quite less frequent). Then, $\mu = 0$ implies that the relevant effects are not present. Hence, for any allocation X_i' of individual i, the function $V^i(X_i')$ defined as

$$V^i(X_i') = U^i(X_i', 0)$$

represents individual i's preferences laundered for her reciprocitarian preferences. Moreover, since U^i is a decreasing function of μ, with $\mu(x) > 0$, in all cases,

$$U^i[X_i + y, \mu(x)] < V^i(X_i + y)$$

and, for surplus-seeking with $\delta(x) = -s(x) < 0$,

$$U^i[X_i + y, \delta(x)] > V^i(X_i + y).$$

Individual i, receiving gift x_j, then chooses the return gift x_i that maximizes U^i (or, if balance is desired with priority and is possible, she achieves $m(x) = 0$ and chooses the x_i that maximizes $V^i(X_i + y)$ on $x \in B$ if there is a choice). Individual j may more or less foresee this move. This leads to the interactions that will be analysed in chapter 22. Her choice may also be described by a maximand U^j. The argument of function U^j that represents this individual's self-interest in the strict sense is $X_j - x_j + x_i = X_j - y$. This is the only argument when the initial giver j aims only at receiving a return gift for a purely self-interested reason – this is the case of self-interested exploitation of the return gift in such a "half-reciprocity." However, the initial giver may also have other concerns and motives of various possible types. If these motives can be represented with the variables x_j, x_i, $X_i + y$ and $X_j - y$ only, then the initial giver's choice is again a "domination" (of the "Stackelberg" type), although it need not be solely and strictly self-interested. These motives for giving can be any of the types noted in chapter 3, including benevolence and any "social effects" (comparison or status for various reasons, and so on). In particular, she may also be concerned about balance, deficit or surplus. These items can have two types of relations with those previously considered. First, the roles of the two agents are reversed: a deficit for one can be a surplus for the other. Second, this being taken into account, the definitions of these items by the two agents may be the same or different ones. When they are the same, this may result from a definition that seems "natural" (a particular case is that in which money values are considered) or from a shared social norm. Among her possible conducts, the initial giver may seek superiority, pride, or being a moral creditor, in hoping that the return-gift will be insufficient for reaching balance and will leave a surplus in the initial giver's net gift (this surplus is a priori according to the initial giver's conception, but, if conceptions of others differ from it – in particular that of the receiver –, these other conceptions may be relevant if the initial giver cares for these other persons' views). The initial giver may again act in taking into account the receiver's foreseen reaction, by adding this concern about balances, deficit, or surplus to her pure and strict self-interest. The initial giver may have yet other concerns and motives. She may simply give out of benevolence. Then, the return giver may act as described, in particular by seeking balance. However, she may also come to like the initial giver because of this benevolent gift, attitude or sentiment, and give because of this liking, with a possible role for gratitude. This may be expected by the initial giver and be a motive for her action. Such interrelations are analysed in the next chapter. The initial giver may also give because this is morally valued or praised or a norm of conduct. She may also seek to establish a social relation that she appreciates. This social relation may be, rather than the domination previously considered, some more egalitarian relation between peers with, in general, also a material appreciation of the mutual transfers. In this case, the return gift is commonly necessary to establish a required balance. The aspect of fairness and some equality in the relation is then usually important for its quality. This equality or balance may, notably, be extended to erasing the difference that can arise from one person being the first giver and the other the second one. Such a desire shows in the strategic choice and cannot be solely described by the structure of the utility function (as mere imbalance aversion can be). Chapter 22 will consider and analyse these issues closely.

19

The theory of liking reciprocity

19.1 Liking reciprocity and comparative reciprocity

Liking reciprocity is reciprocity in which giving in return is motivated by liking. As we have seen in chapter 7, this liking results either from the initial giving, essentially when it is benevolent towards the beneficiary, or directly from the reciprocity in sentiments of reciprocal liking. In both cases, the motivation of the initial giver is essential. In balance reciprocity, in contrast, the motivation for giving in return is thoroughly different, and the motivation of the initial giving is a priori irrelevant. This motive for returning gifts is a "preference" for balance or matching, or deficit aversion (and, possibly, surplus seeking), whereas, in both types of liking reciprocity, giving in return is motivated by liking. These two families of reciprocity are thus inconsistent with one another, at least for strong forms of liking reciprocities: "*L'amour ne compte pas*" (He who loves does not count or "Love counts for all"), the dictum says, and love makes one give without seeking any kind of balance. One is also always "indebted" towards the loved one for her love or for her existence. However, for milder kinds of liking the two reciprocating sentiments and motives can be jointly present in the same person for the same return-gift. There can then be both liking and a preference for balance or for lower deficit – and surplus seeking may not be absent. In fact, balance may be favourable to friendship ("good reckonings make good friends" or "*Les bons comptes font les bons amis*"). There is also a kind of specific deficit aversion about the other's liking in the frustration of being liked less than one likes in mutual likings; however, this compares sentiments rather than gifts *per se*.

19.2 The sentiments of liking reciprocity

Liking reciprocity, therefore, has to consider the motives and sentiments not only of the return giver but of the initial giver too. It associates the following twenty or so families of relations between sentiments and between sentiments and giving.

19.2.1 Giving and liking

You like what you deem to be good for people you like. Hence, you tend to give to someone you like, and you give her if it is possible and not too costly otherwise for you, in order to increase this person's happiness, pleasure, welfare, propriety, status, or anything you deem favourable to her. Other reasons for giving to persons you like, for being liked in return or as information, will be pointed out shortly.

You tend to like to be given to, for several reasons. You often appreciate the gift or favour received in itself. You tend to value favourably the attention towards you that giving with the final aim of benefiting you constitutes or manifests. When this giving results from liking, you value all the more this attention which is appreciative of yourself, kind, and possibly more or less affectionate, and the general appreciation, kindness and liking causing the giving and manifested by it. This attention, this appreciation and this affection are favourable to your sense of self and of social existence. Moreover, when you like the giver you sometimes appreciate the relation and interaction the opportunity for which is provided by the giving. When the giving aims at eliciting liking in return, the effects are somewhat different: this most often reveals and proves that you are liked and hence considered favourably, but this is not the direct cause of the giving.

19.2.2 Liking to be liked, and the altruistic basis of individualism

You tend to like to be liked in itself – independently of any gift. Indeed, you commonly appreciate or enjoy the appreciative judgment, the respect, possibly the affection, implied by this sentiment towards you. Moreover, this liking implies considering you and paying attention to you. As noted, this attention is necessary to your sense of self and of social existence, it is the more favourable to it that it is appreciative of yourself, and all the more so that it is accompanied by some affection.

You tend to like more to be liked in itself by someone when you yourself like this person, and all the more the more you like her. The importance you attach to being liked by some person tends to be greater the more you like her. This is the *complementarity of mutual liking*. The basic reason is that you care (more) about people you like (more), and notably about their views and sentiments about you. Insofar as you like to be liked because the implied attention, favourable attention, and appreciation and affection foster your sense of self and of social existence, this sense is enhanced by your own favourable consideration of the others who like you. You feel you "exist" more – as proven by society – the more you care about these others. However, this complementarity also relates to the fact that friendship or love between persons is in a sense more genuinely social than just a pair of individual sentiments, no matter how interrelated they may be. This is suggested by the very expressions of friendship or love "between" people, and strongly revealed by expressions such as "our (or their) friendship or love." Symmetrically, you tend to suffer if you are not sufficiently liked by persons you like, especially for strong liking or love, and more so the more you like them. In particular, sometimes you resent a deficit in their liking you less than you like them.

The reasons that make you benefit from being liked intervene at three very different levels of depth, from the satisfaction or pleasure elicited by the appreciation of yourself by other people and the more or less warm interaction, to self-evaluation in the realm of self-respect and dignity, and to the "ontological" sense of self and of social existence. These effects increase when you like more the person who likes you. In particular, the resulting self-evaluation, and sense of self and of social existence, are greater, the greater the importance you attach to the consideration, appreciation, and liking of yourself by others, and hence the more you consider, appreciate, value or like these others. Now, the sense of self is the sentiment that founds individualism. Hence, both rest not only on the consideration of the individual by others, but also on the individual's own valuation of others. These mutual other-regarding sentiments are complements in a synergy for each individual. Each of these sentiments so fosters the sense of self at both ends, directly for the person who is the object of the sentiment, and for its holder because it increases the value for her of the other's view of herself. Since, moreover, individuals tend to consider and appreciate more the people who consider and appreciate them more – as we have seen for liking –, the deepest basis of the sense of self, of social existence, and hence in particular of individualism is a reciprocity in which all people are immersed. This shows that superficial oppositions between individualism and altruism miss the most important facts. This intrinsically social basis of individualism is fostered by the tendency to like people who like you (and conversely), by the psychological and psychosocial interaction of all these sentiments, and, in the end, by the practically properly social and collective aspects of mutual liking.

19.2.3 *The two gratitudes and their effects*

You tend to be grateful to someone responsible for something you favour, for this fact, if her final motives for acting in this way include favouring you one way or another. This act can be to give to you with benevolence. This sentiment of hers can manifest liking you (the giving can then be directly for favouring someone one likes or for the information effects considered shortly); but it can also result from the different motives of pity, compassion, or charity. The specific fact eliciting gratitude in this way can be any aspect of gift giving such as the gift or favour in itself, the attention towards you, possibly an appreciation of yourself and positive affects, or the relationship in the process of giving and receiving. You also tend to be directly grateful for someone liking you, towards this person.

However, this gratitude for a sentiment and towards its holder is particular both in itself and by its consequences. Normally, you can be grateful to someone for something she chooses to do with the intention of favouring you or something you like. Now, a person who likes you is responsible for holding or keeping this sentiment to an extent which is often quite limited, as with most sentiments (this subtle but important issue, touched upon in chapter 7, is fully analysed elsewhere).[1] Moreover, insofar as this sentiment is chosen, the intention of this choice is not to please you. Hence, being grateful to another person for her sentiment towards you in itself is a particular type of gratitude. In fact, since this sentiment is a part of the person, the gratitude is for the very existence of the person as she is. Hence, this is not gratitude towards someone responsible for a favourable act but gratitude addressed to nobody for the existence of something – the sentiment – and of someone – the person holding it.[2] This

---

[1] Cf. Kolm 2004, chapter 6.

[2] The sentiment and stance of gratitude in itself, addressed to nobody, is basic in advanced Buddhist philosophy and its practice (see Kolm 1982).

kind of gratitude is very close to directly liking the person who likes you, and can be seen as an aspect of it.

The sentiment of gratitude in general is favourable to liking the person one is grateful to. At least, it seems rather contradictory both to be grateful to someone and to dislike her. One could even see gratitude as one particular type of liking. This can directly entail giving in return. Gratitude, and such a consequence, are very different from a sense of moral indebtedness and the return giving it may induce to reduce imbalance or deficit, although both can coexist as results of the same gift and as motives for the same return gift. Moreover, being grateful because one is liked is being grateful for a sentiment of the other person, and a sentiment is more a part of the intrinsic self of a person than an act of hers is. This tends to be still more favourable to liking this person – then, there is practically an intrinsic direct reciprocity in liking.

In fact, gratitude is in itself a reciprocitarian sentiment. As an appreciative sentiment towards the giver, it performs some of the role of a return gift. In this aspect, its intensity manifests some balance with the initial gift. This is thoroughly different from balance reciprocity, however, since gratitude is a priori a spontaneous appreciative sentiment and not the wilful manifestation of a duty or sense of propriety to establish balance, or this sentiment of duty or propriety itself, as are the return gift and its motive in balance reciprocity. However, there are also the sentiments of a duty or propriety to be grateful and the corresponding reproach or accusation of ingratitude.

19.2.4 Reciprocal liking

You tend to like people who like you. This *reciprocal liking* is a basic reciprocity of sentiments. It has been explained in chapter 7. In brief, since you like to be liked in itself for the noted reasons of attention, favourable attention, and kind attention towards yourself which foster your sense of self and

of social existence, and for the agreeableness of the relationship, simple causal liking makes you like the person who
likes you. Insofar as she can influence her liking sentiment
and hence is responsible for it, you agent-like her. However,
you do not benefactor-like her for this reason since liking you
does not a priori aim at benefiting you (she does not like you
because you like it).

Moreover, since you particularly like to be liked by people you like, for reasons just noted, it is your "interest" to
like particularly people who like you. This tends to make
you like them (more) by a complex but standard process.
The largest part of this process is not voluntary and conscious (only its result is conscious). It is akin to cognitive
dissonance in the field of cognition. However, a part of this
process can be conscious and voluntary. This comes from an
adjustment of your sentiments by reasoning, attention, habit
formation and the like (this is supported by material acts such
as seeing more people who like you). These processes create
or reinforce sentiments, and reallocate the scarce factors of
your liking capacities – capacities for attention, affection and
emotional involvement – among the objects of your liking,
notably towards the people who like you more.

Other phenomena have an effect in the same direction. One
is the imitation of sentiments (Spinoza's *imitatio affectuum*),
applied in mirror-image imitation towards people who like
you, and which is better described as emotional contagion
since this process is largely involuntary. However, the person's will can also intervene, at least in not blocking the influence by the various ways just noted. Therefore, there can also
be the effect of a notion of the propriety of reciprocal liking
and of having mutual likings that are not too imbalanced. In
particular, this reciprocal sentiment can be favoured by social
approval about which the person cares.

The particular gratitude for sentiments described in the
previous section also fosters reciprocal liking. Being liked is
appreciated and may tend to elicit gratitude towards the liker.

However, gathering together a number of previous remarks shows that this gratitude and liking are quite particular. (1) Ordinary gratitude in this case is limited to the extent to which the person who likes can affect this sentiment. (2) It is furthermore limited because the objective of such an influence is usually not to be favourable to the liked person, for instance to please her. (3) Hence, this gratitude is, rather, simply for the existence of this sentiment – rather than towards someone who wilfully causes it. (4) However, this sentiment is a part of the person who likes. (5) Hence, the gratitude, which is not towards this person, is for her existence as she is. (6) Moreover, being liked is essential for self-evaluation, self-esteem, and, by the attention, appreciation, and possibly affection it entails, for the individual's sense of self and of social existence. Finally, in this particular relation, the existence of someone supports the sense of existence of someone else. The corresponding particular gratitude is one of the deepest aspects and bases of liking someone who likes you.

The interrelations and dynamics of these related sentiments are essential. They work at three levels: the psychology of each individual, the interaction between the individuals, and the case of sentiments that are more fruitfully seen as collective and properly social. If you like more someone who likes you, prima facie both of you benefit from it. She benefits from your sentiment by all the effects described. You also benefit because her liking you becomes more valuable for you by all its effects, from agreeableness to self-evaluation and sense of self and of social existence (you also enjoy more what is good for her and her satisfaction, but you may also suffer more from her misfortune or pain). At the level of individual psychology, this increased value of her liking can induce you to like her still more by the described processes which are involuntary for the largest part (this is mostly not a choice). Given all your psychological conditions, your sentiments settle into an affective equilibrium. In the meanwhile, however, the other person reacts to your increased liking by liking you more, with similar effects on her sentiments. This creates an interpersonal positive feedback in liking, with, again, a dynamics and possible stable equilibria. However, such a positive interaction of positive mutual sentiments tends to shift them from the realm of individual sentiments towards that of more specifically collective or social facts. This is indeed how people see it when they speak of "our friendship" or "our love." This primarily social aspect of sentiments that are so basic to the sense of individual existence is the reason for the particular place and importance of this reciprocity.

Finally, and more indirectly, liking tends to elicit giving which can be appreciated for the gift, the attention and consideration that giving constitutes and manifests, their kindness, and the corresponding relation and interaction. This tends to elicit gratitude, which is favourable to liking.

19.2.5 Giving in order to elicit liking

Giving in order to be liked is most common. It is also commonly frustrated, for an obvious reason. Indeed, the objective of being liked is not to benefit the person who is given to. This benefit is also sought, but only as a means to being liked. Hence, this action is not properly benevolent giving. It is akin to giving in order to receive a return gift (although what is sought is being liked, a sentiment and a fact largely beyond the will of the receiver). This does not induce the receiver to benefactor-like the giver. It can only induce her to like the giver as a cause of the benefit she receives (to agent-like her, since the benefit results from an agent's action). This is a much milder sentiment, usually not the one expected by the giver. For the same reason, this act a priori elicits no gratitude from the beneficiary. This lack of gratitude is a common complaint of the giver ("she is not even grateful . . ."). It is, however, necessary because of the lack of any intent to benefit the receiver other than for another objective – to be liked by her. (A truly benevolent giver can be said to give because the receiver's pleasure or other benefit pleases herself in the end, but this cannot be taken to mean that this giver is not genuinely benevolent since this effect defines this benevolence.) Therefore, for the main part, to be liked as a result of giving cannot be obtained purposefully. It can only be a by-product of an action with another intent, giving for the sake of the receiver's good or pleasure.

However, the desire to be liked by someone often implies that one likes her one way or the other (exceptions can result from indirect benefits from being liked, such as material ones, status or political interest). And one generally wants to be liked more by someone, the more one likes her. These relations hold for the giver towards the beneficiary. Then, the situation is that of a person who likes the beneficiary, and gives her something in order to please her, but for another final intent – to be liked by her. The beneficiary is a priori aware of this liking – revealed by this objective. This can induce her to like the giver for a direct reason of reciprocal liking. Moreover, the giver may also give directly because she likes the beneficiary. These two motives may coexist. This is indeed a common case. However, the foregoing remarks remain valid, by applying them to giving in excess to what is directly elicited by liking the beneficiary.

19.2.6 Informational giving

Giving also often aims at revealing that the giver likes the receiver. This is not directly benevolent giving. However, if the giver tries to show the beneficiary that she likes her because she knows the beneficiary likes to be liked, then the intent is in fact benevolent, not by directly pleasing the receiver by the gift, but by pleasing her because of her knowledge that she is liked. The corresponding benefactor-liking exists but is more involved and less clear and direct than the one that results from a simple gift because of liking. However, this information also permits the receiver to develop the sentiment of reciprocal liking that results from being liked – presented above. If the giver wants to show her liking in order to be liked in return, this non-altruistic objective prevents the informational giving from being benevolent, but, most of the time, this objective reveals and proves the giver's liking, and the corresponding reciprocal liking remains.

19.3 The interrelations of liking-reciprocity

19.3.1 The four synthetic relations

For convenience, denote as i and j two individuals, x_i individual i's gift to individual j, and ℓ_i individual i's liking of individual j with the description of its type and intensity, while x_j and ℓ_j similarly denote individual j's gift to, and liking of, individual i. Variables ℓ_i and ℓ_j simply denote sentiments here, without further qualifications for the time being; qualifications and specifications will be introduced below when needed.

The noted influences are synthesized as follows.

Individual j's gift to individual i, x_j, may depend on her liking of individual i, ℓ_j, for the following reasons. Individual j wants to please individual i because she likes her (ℓ_j), by the gift (x_j) and because this giving shows and proves that she likes her (which individual i likes). Moreover, individual j wants more to be liked by individual i the more she likes her (ℓ_j). She tends to elicit this liking by the gift x_j in two ways: by reciprocal liking since the giving can show and prove her liking; and, more or less, by liking the benevolent giver who provides the gift, the attention, and the interaction (even though the aim in question is, ultimately, to be liked, notably since this generally implies liking). Moreover, individual j's gift x_j, when it aims at influencing individual i's liking of individual j, may depend on the present state of this liking, ℓ_i. All these influences can then be epitomized by the functional relation $x_j = x_j(\ell_j, \ell_i)$. Symmetrically, one can have $x_i = x_i(\ell_i, \ell_j)$.

Moreover, individual j's liking of individual i, ℓ_j, depends a priori on individual i's liking of individual j (reciprocal liking), ℓ_i. However, it depends more precisely on individual j's belief about this liking ℓ_i. This belief depends, in particular, on messages that individual i sends to individual j in the form of giving gift x_i, which can show or prove individual i's liking of individual j. This belief may, in addition, depend on actual ℓ_i through information about it which can take various other ways (attitude, communication, and so on). Finally, individual j's liking of individual i, ℓ_j, can also depend on the gift she receives from individual i, x_i, because of the gratification she receives from the intrinsic interest of the gift, the attention of the giving, or the interaction; given that individual i is responsible for this giving and does it notably with benevolence because she likes individual j; and that she gives as a result of this liking either directly or to show and prove this sentiment to please the other and to elicit her liking in return. Individual j's liking ℓ_j may also be fostered by gratitude towards individual i for these effects of giving x_i, for the liking ℓ_i, and for the noted effects that induce liking them. In the end, all these effects can be epitomized in the functional relation $\ell_j = \ell_j(\ell_i, x_i)$. Symmetrically, one can have $\ell_i = \ell_i(\ell_j, x_j)$.

This makes four relations for four variables, x_i, x_j, ℓ_i, and ℓ_j. A dynamics can result. For instance, one can start with levels (and types) of ℓ_i and ℓ_j. They induce giving gifts x_i and x_j, which in turn induce new levels of ℓ_i and ℓ_j, and so on. Alternatively, one giving may begin, followed by the other. There are also equilibria determined by these four independent relations between these four variables.

A notable particular case is that of *pure reciprocal liking* in which each liking depends only on the other, whereas each giving depends on the giver's liking only. Then, discarding also informational giving, $\ell_j = \ell_j(\ell_i)$, $\ell_i = \ell_i(\ell_j)$, $x_i = x_i(\ell_i)$,

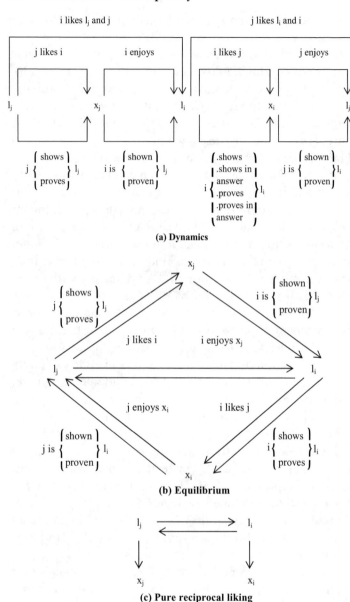

Figure 19.1 The logic of liking reciprocity

$x_j = x_j(\ell_j)$. There is only a reciprocity of sentiments and benevolent givings.

19.3.2 Synopsis and graphs of the relations

The relations discussed above constitute a network represented by figure 19.1. Figure 19.1a represents a dynamic ordered graph, while figure 19.1b epitomizes the relation of general interdependence, and figure 19.1c shows the case of pure reciprocal liking. Note that an individual can like a person, a sentiment, an act, a gift, a relation, and so on. Also, an individual can show or prove her liking not only spontaneously but also in response to a revelation of this type by the other.

19.4 The economics of liking reciprocity

19.4.1 Preferences

The foregoing analysis considers that each individual chooses her gift to the other, x_i for individual i. The main characteristic of standard economic analysis consists in a theory of choice as resulting from a previous preference ordering, often representable by an ordinal "utility function" which is so maximized. Such an ordering or function is also commonly deemed to represent levels of "satisfaction" of the individual – sometimes seen as her happiness or pleasure. They also commonly have a normative use. This ordering or function depends on objects of choice and on parameters that may influence the choice (and the satisfaction). This will be written for utility functions because this is the common case and for convenience in presentation and discussion (the extension to more general preference orderings is straightforward).

Again, x_i, x_j, ℓ_i, and ℓ_j denote individuals' i and j gifts to, and liking of, the other, respectively. The x_i and x_j are vectors of quantities of goods, as the individuals' initial endowments of goods X_i and X_j. Variables ℓ_i and ℓ_j can just represent the likings. However, it is commonly considered that an individual can more or less like the other. Then, the ℓ_i and ℓ_j will be ordinal numerical representations of this intensity (ordinal means that each index can be replaced by an arbitrary increasing function of it). It is even sometimes considered that an individual likes more than the other does. In such a case, the two ℓ_i and ℓ_j are assumed comparable by a relation of more or less, with "co-ordinality" (i.e., they can be transformed by the *same* arbitrary increasing function). However, such structural assumptions – ordinal representation of intensity and interpersonal comparability – are assumed only in the cases in which they are used in the representation of actual conceptions, and are not a priori assumed in the other cases.

Following the general methodology, only the structure of liking reciprocity and of its basic consequences (such as liking the good of people one likes), and pure self-interest, are considered at present. The various relevant effects of variables and parameters are considered. Then, using the relations among the variables pointed out in the previous section, the utility functions will be reduced to functions of x_i and x_j alone, for introduction in the reciprocity games considered in the following chapters.

U^i and U^j will denote the direct utility functions of individuals i and j respectively, and the values of these functions for any given specifications of these ordinal utilities. Then, for individual i,

$$U^i = U^i(X_i + x_j - x_i, U^j, S_j, \ell_j, \ell_i, x_j, x_i), \qquad (1)$$

with the following meanings.

The variable $X_i + x_j - x_i$ is individual i's remaining allocation after the gifts received x_j and given x_i. Its considered effect is pure self-interest (there could also be effects of comparisons with the consumption or incomes of other people).

Individual i liking individual j usually implies that she likes individual j's satisfaction represented by U^j. Hence, U^i is an increasing function of U^j.

More generally, individual i liking individual j implies that she likes what she deems to be good for individual j. This generally includes individual j's satisfaction. It may also include other items that concern individual j, chosen for reasons that are not only that they satisfy her – and which may sometimes even be disliked by individual j. These items may for instance include individual i's income, general or specific consumption, or anything that individual i deems "proper" for individual j. This preference of individual i is usually called "paternalism." These items are the relevant aspects S_j of individual j's situation in a broad sense.

19.4.2 The effects of liking and being liked

Liking and being liked have important "welfare" effects, or effects on satisfaction, or on the structure of preferences about other items. These effects are of four types: *direct, parametric, comparative* and *inducing*. Indeed, people often enjoy being liked and possibly also liking; liking someone more makes one more sensitive to her satisfaction and situation, and to her liking oneself – hence it makes one happier when they are high or good and less happy when they are insufficient; mutual likings are sometimes compared; and liking induces giving and other actions. Let us consider these different effects.

Individuals a priori like and enjoy being liked. This is a priori particularly the case when they themselves care about the other person, notably because they like her. Being liked implies being the object of attention and consideration which increase the sense of self and of social existence, especially since this consideration is appreciative of some sort, and still more since it goes with affection. People generally like and enjoy the benevolence and kindness towards them, and the

warmth of the relationship. Hence, with the proper representation ℓ_j of individual j's liking, U^i tends to be an increasing
function of ℓ_j. Being liked tends to induce liking the other,
with the effects, discussed above, of adjustment of one's sentiment, of gratitude, of the extension of the liked object from
the other's sentiment (and the resulting attitude) to the person
herself, and of imitation (and "contagion").

Liking (or loving) is in itself a positive feeling which is
bound to make the individual happier. However, it makes
the individual (more) sensitive to the object of this sentiment,
and this effect can either favour or hamper the person's satisfaction, depending on the state of this object. Individual i,
liking individual j, is concerned with individual j's satisfaction U^j, possibly with other aspects of her situation S_j, and
with individual j's liking of herself, ℓ_j. When individual i's
liking ℓ_i increases, these effects make individual i more or
less satisfied depending on whether individual j's satisfaction, other relevant aspects of her situation, and her liking
of individual i are satisfactory or not. If the other person is
happy, otherwise in a good situation, and likes you, liking her
more tends to make you appreciate these facts more and a priori makes you happier for this reason. However, if the other
is unhappy, otherwise in a poor situation, or if she likes you
too little, liking her more makes you resent more these insufficiencies and lowers your satisfaction. A priori, this implies
that there is a critical level for each of these items, such that a
higher ℓ_i makes individual i happier if the item is above this
level and less happy if it is below. These levels are U_o^j for U^j,
ℓ_j^o for ℓ_j, and s_j^o for some other parameter of individual j's situation, s_j, that individual i prefers to be higher. This does not
prevent the fact that these representations can be ordinal only,
since a corresponding transformation of these indexes (by any
increasing transformation) is then also applied to the critical
level. If a_j denotes U^j, s_j, or ℓ_j, with a_j^o denoting the corresponding critical level, the increasing curve representing U^i
as a function of a_j passes through a point with $a_j = a_j^o$, and,

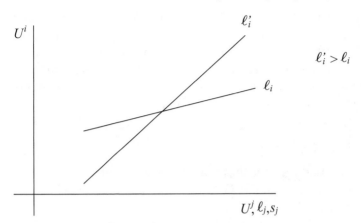

Figure 19.2 Effects of liking on satisfaction

when ℓ_i increases, it becomes higher (larger U^i) for $a_j > a_j^o$, lower (smaller U^i) for $a_j < a_j^0$, while $U^i(a_j^o)$ does not change (figure 19.2). The critical levels can a priori depend on all the parameters of the problem, the individuals in question to begin with. They can even depend on the liking parameter ℓ_i itself in the sense that the noted fixed point of the curve $U^i(a_j)$ is replaced by an envelope of this curve. This discussion need not be pursued here.

Moreover, sentiments commonly attach to the comparison of reciprocal likings by more or less. However, the sentiment and its consequences differ depending on whether a surplus or a deficit is faced. Such comparisons a priori imply such a comparability of these likings. People sometimes resent being liked less than they like. This can notably occur in the strong case of love. Then, individual i resents the fact that $\ell_j < \ell_i$, and this reason tends in this case to make U^i increase with ℓ_j, and decrease when ℓ_i is higher. This effect induces individual i to particularly favour acts that tend to increase ℓ_j, and it produces a relief for her when ℓ_i decreases. The converse situation with $\ell_i < \ell_j$ does not elicit the same type of sentiments for individual i. However, it sometimes elicits a sentiment of guilt for not liking the other more, and a sense of duty to like her more (limited by the limits of the possibilities to influence one's sentiments), to diminish the imbalance, sometimes with some corresponding sentiment of fairness and unfairness. All these effects combine with the other noted reasons and sentiments.

19.4.3 Gifts and actions

Individual i appreciates the gift she receives, x_j, for various possible reasons: its effect on her allocation $X_i + x_j - x_i$; its manifestation of individual j liking her, ℓ_j, and its showing and proving its intensity; the attention and consideration that giving constitutes; the favourable appreciation it implies; the benevolence and kindness associated with it; the effects of this attention, consideration, and appreciation on her sense of self and of social existence; and the relation established in the process of giving and receiving.

Individual i's basic choice is the gift x_i that she gives. With the conception retained at present, she does that with the aim of maximizing U^i. However, her motivation in question is her liking individual j (ℓ_i). The resulting effect of x_i on U^i passes through various channels: it increases individual j's allocation $X_j + x_i - x_j$ and hence her satisfaction U^j; it may relevantly improve aspects of individual j's situation S_j; it shows and proves individual i's liking and its intensity – which may augment U^j and induce a higher ℓ_j; it manifests attention, consideration, appreciation, benevolence and kindness that individual j appreciates – which again tends to augment U^j and ℓ_j; and it may create a relationship appreciated by any individual or by both in the process of giving. These values are compared with cost in terms of self-interest in $X_i + x_j - x_i$.

Gifts x_i and x_j can also have other effects, for instance demonstration effects of showing liking or being liked to third persons whose opinion may be appreciated by the individuals in question.

Showing one's liking, in particular for eliciting reciprocal liking, is, of course, done mostly by communication and
the appropriate interaction. Moreover, likings are sentiments
and common individuals exercise only a limited choice over
their own sentiments. Nevertheless, such actions exist more
or less, through various devices including reasoning, getting
used to, meeting or avoiding, focusing attention on particular sentiments or on their object, or diverting attention from
them, and so on.

19.4.4 Reduced forms

Considering equation (1) and the similar one for individ-
ual j, the two relations previously discussed $\ell_i = \ell_i(\ell_j, x_j)$
and $\ell_j = \ell_j(\ell_i, x_i)$, relations $S_i = S_i(x_j, x_i)$ and $S_j = S_j(x_i, x_j)$
that express effects of the gifts x_i and x_j, and solving for
the levels U^i, U^j, ℓ_i, ℓ_j one notably obtains $U^i = u^i(x_i, x_j)$ and
$U^j = u^j(x_j, x_i)$ for given initial individual allocations X_i and
X_j. These reduced forms can then be used for the analysis of
the reciprocity game in the next chapters.

Then, the choices of x_i and x_j, and the relations discussed
above $\ell_i = \ell_i(\ell_j, x_j)$ and $\ell_j = \ell_j(\ell_i, x_i)$ give levels $\ell_i = \tilde{\ell}_i(x_j, x_i)$
and $\ell_j = \tilde{\ell}_j(x_i, x_j)$.

However, since one relation is reciprocal liking, and liking
the giver is the strongest when this giving is motivated by liking which can be determined in reciprocal liking, an important simple case is described by pure reciprocal liking. When,
moreover, gifts have no role of information about liking, the
liking relations become simply $\ell_i = \ell_i(\ell_j)$ and $\ell_j = \ell_j(\ell_i)$. This
can be an actual case or an interesting acceptable approxima-
tion of real cases. These relations may be solved as $\ell_i = \tilde{\ell}_i$
and $\ell_j = \tilde{\ell}_j$. Then, simple giving from liking can yield the
gifts $x_i = x_i(\tilde{\ell}_i)$ and $x_j = x_j(\tilde{\ell}_j)$.

However, the cases of multiple solutions, and, if an adjustment process is considered, of multiple equilibria and of multiple stable equilibria, are not rare. There are often dynamics

that lead to either mutual high liking or mutual low liking according to the conditions.[3]

19.4.5 Group sentiments

Finally, although reciprocal liking constitutes a close, integrative relationship between the individuals, the foregoing analysis has ultimately considered distinctly individualized items. However, there are limits to this "methodological individualism." Norms and social opinions, notably for comparative reciprocities, are already not always being considered in the most fruitful way when they are seen only as related individual views or sentiments. In a different way, but sometimes very strongly, interdependent mutual liking is not just a pair of individual sentiments but is often more fruitfully viewed as a properly collective sentiment of the considered micro-society.[4] Indeed, we have noted that people consider it this in way when they speak of "our friendship", or "our love." However, an analysis from this point of view, possibly based on a phenomenology of intersubjectivity, would take us quite far away from the traditional methods of economics followed here. From a formal point of view, however, the full realization of this fusion and commonness of sentiments can be described in writing $\ell_i = \ell_j = \ell$ in the foregoing equations.

[3] This issue is analysed fully in Kolm 1984a.
[4] See Kolm 1984a.

20

Strategic interaction and process preferences: games of reciprocity

20.1 Objects of preferences

Given possible motives and their relations with actions, there remains, to explain reciprocity, to consider the effects of the interaction of the participants that leads them to the choice of actions. In so choosing, participants often take into account their anticipation of others' reaction. Thus, they consider the thinking of others, and they may have to consider what others think they themselves think. This gives a game-theoretic form to the interaction leading to the choices of actions. In addition, people also often directly care about the nature of the intentions, attitudes, judgments and views of others, notably concerning themselves. And they also have judgments about their own intentions, attitudes, judgments, and views towards others. This is notably important for most genuine reciprocities. It is self-evident for reciprocities based on liking, but it also holds for the balance or fairness of balance reciprocity. Hence, the strategic game-theoretic dimension of the relation is not only present but also correspondingly enriched by these other concerns. Therefore, beyond the general properties of game theory, there will be major differences with other games, due to the type of motives and concerns. These specific properties of games of reciprocity influence both the preferences and the concepts of solution (in the sense of game theory) – as will shortly be seen.

These motives refer to social relations, which determine a type of process for the interaction such as, notably, a type of reciprocity, a purely self-interested exchange, or imposition by force. This reciprocity can be of a pure or mixed kind of any type (liking, balance with some liking, normatively oppressive balance, with any kind of combination and of role for self-interest). The definition of the process determines the game and in the end the outcome. It is a parameter of the game and in particular of the preference (utility) functions and of the type of "solution" retained – as will be discussed soon. Moreover, the comparison of processes and hence of types of social relations, given their intrinsic values or defects and their consequences, is an essential issue. In particular, explaining the existence of processes (and types of social relations), and their choices or the choices that lead to them, is a most important question. As is the normative comparison of the alternatives.

Then, in particular, we have to consider that people have preferences about processes independently of their effects on transfers and on the resulting economic allocations. Indeed, a type of process goes along with a type of social relation, and people are generally not indifferent about being liked, appreciated, trusted, treated fairly, or instrumentalized, reified, exploited or forced. When there are two transfers – one in each direction – between two persons, it is not indifferent for these persons (and for many observers) whether these transfers result from a selfish but respectful exchange, a reciprocity induced by mutual liking, a reciprocity motivated by balance or fairness, or a theft or forceful appropriation followed by retaliation. Besides the style of relations, types of processes entail more or less freedom, for the actor, from the acts and choices (and judgements) of others. People often like this freedom in itself, although the costs of choosing, the anguish of choice (as Sören Kierkegaard and Jean-Paul Sartre put it), and a possible aversion to responsibility, can have the opposite effect. These preferences for the type of process in itself are the *intrinsic process preferences*, or "preferences about the

process in itself or per se". The association of these preferences with the preferences about the effect of the process on
the transfers and allocations, that is, the preferences about
the process both in itself and because of its consequences,
constitute the *full process preferences*, or, for short, simply
process preferences.

The other relevant variables and objects of preferences are
of two kinds: the "transfers" and the "allocations." A "transfer" is a change of the world that is both favourable to an
agent and unfavourable to another – this is a transfer from
the latter to the former. This can be a physical transfer of a
good, or a service from an agent to the other (costly in some
sense for the former). The transfers are for instance the gifts
or the items exchanged or taken by force. The gifts x_i and x_j of
the previous sections are such transfers. The allocation is the
resulting allocation of goods and services (for instance, the
$X_i + y$ in the previous sections). The transfers influence
the allocation. They determine the allocation resulting from
the process, given the initial allocation. The following analyses take the initial allocation as given. Hence, the allocation resulting from the processes can be fully described by
the transfers alone. These transfers are also the acts under
consideration. Therefore, they will be the variables of the
analyses, in addition to the nature of the processes. The preferences concerning these variables, which aggregate preferences about the transfers per se and preferences about the
resulting allocation, are the *allocative preferences.*

This simple form will permit the most general analysis.
However, of course, allocative preferences can a priori result
from a variety of motives, depending on the process, and
which can be directly concerned either with transfers or
with the final allocation (hence indirectly with transfers).
For instance, in a process of balance reciprocity, the agents
compare transfers (they are also sometimes concerned with
transfers relative to some allocation, when giving according
to the giver's means or to the receiver's needs). In liking reciprocity, the benevolent favours are primarily concerned with

the receiver's allocation, for her self-interest or for improving some other aspect of her situation. And yet, transfers of gifts or favours also matter for their information or demonstration effect about the giver's sentiment. In a standard exchange, people are concerned with their interest for their final allocation, although this process establishes some equality in the (market) value of the transfers. Transfers may also matter for other effects of social nature, such as establishing or manifesting statuses. Concerns about the final allocations can have many motives: in addition to self-interest, there are motives for being concerned with the allocations of other people in themselves (altruism, justice, other views) or comparatively (comparative justice, envy, jealousy, sentiments of inferiority or superiority, preferences for conformity or for distinction). In particular, comparative justice can be concerned with transfers in a balance reciprocity, and also with final allocations (then, the former comparison is in a sense more "local" than the latter). It is even concerned with a mixture of both when the gifts are compared according to the giver's means or the receiver's needs. One could distinguish, in the allocative preferences, "transfer preferences" directly concerned with transfers, and "allocation preferences" directly concerned with allocations (hence concerned with transfers only indirectly). However, this is not needed in the most general theory in which final allocations are represented by the given initial ones plus or minus the transfers.

In addition to individuals' preferences, the game is determined by concepts of "solution" of the strategic interaction – in the sense of game theory. In this respect as well, relations of reciprocity bring in something new.

20.2 Interaction and solution

In the simplest reciprocity in which a gift elicits a return gift, the initial giver may be concerned with the overall reciprocity and, rather than provide a gift irrespective of the reaction it entails, she may also consider the return gift when choosing her gift. Then, she more or less foresees the other's reaction and chooses accordingly. This Stackelberg-type solution is a *domination*. In so doing, the initial giver may be purely self-interested and hence give in order to receive the return gift. This is "exploitation of the return gift." However, the initial giver may also perform this domination with any other motive or mix of motives, including altruism, liking and kindness, any of the reasons noted above for being concerned with the resulting allocation, justice and fairness in the comparison of the two gifts, or their proper balance per se, and so on.

Nevertheless, justice, fairness, balance and equality may be among the concerns, and yet the very fact that there is a first and a second giver, and hence a domination, is in itself an inequality. Hence, the initial giver may want to remedy this basic imbalance in her giving. That is, she may be concerned about fairness not only for the transfers or the allocation, but also for the process, in seeking the corresponding *procedural fairness*. This is done when *the initial gift elicits a return gift such that, if the return giver were the initial giver and handed out this return gift as initial gift, the former initial giver would then react with a return gift identical to her initial gift*. This leads to a solution formally analogous to a Cournot-Nash solution, yet with the preferences and hence reaction functions corresponding to the type of relation under consideration. Note that Cournot-Nash solutions have no valid justification in usual one-shot or two-move games. Therefore, the described motive of procedural fairness constitutes the only justification proposed so far for a Cournot-Nash solution to one-shot or two-move games. A solution with this structure will be called an *equilibrium*.

Equilibrium solutions are also interesting because solutions with the same structure result from important cases of longer relations of reciprocity. In these relations, there is a large number of iterative givings, either alternately from each side, or simultaneously at successive dates. The equilibrium structure can notably result from two rationales, the "myopic" and the "cumulative." In the former, each individual gift is the return-gift corresponding to the last gift received by the giver. In the latter case, each individual gift is an adjustment that reacts to the stocks of previous gifts both ways.[1]

Yet other solutions with plausible rationales will be pointed out, but the structures of domination and of equilibrium seem to be the main ones and will be particularly considered, and compared. The comparisons will also extend to processes that are not reciprocities, such as standard exchanges or the imposition of an outcome.

The usual considerations of situations of such dominations and equilibria in the space of transfers suggest that the outcome is such that other sets of transfers satisfy both participants better, i.e., it is not Pareto-efficient. However, reaching another set of transfers requires another type of process and of social relation, and, hence, other preferences between sets of transfers or utility functions as function of the transfers. For instance, a standard exchange may lead to a Pareto-efficient state, but one with utility functions corresponding to this process and type of social relations. In comparing processes and their outcomes, a seemingly allocatively inefficient reciprocity may be preferred by all participants to another process that is allocatively efficient (e.g. exchange or force), if this reciprocity is sufficiently preferred intrinsically because of the social relations it implies (e.g. kindness, liking, fairness, freedom from others' actions, and so on). The logic of this kind of issue will be analysed closely.

Particularly important properties exist when the transfers are quantities of a good (e.g. a good the yielder produces or possesses, possibly her labour, or the value of aid in case of particular needs of the receiver or means of the yielder) – in fact, it suffices, for these properties, that the transfers or favours from the same agent can be ranked by a relation

---

[1] See Kolm 1984a, 1984b, 1994, and appendix A of chapter 22.

of more or less, and even only that they can be so classified according to their desirability by the receiver. In this
quantitative case, preferences about processes are related to
the fact that more or less of the goods are transferred – an
observable property. This leads to a number of notable properties with meaningful and important applications, including
counter-intuitive logical results that explain some paradoxes
observed in processes of social change and development (for
instance, larger transfers of goods accompany processes with
lower intrinsic relational quality).

Important applications of the results obtained are found in
the analysis and comparison of various types of economic
realization (including of organizations), with various kinds
of intrinsic motivations and extrinsic incentives, and results
concerning their economic performance and participants'
satisfaction. This applies to the choice of social and economic
design, and to the analysis of competitions between forms
of economic realization and of the resulting evolution. This
includes the comparison of economic systems, and in particular the properties of the process of "development," since the
latter has consisted largely of substituting markets and command systems for economic relations that were essentially
based on various types of reciprocity.

The logic of process preferences, notably the relation
between intrinsic and full process preferences, and the general resulting properties of interactions between two agents,
will be considered in chapter 21. Chapter 22 then considers
the interactions between two agents engaged in some type of
reciprocity or other process, and it relates the types of process, preferences about them, their results in transfers and
allocations, and the comparisons of the resulting amounts
transferred and of participants' satisfaction. In particular, the
"reciprocity games" lead to the consideration of specific rationales for the relevant concepts of "solutions" of the game.
Reciprocity is then compared with other processes (this
explains, among other things, the "paradox of development").

21

General properties of processes

21.1 General preferences

21.1.1 Transfers, process and preferences

Let variable $x \in X$ denote the set of transfers, from and to any agent (these distinctions will come later). As noted, x also entails the final allocation, and the "allocative preferences" can be about both the transfers per se and the resulting allocation. Variable $z \in Z$ denotes a type of process, and hence both a type of "mechanism" leading to a solution, and the type of social relations that accompany it. An agent's (overall) preferences are concerned with the pairs (x, z).[1] Classically, these preferences will be assumed to constitute a preordering with pairwise relations denoted as $\succ$ (preference), $\sim$ (indifference), and $\succsim$ ($\succ$ or $\sim$). These preferences are often representable by an ordinal utility function $u(x, z)$, and we will often consider this representation for convenience. These preferences, considered for all involved agents, will be used to explain the outcome x of each type of process z; the emergence of a specific process z; the normative evaluation and comparison of

---

[1] By comparison (full) process preferences are preferences among processes (and the corresponding social relations) z that derive from (overall) preferences among pairs (x, z) by being the preferences among pairs $[x(z), z]$ where $x(z)$ denotes the transfers (and the allocation) that are determined by the working of process z.

the processes; and the evaluation of the realized solution among them.

21.1.2 Intrinsic process preference and a basic lemma

Let us first point out a basic general property. Assume that x and $x' \in X$, z and $z' \in Z$, and $(x', z') \gtrsim (x, z)$. Then, $(x, z) \succ (x, z')$ implies $(x', z') \succ (x, z')$, and $(x', z) \succ (x', z')$ implies $(x', z) \succ (x, z)$. In particular, $(x, z) \succ (x, z')$ and $(x', z) \succ (x', z')$ may result from $(\xi, z) \succ (\xi, z')$ for all $\xi \in \overline{X} \subseteq X$ and $x \in \overline{X}$ and $x' \in \overline{X}$. Hence the following definition and properties.

Definition
Process z is *intrinsically preferred* (or *preferred per se*) to process z' in the relevant domain $\overline{X} \subseteq X$ if $(x, z) \succ (x, z')$ for all $x \in \overline{X}$. Weakly intrinsically preferred (or weakly preferred *per se*) is similarly defined in replacing $\succ$ by $\gtrsim$.

The domain $\overline{X}$ will usually be kept implicit for simplicity, and hence it will be assumed to be the one relevant for the specific issue under consideration. Intrinsic preference, or preference *per se*, for process z over process z' will be denoted as zPz'.[2]

Proposition 1
Assume process z to be intrinsically preferred to process z'. Then, $(x', z') \gtrsim (x, z)$ implies both $(x', z) \succ (x, z)$ and $(x', z') \succ (x, z')$; that is, x' is preferred to x with both processes. And $(x, z) \gtrsim (x', z)$ or $(x, z') \gtrsim (x', z')$ implies $(x, z) \succ (x', z')$; that is, the latter relation holds if x' is not preferred to x with either process.

---

[2] Similarly, x is (weakly) intrinsically preferred to x' in the relevant domain of processes $z \in \overline{Z} \subseteq Z$ if $(x, z) \succ (x', z)$ (or $(x, z) \gtrsim (x', z)$) for all $z \in \overline{Z}$. This property will be less used, however. A proposition dual to proposition 1 but inverting x and z (and x' and z') then holds.

These properties are particularly meaningful. The former says that for (x', z') to be weakly preferred to (x, z) in spite of the intrinsic preference for z over z', x' should be preferred to x with both processes; this can result, for example, from the fact that the allocation implied by x' is intrinsically much more favourable than the allocation implied by x and this compensates for the intrinsic preference for z over z'.[3] For example, z can be a reciprocity that yields x, and z' can be a very efficient exchange that yields x'. In the second, converse, property, $(x, \zeta) \succsim (x', \zeta)$ can mean that x is freely chosen by the agent with process ζ while x' is a possibility, and the property implies that if this is the case for ζ being either z or z', then $(x, z) \succ (x', z')$. For example, z can be a reciprocity and z' an exchange, and x can be the choice in either process.

21.1.3 Process-dependent allocative preferences

Allocative preferences may be the same for different types of processes, but this is certainly not the general case, because a number of reasons for preferences about processes depend on transfers. This happens notably for reasons based on the quality of social relations or on the activity. For example, such reasons are absent if there is no transfer, which will be denoted as $x = 0$. If process preferences rely only on such reasons for the comparison of processes z and z', then $(0, z) \sim (0, z')$. If, furthermore, allocative preferences are the same for processes z and z', and if there exists one $x \neq 0$ such that $(x, z) \sim (0, z)$ (or the same with z'), then $(x, z') \sim (0, z') \sim (0, z) \sim (x, z)$. Hence, process z' cannot be better or worse than process z for x. In particular, none of these processes can be intrinsically preferred to the other for all $x \neq 0$. Of course, when $(0, z) \sim (0, z')$, the case $x = 0$ is to be excluded for proposition 1 which, hence, considers only situations with transfers. However, other reasons for process preferences may

---

[3] This can result from intrinsic preference for x' over x.

exclude $(0, z) \sim (0, z')$. For example, z may denote some process with much freedom (exchange or reciprocity) that ends up in $x = 0$, while z' may be command that imposes $x = 0$, and preference for freedom may then lead to $(0, z) \succ (0, z')$. In yet other cases, the mere attitudes towards others may make the difference between z and z' even when $x = 0$.[4]

21.1.4 Preferences and intrinsic preferences among processes

If the type of process $\zeta \in Z$ is defined with sufficient specification, it fully determines its outcome $\xi = \xi(\zeta) \in X$. One can say that process z is fully preferred or, for short, preferred, or indifferent, to process z' when $[\xi(z), z] \succ [\xi(z'), z']$ or $[\xi(z), z] \sim [\xi(z'), z']$. Proposition 1 can be written in this case, and it then gives:

Proposition 2
A process that is intrinsically preferred to another is also preferred to this other if the transfers and allocations it induces are preferred to those induced by the other in either of the two processes.

If a process is preferred to another although this other is intrinsically preferred to it, then the transfers and allocations it induces are preferred to those induced by the other in both processes.

---

[4] If $(0, z) \sim (0, z')$, system z is said to be intrinsically preferred to system z' if $(x, z) \succ (x, z')$ for all $x \neq 0$, and proposition 1 becomes the following set of properties:

$$(x', z') \succ (x, z) \Rightarrow (x, z') \succ (x, z) \text{ and } (x', z') \succ (x, z'),$$
$$(x', z') \succsim (x, z) \Rightarrow (x, z') \succsim (x, z) \text{ and } (x', z') \succsim (x, z'),$$
$$(x', z') \succsim (x, z) \text{ and } x' \neq 0 \Rightarrow (x', z) \succ (x, z),$$
$$(x', z') \succsim (x, z) \text{ and } x \neq 0 \Rightarrow (x', z') \succ (x, z'),$$
$$(x, z) \succsim (x', z') \text{ results from } (x, z) \succsim (x', z) \text{ or } (x, z') \succsim (x', z'),$$
$$(x, z) \succ (x', z') \text{ results from } (x, z) \succ (x', z) \text{ or } (x, z') \succ (x', z'),$$
$$\text{or } (x, z) \succsim (x', z) \text{ and } x' \neq 0, \text{ or } (x, z') \succsim (x', z') \text{ and } x \neq 0.$$

For instance, if an exchange is preferred to a reciprocity while the latter is intrinsically preferred to the former, then the outcome of exchange is preferred to that of reciprocity with both modes of realization. With exchange, this can be manifested by the choice of this outcome rather than that which would result from reciprocity. With reciprocity, it is regretted that the resulting outcome is not, rather, the one of exchange.

21.2 Dyadic processes

21.2.1 *General concepts*

Consider now a society made of two agents denoted as 1 and 2. Write $i = 1$ or 2. Agent i's preference, indifference, and ordinal utility function will be denoted as $\underset{i}{\succ}$, $\underset{i}{\sim}$, $\underset{i}{\succsim}$ (either $\underset{i}{\succ}$ or $\underset{i}{\sim}$), and $u_i(x, z)$. Write also $j = 1$ or 2 with $j \neq i$. Let x_i denote a transfer from agent i to agent j, and x_j a transfer from agent j to agent i, and write $x = (x_i, x_j) \in X$ (the set of possible x_i may depend on both agents and on x_j, and similarly for x_j).

In a free-transfer process, agent i freely chooses her transfer x_i to agent j, but this can be under various possible conditions. One of these conditions is that x_j is given. The two following concepts will be needed later:

Agent i's *best response* to x_j is
$$r_i(x_j, z) = \arg\max_{x_i} u_i(x, z),$$

and this function of x_j is agent i's *best-response or reaction function*.

Agent i's *preferred response of the other agent j* to x_i is
$$p_i(x_i, z) = \arg\max_{x_j} u_i(x, z),$$

and this function of x_i is agent i's *preferred response function* of agent j.

The x such that $x_i = r_i$ (x_j, z) for both $i = 1$ and 2 (and $j \neq i$) are formally "Cournot-Nash equilibria" (whether they actually result from process z constitutes a major issue).

The x such that $x_j = r_j(x_i, z)$ and
$$x_i = \arg \max_{\tilde{x}_i} u_i[\tilde{x}_i, r_j(\tilde{x}_i, z); z]$$

are the dominations of agent j by agent i (Stackelberg solutions) – x_i denotes this particular value of the generic $\tilde{x}_i$.[5]

The functions r_i and p_i are written here as single-valued. When they describe an agent's choice (which is always the case for r_i), this can justify this assumption. This assumption also permits a simpler presentation. It will have a consequence only for the r_i for a single particular property.

21.2.2 The quantitative case

A further specification is the quantitative case in which x_i is a quantity of a good, hence $x_i \in \Re^+$, for all i. Then, x_i and x_j are quantities of different goods. For example, each agent can provide to the other services corresponding to their particular skills, endowments, information, or situation in the social structure. Or each good corresponds to the receiver's specific tastes or needs. Or the transfers or services are contingent aid provided in particular cases of need of the receiver or of a relatively favourable situation of the giver. Or, again, the agents may own different resources of any other type.[6] This quantitative case is thus a rather frequent occurrence, and it will be shown to entail particularly remarkable properties (moreover, it suffices, for these results, that the $x_i \in \Re$ represents an ordering of the transfers in order of desirability for the receiver j). The graph of the reaction function

---

[5] Other solutions are defined by $x_j = r_j(x_i, z) = p_i(x_i, z)$, considered later.

[6] In particular cases in which the relational or symbolic value of the transfers predominates, the goods can have, as sole differentiation, the agent who is the origin or the receiver of the transfer, and hence the direction of the transfer.

$x_i = r_i(x_j, z)$ in the plane (x_i, x_j) is the *reaction curve R_i^z* of
agent i for process z.

Definition

Agent i is said to *appreciate the other's transfer* at (x, z) when
the function $u_i(x, z)$ is increasing in x_j.

Mention of this property will implicitly assume it to hold
in the domain relevant for the specific issue considered.

Proposition 3

*If agent j appreciates the other's transfer and $x_j = r_j(x_i, z)$,
then $(x', z) \underset{j}{\succ} (x, z) \Rightarrow x_i' > x_i$.*

Indeed, if, with the assumptions, $x_i' \leq x_i$, then (x', z)
$\underset{j}{\precsim} (x_i, x_j'; z) \underset{j}{\precsim} (x, z)$, from agent j's appreciation of the other's
transfer and from the definition of r_j.

The same result holds, with agent j's appreciation of the
other's transfer, if agent j can dispose of any part of the transfer
x_i she receives, that is, with r_j defined as follows with $\xi = (\xi_i, \xi_j) \in X$:

$$r_j(x_i, z) = \{\xi_j : \xi = \arg\max_\xi [u_j(\xi, z)/\xi_i \leq x_i]\}.$$

The foregoing results entail the following property:

Proposition 4

*If $(x', z') \underset{j}{\succ} (x, z), x_j = r_j(x_i, z)$, and agent j intrinsically weakly
prefers process z to process z' and appreciates the other's
transfer, then $x_i' > x_i$.*

Indeed, from proposition 1, the conditions imply $(x', z) \underset{j}{\succ}$
(x, z) and proposition 3 then provides the result.[7]

---

[7] Results analogous to propositions 3 and 4 hold in replacing r_j by p_j.

There result the following properties, which will be applied to the comparison of various types of reciprocities, and of reciprocities and other processes (such as exchange or coercion), in chapter 22.

Proposition 5

If a process is unanimously preferred to a Cournot-Nash equilibrium of another in which the agents appreciate the other's transfer, although this process is found to be intrinsically inferior to the other by both agents, then it achieves larger transfers than the other does.

Proposition 6

If a process is unanimously preferred to a domination with a nondecreasing reaction function of the dominated agent and in which the agents appreciate the other's transfer, although this process is found to be intrinsically inferior by both agents to that which leads to the domination, then this process achieves larger transfers than does the domination.

Proof

Proposition 5 results directly from proposition 4. Let us now prove proposition 6. Let $x \in R_j^z$ denote the transfers of the domination of agent j by agent i with process z. Denote as x' and z' the transfers and process such that $(x', z') \underset{k}{\succ} (x, z)$ for $k = 1$ and 2, with z' being intrinsically inferior to z for both agents. Then, from proposition 4 applied to agent j, $x_i' > x_i$. Furthermore, $(x', z') \underset{i}{\succ} (x, z)$ implies $(x', z) \underset{i}{\succ} (x, z)$ from proposition 1. Denote as ξ the $\xi \in R_j^z$ such that $\xi_i = x_i'$. We have $(x, z) \underset{j}{\succsim} (\xi, z)$ from the domination of agent i. Thus $(x', z) \underset{i}{\succ} (\xi, z)$. Hence, $x_j' > \xi_j$ from agent i's appreciation of the other's transfer. Then, if the function $r_j(x_i, z)$ is non-decreasing in x_i, and since $\xi_i = x_j' > x_i, \xi_j \geq x_j$. Therefore, $x_j' > x_j$. Q.E.D.

22

Solutions of reciprocity games; comparisons

22.1 The three solution concepts

22.1.1 Setting

In reciprocities, the transfers are gifts. In the simple gift/return-gift processes, there are two agents, and agent i hands out gift x_i to agent j who reciprocates with the return gift x_j to agent i. The x_i and x_j can a priori be of any nature, but we will consider later the "quantitative case" in which each gift is a quantity of a good. A notable issue is that of gift refusal, the possibility of refusing a gift in totality or in part, and its consequences. This can apply to the initial gift, to the return gift, or to both. The issue of gift refusal is disregarded in this section for simplicity and because, in a number of cases, it does not matter, or does not occur, or even cannot occur. (It may be that the agents do not refuse because they appreciate the other's gift, or only the gifts offered matter, or refusing the gift or returning it back may not be possible for a material reason or because of a norm internalized or imposed by social pressure, or the giver may be able to refuse the refusal – for instance in not "taking back" something refused –, and so on).[1] Then, the return gift is the receiver's best response,

---

[1] There can be many reasons for refusing a gift (including a return gift) in totality or in part: benevolence towards the giver (which can induce refusing or accepting), norm-following in specific situations, dignity and

$r_j(x_i, z)$ for the relevant type of process z, and it terminates the game for relevant purposes. A function $r_j(x_i, z)$ is now called a *return-gift function*. Given this function for the return giver and the type of process z, the outcome is fully determined by the initial giver's choice of x_i.

If the return giver were strictly self-interested in her allocation, she would return no gift. Then, if the initial giver were similarly self-interested, she would not provide a gift in the first place. Both the initial and the return giving can be influenced by the usual motivations for giving, such as kind or duty-bound altruism, norm following induced by duty or habit, caring for other people's opinion (or pressure), moral self-gratification, and so on. Moreover, return giving can also be influenced by the initial gift for reasons

self-respect, avoidance of the requirement to provide a return gift or of moral indebtedness towards the giver, showing the giver or other people that the gift or the return gift is not sufficient (for the sake of it, or in order to induce higher future gifts), humiliating the giver, and so on. An anticipation of refusal may influence the gift. Expecting partial refusal (when this is a possibility) may lead the giver to offer more a priori. The gift offered may try to influence the amounts accepted or refused when they depend on the offer. Refusal may lead the giver to offer more so as to appear more generous at no cost, or less (or nothing) so as to avoid the humiliation of rejection. And so on. As a reaction to a gift and towards the giver, gift refusal is in some sense akin to return giving (the refused part is in a sense given back when this is possible and accepted, and refusal is sometimes materially performed precisely in this way), but it is also quite different because the initial receiver is imposed straightforwardly to have to choose explicitly whether to accept or refuse, and the various modalities may differ (for instance, the initial giver may be unable to refuse the refusal, and so on).

With the possibility of gift refusal, agents have two types of acts: giving and refusing or accepting gifts. Each gift is then described by two entities: the offered gift x_i and the corresponding accepted gift $\tilde{x}_i$, the latter being limited by the former ($\tilde{x}_i \leq x_i$ in the quantitative case). According to the case, one or the other, or both, can matter. A single gift giving now has two moves: giving, and accepting or refusing. And a gift/return-gift reciprocity has four variables and three moves: the initial giver i offers x_i, the other agent, j, chooses both the accepted gift $\tilde{x}_i$ and the offered return gift x_j, and then the initial giver accepts $\tilde{x}_j$. This last move renders the game fully strategic if the return giver cares about the accepted $\tilde{x}_j$ and not only about x_j. Longer reciprocity processes can also be modelled by taking into account the possibility of gift refusal. The various concepts of solution can be extended to this case.

of gratitude, induced liking, a sense of social balance or fairness, a sense of moral indebtedness, imitation, conformity, and concern for status, with the same possible role for norms, duties, opinion or pressure, or judging oneself. Hence, the initial gift can also be strictly self-interested in exploiting the other person's return-giving behaviour (see below). If $x_i = 0$ denotes the absence of gift from agent i, $r_j(0, z)$ is the pure gift of agent j (if agent j, who may return gifts, does not singly give, then $0 = r_j(0, z)$).

22.1.2 Solutions

The initial giver can follow several possible paths of logic, with three pure rationales and possible compromises between them. Each logic determines a type of process z, and the three pure rationales and the resulting processes will be denoted respectively, when agent i is the initial giver, as δ_i for domination (or exploitation), ε_i for equilibrium, and φ_i for non-frustration.

The formal definitions of these three polar solutions are the following, when the initial giver knows the other's return-gift functions (see the definitions in chapter 21, section 2.1):

> *domination-exploitation:* $x_i = \arg\ \max_{\tilde{x}_i} u_i[\tilde{x}_i, r_j(\tilde{x}_i, \delta_i); \delta_i]$;
> *symmetrical reciprocity equilibrium:* $x_i = r_i(x_j, \varepsilon_j)$ and
> $$x_j = r_j(x_i, \varepsilon_i);$$
> *non-frustration:* $x_j = r_j(x_i, \varphi_i) = p_i(x_i, \varphi_i)$.

What matters most, however, are the reasons for these solutions.

22.1.3 Rationales

In a *domination* solution, the initial giver is concerned only with obtaining the best pair of gift and return gift given the reaction function of the return giver. This solution is formally of the Stackelberg type. Of course, the initial giver's allocative preferences may be concerned with any of the moral, normative, comparative or altruistic reasons, in addition to strict self-interest. However, the initial giver may also be strictly self-interested, and then she can be said to self-interestedly exploit the receiver's return gift behaviour (then, she is interested in the allocation only, and not in the transfers for any other reason). Such a non-benevolent motive basically prevents liking reciprocity, as we have seen; this is an example of how the reaction function depends on the type of the relation.

In other solutions, the structure of the process itself is also of concern for the initial giver. In particular, the two other polar solutions are more elaborate by being based on rationales of *non-regret*, associated with the rationality of foreseeing the outcome (if possible).

In the case of *symmetrical reciprocity*, the initial giver holds that the solution should be neutral with respect to the order of the gifts. The reason refers to procedural justice, or process fairness, and consists of equality with respect to the roles in the interaction.[2] If the initial giver i gives x_i and receives in return $x_j = r_j(x_i, \varepsilon_j)$, then she thinks she should have given $r_i(x_j, \varepsilon_i) = r_i[r_j(x_i, \varepsilon_i), \varepsilon_j]$. If this differs from her initial gift, she regrets this initial gift. There is no such regret only if this initial gift satisfies $x_i = r_i[r_j(x_i, \varepsilon_i), \varepsilon_j]$. That is, this solution satisfies both $x_i = r_i(x_j, \varepsilon_j)$ and $x_j = r_j(x_i, \varepsilon_i)$. This outcome is independent of which of the participants is the first giver and which is the second. And the same outcome is reached if both participants play simultaneously this symmetrical non-regret strategy. In this case, furthermore, if any participant knows that the other is playing this way, she is justified in choosing the corresponding gift either as a simple

---

[2] Ideal equality results from impartiality and basic rationality (see Kolm 1998, English translation of Kolm 1971, foreword, section 5).

reaction or because she herself also plays this way (this holds if there is a single such equilibrium, or otherwise if she knows in addition which equilibrium the other selects, which can be an equilibrium that is better than the others for both agents – see below).

This solution is formally a Cournot-Nash equilibrium, and the foregoing considerations provide *the only reason known to date for reaching a Cournot-Nash equilibrium in a two-move or one-shot game*. In the other views of such an equilibrium, indeed, the fact that it is self-enforcing (in the sense that no agent wishes to depart from it if the other does not) does not suffice to preclude unanimously beneficial correlated deviations. However, Cournot-Nash equilibria can also be the convergence states of longer processes (as with Cournot's original theory), and this can also be the case for longer processes of reciprocity (see appendix A).

Moreover, it is likely that, when the process and its rationale are such a symmetrical reciprocity, the participants evaluate its intrinsic moral and relational value, referring to its fairness, equity or justice, or to the attitudes and sentiments it involves (equality, respect, concern for others), by comparison with the other types of processes, independently of who initiates the process and chooses it. In these cases, it makes no difference whether ε_i or ε_j is in the functions u_i, u_j, r_i, r_j, and they can be replaced with the sign ε. The outcome is then a solution of the pair of equations $x_i = r_i(x_j, \varepsilon)$ and $x_j = r_j(x_i, \varepsilon)$.

In the third type of solution (*non-frustration*), the first giver, agent i, knows that if she gives x_i, then the return gift she prefers to receive is $x_j = p_i(x_i, \varphi_i)$. But she actually receives $x_j = r_j(x_i, \varphi_i)$. If these values are not the same, she is frustrated and regrets this divergence. She can avoid this frustration and regret, however, by choosing an x_i that satisfies the equation $r_j(x_i, \varphi_i) = p_i(x_i, \varphi_i)$, and then the other agent chooses this return gift $x_j = r_j(x_i, \varphi_i)$.

22.1.4 The return-gift game

The initial giver i chooses her gift x_i and also, by her intention (possibly also manifested by attitudes or otherwise), the type of gift/return gift process. The receiver a priori cares about the other's intention and attitude, which are crucial for the quality, value and appreciation of the relationship. It may be that the return gift does not depend on these intentions and attitudes, but this is not a priori the general case (recall that a strictly self-interested return giver caring about her allocation only would not provide any return gift at all in such a two-gift game). Issues of information are not discussed here. For example, if the initial giver prefers domination to symmetrical reciprocity equilibrium, then it turns out that she would generally benefit from the other reacting according to symmetrical reciprocity, and she might be able to induce this behaviour in making the other believe that her intention and behaviour correspond to this process (in the quantitative case considered shortly, this benefit results from the relative disposition and the shapes of the return gift curves in these two cases).

22.2 The quantitative case

Let us now consider the specific case in which both the gift x_i and the return gift x_j are quantities, each of a given good. They can be the goods that the individuals particularly own or produce, or the durations during which each works for the other, or goods that the receivers particularly enjoy, or gifts contingent on some occurrence of an agent's need or gain, and so on. These quantities will be treated as being divisible. The $x_i \in \Re$ could also more generally represent orderings of the possible gifts in order of desirability for the receiver (only this aspect of quantities will be used). The return-gift functions $x_i = r_i(x_j, z)$ can be represented by graphs R_i^z in the plane

(x_1, x_2) – as can be the preferred other's return-gift functions $x_j = p_i(x_i, z)$.

The return-gift functions $x_j = r_j(x_i, z)$ are, in general, increasing functions (or at least non-decreasing functions): if you provide a return gift, you tend to return more (at least no less) if you are given more. This results from the foregoing analyses of the motives of reciprocity, notably of liking reciprocity and balance reciprocity, with the considered effects of induced liking, gratitude, fairness, moral indebtedness, imitation and conformity, norms, duties, and the opinions and – possibly – pressure of others. Of course, several particular reasons can also lead to decreasing return gifts. For example, if the other person gives you little (versus much), this may mean that she is poor (versus wealthy), and hence you will give her much (versus little) out of benevolence – the gift then has this role of information or supposed information. Alternatively, if she gives you little, this may mean that she is a miser, and you may give her much in order to show and emphasize her meanness to herself or to others. The list of possibilities can go on. Nevertheless, increasingness can doubtlessly be considered to be the "normal" case. An agent with an increasing (or, at least, non-decreasing) return-gift function as function of the other's gift is called a "gift-consistent return giver".

"Appreciation of the other's gift" is the application of appreciation of the other's transfer. If an agent can refuse to take part of the other's gift but does not do so, this implies that – everything considered – she appreciates the other's gift. Of course, norms or the opinions of other people may induce someone to accept a gift, or a larger gift, when she would have preferred not to do so, especially if they also demand that she gives in return. However, this is on the whole a secondary phenomenon in the whole field of reciprocity. In particular, it is not present in steady reciprocities, notably related to economic productive or consumptive activities, or to ongoing life in organizations or in collectivities of all types. Now, these latter situations will, in particular, be the ones considered when the present results will be used for comparing economic systems and for considering their transformations.

Of course, individual i's appreciation of the other's gift at (x, z) – that is, the function $u_i(x, z)$ is increasing in x_j – implies that the function of x_j defined by $u_i[r_i(x_j, z), x_j; z]$ is also an increasing function of x_j, from the definition of r_i (if u_i is differentiable at (r_i, x_j), $\partial u_i / \partial r_i = 0$ and hence $du_i / dx_j = \partial u_i / \partial x_j > 0$). That is, u_i increases along the curve R_i^z when x_j increases. Therefore, with non-decreasing return-gift functions and appreciation of the other's gift by both agents, if there exist several symmetrical reciprocal equilibria, one is preferred to the others by both agents.

The quantitative case permits further discussion of the existence of solutions. Assume that individual k's initial endowment of the good she yields (labelled good k) is quantity X_k. Then, individuals i and j's final endowments of goods i and j are, respectively, $(X_i - x_i, x_j)$ and $(X_j - x_j, x_i)$, and this can be described in an Edgeworth box (see appendix B).[3] All the relevant motivations (and the fact that an individual may already have some amount of the good that she receives) may still be present. Consider the return-gift functions and curves $x_i = r_i(x_j, \varepsilon)$ and $x_j = r_j(x_i, \varepsilon)$, defined on $[0, X_j]$ and $[0, X_i]$, respectively. Then, *if these functions are either continuous or non-decreasing, there exists at least one symmetrical equilibrium.*[4]

Proposition 4 entails the following result:

Proposition 7
If the initial giver of a gift/return-gift chooses a domination while she intrinsically weakly prefers a symmetrical equilibrium, and she appreciates the other's gift, then the return gift is higher than it would be at this equilibrium.

---

[3] And also Kolm 1973, 1984a, 1984b, 1994.
[4] See appendix B and the same references, particularly 1994. If these functions are increasing, there also exists one "stable" such equilibrium.

Indeed, if d^i and e denote the x of this domination when agent i is the first giver and of this symmetrical equilibrium, respectively, then $(d^i, \delta_i) \underset{i}{\succ} (e, \varepsilon)$ from agent i's choice, and $e_i = r_i(e_j, \varepsilon)$ from the definition of e, while agent i intrinsically weakly prefers process ε to process δ_i. Then $d_j^i > e_j$ from proposition 4.

Agent j is said to be a *gift-consistent return giver* and a *process-consistent return giver* if, respectively,

$$x_i > x_i' \Rightarrow r_j(x_i, z) > r_j(x_i', z) \ (\text{or } r_j(x_i, z) \geq r_j(x_i', z))$$

and

$$zP_j z' \Rightarrow r_j(x_i, z) \geq r_j(x_i, z')$$

where $zP_j z'$ means that agent j intrinsically weakly prefers process z to process z'. These properties hold for a relevant domain of z in the former case and of x_i in the latter. Gift consistency means the increasingness (or non-decreasingness) of the return-gift function, just discussed. Process consistency can result from gratitude for the type of process initiated by the initial giver (and not only for the gift), and from the return gift being a good complementary to the quality of the social relation (this will be applied for comparing symmetrical reciprocities with dominations). An agent is a *consistent return giver* if she is both gift-consistent and process-consistent.

These definitions imply:

Lemma
If agent j is a consistent return giver,

$$zP_j z' \text{ and } r_j(x_i, z) = r_j(x_i', z') \Rightarrow x_i \leq x_i'$$

Let us, in addition, specify that return-gift functions are single-valued, because they describe actual behaviour (this will be used for the function $r_i(x_i, \delta_i)$ as function of x_i at point d^i).

The following result then holds:

Proposition 8
If both agents intrinsically weakly prefer symmetrical reciprocity to domination, the initial giver appreciates the other's gift, and the return giver is consistent, then the gift is higher in a chosen domination than in an alternative symmetrical equilibrium.

Propositions 7 and 8 together make up:

Proposition 9
Both gifts are higher at a chosen domination than at an alternative symmetrical equilibrium if both agents intrinsically weakly prefer symmetrical reciprocity to domination and appreciate the other's gift, and if the return giver is consistent.

This result has the flavour of a paradox, since both agents intrinsically prefer the symmetrical reciprocity to the domination and a noted consistency property (satisfied for at least one of them) tends to make them give more in processes that they intrinsically prefer.

Proof
However, Proposition 7 has obtained $d_j^i > e_j$. Denote as a the x such that $a_j = e_j = r_j(a_i, \delta_i)$ (see figure 22.1). Then, if agent j is a consistent return giver and $\varepsilon P_j \delta_i$, $e_j = r_j(e_i, \varepsilon)$ and the lemma implies $a_i \geq e_i$. But $d_j^i > e_j = a_j$ (proposition 7), and the function $x_j = r_j(x_i, \delta_i)$ is increasing or non-decreasing in x_i (gift consistency of agent j), single valued, and satisfied by the coordinates of both a and d^i. Hence $d_i^i > e_i$. Q.E.D.

Let us now turn, when comparing domination and symmetrical equilibrium, from the quantities of gifts to the preferences of agents.

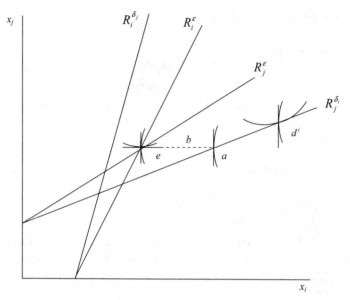

Figure 22.1 Domination and symmetrical reciprocity solutions of the return-gift game

If domination d^i is chosen rather than symmetrical equilibrium, then $(d^i, \delta_i) \underset{i}{\succ} (e, \varepsilon)$. Assume the dominated agent, agent j, appreciates the other's gift. Then, if she is also gift-consistent, $(d^i, \delta_i) \underset{i}{\succ} (a, \delta_i)$ along the dominated return-gift curve $x_j = r_j(x_i, \delta_i)$ since $d_j^i > a_j$. And $(a, \delta_i) \underset{j}{\succ} (b, \delta_i)$ for any $b \in X$ such that $b_j = e_j = a_j$ and $e_i \leq b_i < a_i$ (see figure 22.1). Hence, $(d^i, \delta_i) \underset{i}{\succ} (b, \delta_i)$. Furthermore, $(b, \varepsilon) \underset{j}{\succ} (e, \varepsilon)$ if $e_i < b_i \leq a_i$. Therefore, if $(b, \delta_i) \underset{j}{\sim} (b, \varepsilon)$ for any b with $b_j = e_j = a_j$ and $e_i \leq b_i \leq a_i$, then $(d^i, \delta_i) \underset{j}{\succ} (e, \varepsilon)$. But weak intrinsic preference for symmetrical reciprocity implies $(b, \varepsilon) \underset{j}{\succ} (b, \delta_i)$. Hence, it is possible that the dominated agent prefers the domination to any symmetrical equilibrium. More generally, this will happen if there exists a point b on the closed segment $[e, a]$ such that at this $x = b$, this agent's preference for the symmetrical reciprocity process over the domination process is sufficiently weak.

In this case, the following property is an application of proposition 5 (or of the proof of proposition 7 to both agents):[5]

Proposition 10

If both agents prefer a domination to a symmetrical equilibrium while they hold the reverse intrinsic preference for these processes, and they appreciate the other's gift, then both gifts are larger with the domination than with the symmetrical equilibrium.

This is the same result as that expressed in proposition 9, but without assuming return giver's consistency (which is replaced by her preference for the domination).

Finally, the preference between the two domination solutions for any agent can a priori be anything (in particular, an agent may prefer to be dominated rather than to dominate).

This choice between gift/return-gift processes is a priori Pareto efficient among these processes and in considering the whole preferences, because it amounts to a choice by the initial giver.[6] Yet, all these solutions of the reciprocity or return-gift game generally fail to be Pareto efficient with respect to allocative preferences alone. However, switching from one of these solutions to a unanimously preferred set of transfers requires realization by another process. This, in general, changes the allocative preferences (see chapter 21, section 1.3), and it introduces another process (such as exchange or force) which may be considered inferior to reciprocity for its intrinsic value (intrinsic process preferences).

---

[5] The results of proposition 6 would apply to a process intrinsically worse than domination for both agents.

[6] If several possible solutions are equivalent and best for the initial giver, Pareto efficiency requires choosing one of them that is preferred by the return giver.

22.3 Comparison of reciprocities with other processes

Reciprocities are often compared with other systems of mutual transfers, such as markets, or coercion and planning. In such comparisons, reciprocities are often intrinsically appreciated for the quality of the relations, attitudes and sentiments they embody and that induce them, including the warmth of the relation, freedom and equity and the free realization of fairness and social balance, a sense of community, and so on (although other types of reciprocities can rest on rather oppressive norms and social opinion). However, other systems are often chosen over reciprocity, sometimes – when they are exchanges and markets – apparently freely and by unanimous agreement. Such changes can in particular be said to constitute the essence of the process of economic development and modernization. In these cases, when the change occurs, there often seems to be an increase in the amounts transferred. This increase may seem paradoxical, since people transfer more in the system in which the intrinsic social and relational value of the transfers has been lost. However, this paradox of the relative "autarky of reciprocity" is waved by the following application of propositions 5 and 6:

Proposition 11 (the "autarky of reciprocity")
If two people who transfer to each other both prefer – and possibly freely choose – a system that they deem to be intrinsically inferior to a reciprocity leading to a symmetrical equilibrium or to a return-gift domination, while they appreciate the other's gift and the dominated return-gift function is non-decreasing, then they transfer larger amounts in the former system than in the reciprocity.

The evaluation of reciprocities by the participants can be influenced by two opposing tendencies: the value of social relations and the possible presence of oppressive norms.

Intrinsic preference for reciprocity and appreciation of the other's gift are related to a predominance of the former effect. The foregoing remark and result may suggest that this tends to be the prevailing case for steady reciprocities that can have an important role in ongoing economic life. Many things, however, can occur in historical situations: the choice of some people may induce that of others who lose out in the change; people commonly anticipate imperfectly their evaluation of another system which is often another world; it may be difficult to compare things as different as commodities and social relations; the nature of the goods and the type of division of labour may radically change; and so on.[7]

Appendix A. Longer reciprocity processes

1.   Longer reciprocities

The two-move gift/return gift processes constitute a very important type of social relations, and they constitute one type of reciprocity – the simplest type as regards the number of gifts –, and yet a genuine relation of reciprocity is more typically a longer relation, made up of a larger number of gifts

---

[7] In fact, in certain cases, switches from gifts and reciprocities to markets reduce transfers. In these cases, however, the previous transfers were often within the extended family (an extreme case is provided by a rather common behaviour in hunting societies in which the hunter keeps no share of his catch for himself – in Australia, with the Inuits, etc.). However, the main issue is probably the formation of preferences. A type of economic system provides a global experience, which is evaluated by people but also shapes their preferences, and a lack of evaluation of this influence can lead to inconsistent or suboptimal free choices. For example, denote as $U(s', s)$ the ordinal utility function of an individual evaluating system s (both *per se* and for its consequences) when she is in system s'. One can have $U(s', s) > U(s', s')$, thus inducing a change from system s' to system s, and $U(s, s') > U(s, s)$, thus leading one to regret this change and inducing the reverse one. However, the last inequality can also be reversed into $U(s, s) > U(s, s')$, making system s a stable choice, and yet one may have $U(s', s') > U(s', s)$ – that is, this choice may not be the one actually preferred by the individual if she were fully conscious of the effects of systems on her preferences (see Kolm, 1984a).

than just two. The length of the relation (in terms of the number of gifts both ways) tends to have several consequences. Longer relations permit strictly self-interested motivations to play a role for both individuals, whereas this motivation is necessarily absent from a return gift in itself (and, more generally, for a last gift). On the other hand, longer reciprocity relations are more favourable to sustaining steadier and more integrated social interaction. Moreover, the multiplicity of gifts in each direction tends to force symmetry in the relation, and hence to lead to solutions of the equilibrium type. The two simplest and polar instances of this situation are those of myopic and cumulative reciprocities.

2.   Myopic reciprocities

Myopic reciprocities consist of a series of alternate *myopic* gifts, the adjective myopic meaning that each gift is considered the return gift of the previous gift of the other person: if $n = 1, 2, \ldots$ denote successive dates, $x_{i, n}$ denotes individual i's gift to the other at date n, with $i = 1, 2$, and $x_{i, n} = 0$ denotes the absence of a gift from individual i at date n, then an *alternating myopic* reciprocity process is defined as

$$x_{2, n+1} = r_2(x_{1, n}), \, x_{1, n+2} = r_1(x_{2, n+1})$$
$$\text{and } x_{1, n+1} = x_{2, n} = 0, \text{ for odd } n,$$

and a *simultaneous myopic* reciprocity process is defined as

$$x_{2, n+1} = r_2(x_{1, n}) \text{ and } x_{1, n+1} = r_1(x_{2, n}) \text{ for all } n.$$

A *reciprocal equilibrium* is a pair of gifts (x_1, x_2) that satisfies the two equations $x_1 = r_1(x_2)$ and $x_2 = r_2(x_1)$. If, for some $n = \nu$ (possibly $\nu = 1$), either $x_{1, \nu}$, or $x_{2, \nu+1}$ in the alternating case, or $x_{1, \nu}$ and $x_{2, \nu}$ in the simultaneous case, are gifts of a reciprocal equilibrium, the subsequent gifts are those of this reciprocal equilibrium.

If, moreover, a metric is defined in the sets of the gifts $x_{1, n}$ and $x_{2, n}$ (this is the case, for instance, if the gifts are constituted of quantities of goods, and thus are defined in

$\Re^m$), then convergence $x_{i,n} \to \bar{x}_i$ is defined. The pairs of gifts that are possible limits of such a convergence when n increases are the stable reciprocal equilibria.

3. Cumulative reciprocity processes

In more general cases, in a process of successive alternating or simultaneous reciprocal gifts, each gift depends on a larger number of past gifts from both sides. Each gift may be seen by its giver as an adjustment of the pending stock of past gifts, and these stocks are seen as the relevant variable of the reciprocity relation. Denote as $\xi_{i,n}$, with $i = 1, 2$ and $n = 1, 2, \dots$, the gift given by individual i to the other individual at time n, as $\xi_{i,n} = 0$ the absence of gift from individual i to the other at time n, and as $x_{i,n} = (\xi_{i,1}, \xi_{i,2}, \dots, \xi_{i,n}, 0, 0, \dots)$ the set of the first n $\xi_{i,v}$ completed with zeros for $v > n$. The $\xi_{i,n}$ are the *elementary gifts* and the $x_{i,n}$ are the *cumulated gifts*. An *alternating cumulative* reciprocity process is defined as

$$x_{2,n+1} = r_2(x_{1,n}), \ x_{1,n+2} = r_1(x_{2,n+1})$$
$$\text{and } \xi_{1,n+1} = \xi_{2,n} = 0, \text{ for odd } n,$$

and a *simultaneous cumulative* reciprocity process is defined as

$$x_{2,n+1} = r_2(x_{1,n}) \text{ and } x_{1,n+1} = r_1(x_{2,n}), \text{ for all } n.$$

We have $x_{i,n+1} = x_{i,n}$ when $\xi_{i,n+1} = 0$.

Let us again call a pair of gifts (x_1, x_2) that satisfies the equations $x_2 = r_2(x_1)$, $x_1 = r_1(x_2)$ a *reciprocal equilibrium*.

If for some $n = v$ (possibly $v = 1$), either $x_{1,v}$ or $x_{2,v+1}$ in the alternating case, or $x_{1,v}$ and $x_{2,v}$ in the simultaneous case, are gifts of a reciprocal equilibrium, the subsequent *cumulated gifts* $x_{1,n}$ and $x_{2,n}$ for $n > v$ are those of this reciprocal equilibrium, and $\xi_{1,n} = \xi_{2,n} = 0$ for all $n > v$.

If, moreover, a metric is defined in the sets of the gifts $\xi_{1,n}$ and $\xi_{2,n}$ (this is the case, for instance, if these gifts are constituted of quantities of goods, and thus are represented in $\Re^m$), then convergence $\xi_{i,n} \to 0$ is defined. The pairs of cumulated gifts that are possible limits of such a convergence when n increases are the stable reciprocal equilibria.

4.   Other phenomena and modalities of reciprocity

These longer reciprocity processes lead to reciprocal equilibria of the return-gift functions $r_i(x_j)$ ($i \neq j$ and $i, j = 1, 2$). They are homomorphic to the gift/return-gift processes with symmetrical equilibrium solutions. Hence, they can largely be analyzed with the same analytical apparatus based on the return-gift functions. In particular, the analyses of the quantitative case can thus be given several interpretations.

Many other aspects and phenomena of reciprocity relationships with more than two moves can be introduced, and other specific structures of processes can be considered (the study of classical exchanges proceeds similarly). This includes, in particular: the use of strategies (and not only reactions) by both participants, through their considerations of unknown gifts in the future or in simultaneous givings; gift refusal (either for gifts or for return gifts), with its many possible reasons, availabilities and consequences;[8] the role of time through time preference and oblivion; continuous processes;[9] income effects; aid in case of need in relations of mutual insurance based on reciprocity; and various aspects of the value of the reciprocity relationship in itself.

Appendix B. The existence of equilibria

Consider the quantitative case of section 22.2 for symmetrical equilibria, with return-gift functions $x_2 = r_2(x_1)$ and $x_1 = r_1(x_2)$ with respective graphs R_1 and R_2 ($y = \varepsilon$ is kept implicit). The transfers x_1 and x_2 are quantities of a divisible good

---

[8] See Kolm 1984a, chapters 14 and 15.
[9] Id., chapter 14.

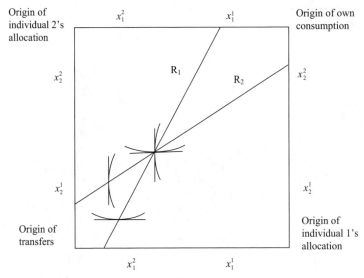

Figure 22.2 Reciprocity equilibrium

(possibly a duration of labour services), and the total amount that one individual i can transfer to the other is limited by the quantity X_i. Hence, $0 \le x_i \le X_i$ for $i = 1, 2$. The functions r_i are defined on the intervals $[0, X_i]$, and a x_i can be 0 or X_i, for $i = 1, 2$.

Symmetrical equilibria of gift/return-gift relations or reciprocal equilibria of longer reciprocity processes (see appendix A) are the solutions of the system $x_2 = r_2(x_1)$ and $x_1 = r_1(x_2)$, represented by the intersections of the curves R_1 and R_2 in the Edgeworth box of figure 22.2 where x_j^i denotes the quantity of good j (originating from individual j) held by individual i, with $x_i = x_i^j = X_i - x_i^i$: individuals' allocations of the two goods are $x^i = (x_i^i, x_j^i)$ with $j \ne i$ for individuals $i = 1, 2$; transfers are x_j^i for $j \ne i$; and "own consumptions" are x_i^i for $i = 1, 2$. For a myopic reciprocity process, such an equilibrium is (locally) stable when $|r_1' \cdot r_2'| \le 1$ in which r_i' is the derivative of the function r_i (an easy discussion can take

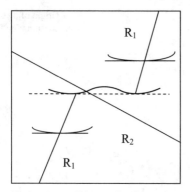

Figure 22.3 Discontinuity

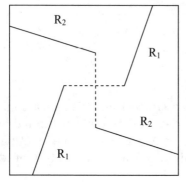

Figure 22.4 Double discontinuity

care of the cases when these derivatives do not exist – or are
not unique – and when the product is equal to 1). The results
concerning the existence of symmetrical and reciprocal equilibria are the following:

Proposition 12
*With nondecreasing return-gift functions, there exists a recip-
rocal equilibrium, and there even exists a stable reciprocal
equilibrium.*

Proposition 13

With continuous return-gift functions, there exists a reciprocal equilibrium.

Return-gift functions are continuous if reciprocity preferences about (x_1, x_2) are strictly convex (a utility index is strictly quasi-concave).

The proofs are rather simple and are omitted. Note, however, that when neither the monotonicity of proposition 12 nor the continuity of proposition 13 holds, one return gift curve can pass through a "hole" in continuity of the other, or two such "holes" of these curves may meet, as shown in figures 22.3 and 22.4.

There can also be multiple equilibria. In this case, in a gift/return gift with symmetrical equilibrium (and non-decreasing return-gift functions), the initial giver will choose the equilibrium that is the best for both agents.

23

Reciprocity in the understanding of society and its economy

23.1 Further studies

The relationship of reciprocity and, more generally, the basic reciprocal dimension of human relations, have been presented and analysed in the foregoing chapters. This included the consideration of the very different types and motives of reciprocity; the explanation of these motives from basic psychological phenomena; the analysis and comparison of the various types of reciprocal interaction; the presentation of the relations between reciprocity and the various social sentiments (with which it should not be confused, short of complete misunderstanding – for instance, reciprocity is neither altruism nor fairness); the presentation of the place of reciprocity among the various types of social relations and the comparison with the others; and the presentation and explanation of the various types of extended reciprocity. This has then been applied in the presentation and analysis of the role of reciprocity in various very important aspects of social and economic life, such as the family; relationships, groups, and communities; general respect permitting a peaceful and free society; honesty, truth-telling, promise keeping, trustworthiness and trustfulness in exchanges and cooperations; life in organizations and notably firms, and at the workplace; the common reciprocitarian corrections of market failures (difficulties in information and exclusion, asymmetric information, incomplete and missing contracts, the voluntary provision of public goods and participation in collective action, externalities, ending sequential exchanges, etc.); the political and public sector, its structure and its social policies; the effects of reciprocity on the efficiency of groups and societies; and the intrinsic value of reciprocitarian relations.

These explanations, understanding, analyses and applications should be pursued, specified and developed. This advance can occur in various directions, and the discipline to which a particular analysis relates should be completely irrelevant, so long as this thought improves our understanding of important facts. In particular, very important roles of reciprocity in economic life can be understood better only by some of the various types of psychological analysis. For instance, a phenomenology of reciprocity could probably help us greatly to understand its psychology and, more generally, the general nature of human relation and interaction. Interactionist sociology is particularly suited to the analysis of reciprocitarian relationships. In particular, symbolic interactionism could probably add finesse and subtlety to our understanding of reciprocity. The game-theoretic-like analysis of reciprocity of previous chapters can be elaborated. For instance, the standard consideration of information has a specific and important application in reciprocity analysis, concerning each player's information about the intent and motivations of the other, since her belief in this respect is an important determinant of her action.

Before presenting, as conclusion, an overview of the specific roles of reciprocity in the life of societies, let us note here a few remarks about the methodology of its analysis.

23.2 Remarks on methodology[1]

The existence of reciprocity – indeed, of its different types – is obvious from any kind of observation. Economic models

---

[1] These remarks are motivated by a number of studies shortly to be noted.

of reciprocity have been studied since the 1970s and early 1980s (without falling into the pitfalls that will soon be highlighted). Of course, the omission of reciprocity is perfectly legitimate when its consideration is not relevant to the topic under study – in a relationship, reciprocity could be negligible or, more often, taken for granted in the analysis of something else (e.g. an exchange between people reciprocally respecting each other's property). The relevant perceptiveness consists in seeing that conducts of reciprocity explain a number of important aspects of social and economic life (e.g. the life and economy of families, the remedy to a number of market failures, the functioning of organizations, the possibility of a peaceful and free society, a number of motives for "welfare state" policies, and so on). The essential thing, in this respect, is to distinguish the various motives and sentiments and the corresponding objects and relations, in particular to distinguish reciprocity from various sentiments and conducts related to it or not, and to distinguish the very different types of reciprocity. Reciprocity is not everything that is not purely self-interested! Reciprocity is not altruism or "interdependent preferences or utilities." Liking reciprocity is one cause of altruism, and balance reciprocity is another cause of giving (it is debatable whether this giving should be considered to result from a type of altruism). Reciprocity is not even giving because a gift received has increased one's wealth; it is, rather, either a benevolent answer to benevolent giving or a match to an initial gift (balance), and in the latter case it depends directly on this initial gift rather than on the resulting wealth. Reciprocity is not inequality aversion, although balance reciprocity is a very particular kind of inequality aversion between the two gifts (and not between the agents' overall situation as with the standard case of a sentiment of distributive justice). Promise-keeping, truth-telling, honesty, trustworthiness or trustfulness are not reciprocity but can be its object. Preference for conformity, norm following, and sentiments of inferiority are not reciprocity but can induce balance reciprocity. Gratitude is related to both basic reciprocities, balance and liking, but it differs from them. All these motivations a priori elicit different behaviours. They do not even attach to the same items. For instance, balance reciprocity is directly concerned with acts or transfers, whereas liking reciprocity or altruism are concerned directly with the overall allocations or satisfactions (although a transfer can be relative to the allocations of the giver or the receiver, and a transfer can provide information on liking). These different motivations are described by different models which should encompass all the characteristic properties of the case, and should not be arbitrarily and unwarrantedly specified or introduce arbitrary or meaningless properties. These various motivations are explained by different psychological and other theories. They have different consequences. And they require different enquiries and experiments when they are studied in this way.

The use of formal models is useful, and even necessary, for describing and understanding the relations among the various psychological and behavioural facts and the interaction among persons. The general modelling and use of models for reciprocity have been presented in foregoing chapters. This can be continued by introducing other facts or specific situations. However, models are useful – or, even, make sense – only if they respect the basic epistemic moral of modelling.

This rule says that the model should not have properties that are absent in the facts it describes and the presence of which influences its working and conclusions. Let us hasten to point out that, in the field under consideration, such properties cannot be tentatively justified by the fact that they would make the model simpler: on the contrary, the models properly built happen to be simpler. These faulty properties can be so in various ways.

A property is absurd (meaningless, nonsensical) when it cannot be a property of the phenomenon it purports to describe, by nature of the facts and concepts (this differs from purely logical or mathematical meaning). An example would be to describe notions such as happiness, pleasure, fairness, kindness, altruism, etc. by quantities, under the influence of the fact that relations of more or less may be meaningful for them as they are for quantities, and then to perform, on measures of these "quantities," operations of adding numbers to them or multiplying them by numbers, the use of ratios, level zero or powers, etc., whereas these operations or levels, which are meaningful for quantities, are not for the concepts under consideration.

A property that is not a priori absurd but is certainly not the case in the situation under study simply makes the model false. However, a more common slip is arbitrariness or over-specification. It consists in using a more or less specific property that may or may not be the case, a priori. The slip is the more serious the less likely this property is to be actual. For a very specific property, this likelihood may be null (an a priori probability of measure zero). Then, the model is almost certainly false (such models can be useful only in reasonings by counter-examples, in which the likelihood of the property may or may not matter depending on the question).

The only way to determine how detrimental such modelling slips are is to compare with the model properly built. Then, however, the later model alone should be retained. As we have noticed, for the issues in question this model is not more complicated and is in fact simpler. For instance, an ordering or an ordinal index of some notion fully and sufficiently describes comparisons by more and less (which generally imply this ordering property). Properties of functions can describe all the needed properties of influence, sense of variation, complementarities, and the like, without arbitrary specifications. The foregoing models of reciprocity provide instances of formalizations of this type.

Such slips of formalization have, unfortunately, spoiled many works that were otherwise interesting. This includes representing facts or concepts by variables having properties that are meaningless and absurd for this role but that are used by the model. This has been found in works in social psychology for a long time. It is more surprising in more recent works presented in the institutional framework of economics, because the efficiency and – one might say – the honour of economics has largely consisted in being particularly keen about such issues (see, for instance, the lengthy historical birth of ordinal utility and preference ordering). Concepts that have been so treated, or derived from such variables, have been happiness, satisfaction, equity, fairness, altruism, kindness, goodwill, and so on.

Reciprocity is a priori a phenomenon of the general type studied by game theory, but the various specifics are quite particular, concerning the relevant variables, players' preferences and information, and the concepts of solution (all depend, in fact, on the type of reciprocity). In particular, the concepts of solution for games of reciprocity should be carefully chosen, notably by taking into account the aspects that are specific to relations of reciprocity. For instance, the concept of procedural fairness leads to a solution of the Cournot-Nash type ("equilibrium"), even in short games (one-shot or two moves). Note that no other general reason for Cournot-Nash solutions in short games has ever been proposed. The argument that such solutions are self-sustainable solutions of agreements rests on a particular and tautological definition of sustainability, it is not general (there may be other ways to sustain the agreement), and, to begin with, it does not apply to reciprocities and reciprocations because they are not agreements. The "domination" solutions of the Stackelberg type are ordinary in relations of reciprocity. The initial player can have motives of various types. She can, in particular, be solely self-interested and thus "exploit" the return-gift; then, however, the return gift cannot be motivated by liking reciprocity, and it may minimally seek balance – if the initial receiver accepts the gift and knows the motive. However, the most characteristic relationships of reciprocity are longer, with sequences of helping or favours in both directions.

The type of relation – for instance a reciprocity of some kind or an exchange in the strict sense – generally matters for the participants, sometimes very much. Hence, it should be an object of their preferences (intrinsic preference), and it also generally influences their preferences about the transfers or favours (therefore, it constitutes a parameter of these latter preferences). This explicit formulation is important for explaining which type of relation prevails, and for normative judgments about this issue.

23.3 Reciprocity in social science

23.3.1 Sociology and anthropology

Reciprocity, its pervasiveness, generality and universality, and its importance for constituting a society, have, of course, not escaped perceptive observers of societies (although they did not distinguish and explain its various motives). Cicero notes: "There is no duty more indispensable than that of returning a kindness," and adds: "All men distrust one forgetful of a benefit." The Christian gospels state: "Give and you will be given to" (Luke). Jumping centuries, one finds René Descartes explaining reverse reciprocity in a letter to Queen Christine of Sweden. Adam Smith naturally emphasizes direct and reverse reciprocity in his *Theory of Moral Sentiments* (1759). Morelly (1775) also discusses reciprocity. Bentham considers reverse reciprocity again. Proudhon (1853) emphasizes the generality and importance of reciprocity, as do Marx and Durkheim. For L. T. Hobhouse (1906), "Reciprocity is the vital principle of society." Richard Thurnwald (1916, 1921, 1922, 1932), the anthropologist student of the economist Karl Menger, sees the "principle of reciprocity" as a primordial imperative which "pervades every relation in primitive life" and "is the basis on which the entire

social and ethical life of civilizations rest." Bronislaw Malinowski (1932), Raymond Firth (1950, 1957), and Claude Lévi-
Strauss (1949) endorse, develop and apply this view. Indeed,
reciprocity became a (or, rather the) central concept in all
anthropology, with applications, notably, as the explanatory
principle in economic anthropology and in kinship systems
(Lévi-Strauss's famous "exchange of wives" is already noted
by Thurnwald). Marshall Sahlins (1968) and Elman Service
(1966) classify all social relations as types of reciprocity. Karl
Polanyi (1944) emphasizes reciprocity as an economic system, along with market exchange and "redistribution" (by a
central power). However, sociologists such as Georg Simmel
(see Wolff, 1950), Howard Becker (1956b), George Homans
(1958), and Alvin Gouldner (1960) put forward that the interpersonal relation of reciprocity is essential in all societies
and present in all individual interactions. As Gouldner wrote,
"Simmel remarks that social equilibrium and cohesion could
not exist without 'the reciprocity of service and return service,' and that 'all contacts among men rest on the scheme of
giving and returning the equivalence.'"

Sociologists explain reciprocity by its contribution to the
stability – and hence the existence – of social systems, or
its necessity for this result. They particularly emphasize the
norm of reciprocity, and the corresponding duty or propriety of reciprocation (they thus focus on the "balance reciprocity" of the preceding analysis). Whereas Talcott Parsons
(1951) and Robert Merton (1957) focus on the reciprocity
of complementary duties and the corresponding reciprocal
expectations, Alvin Gouldner considers, more generally, all
situations of such reciprocity. He emphasizes that individuals are made to internalize the norm in the process of their
socialization. The norm of reciprocity can thus be beneficial
to mutual interest – a suggestion reminiscent of the reciprocitarian corrections of market failures of the foregoing analysis.
Reciprocity may soften abuse of power – which is reminiscent of the foregoing remark about general respect maintained

by generalized or general reciprocity. The pending obligation constituted by the indebtedness before the presentation of the return gift or favour is favourable to social peace (a remark also common in the studies of anthropologists and psychologists). Sequential exchange is also hinted at. A main reason for the importance of the norm of reciprocity lies in its generality, since it applies to many types of specific relations and interactions. In order to explain reciprocity, Gouldner naturally considers the possibility of a functionalist explanation. However, a functionalist theory is a proposal of a way of explanation, rather than a full explanation in itself. The full explanation should make precise the specific "mechanisms" that lead to the item to be explained. Assuming that it has explained sufficiently why the system needs the item (here the norm of conduct), it should also explain two facts. First, how does the system induce the item – that is, here, how is the norm "put in" the individuals? There can be various ways of cultural formation, with the formation of habits, traditions and judgments, with roles for social selection described previously, and for conscious processes in education. Second, the historical origin of the system and the item – and not only their continuation – should be explained. Gouldner suggests that reciprocal behaviour may start systems relying on it (but does the conduct appear as mutant genes do, or, as is likely, has there been some of it since the beginning of society – hence of the species?).

23.3.2 Social psychology

Social psychologists are no less convinced of the pervasiveness and importance of reciprocity than anthropologists and sociologists are – as is the case with all perceptive observers of societies. Since the 1950s, they have studied reciprocity with abundant laboratory experiments and investigations, and often simplistic formulas describing behaviour (see section 23.2). They have focused on major domains of manifestation of this conduct, notably two of them, labour relations and pay on the one hand, and the generalized (or general) reciprocity of "helping behaviour" on the other hand.

The main topic in the field of labour and pay was an explanation of labour productivity as employees' voluntary adjustment of their labour and effort to the pay supplied by the employer. Among early landmark studies were the much-discussed and influential experiments and discussions of Adams (1963, 1965) and Adams and Rosenbaum (1964). The employee is seen as reacting in reciprocity to the pay. This was related to the so-called "equity theory," in an application saying that the employee tends to work in such a way that the pay seems to her to be a fair reward for her effort. This is a type of balance reciprocity.

Under the name of "helping behaviour," generalized reciprocity has been the object of numerous studies in laboratory experiments and empirical investigations, notably since the mid-sixties in a framework noted in chapter 2. This includes many articles, and the famous collective book edited by Macaulay and Berkowitz (1970).[2]

23.3.3 Economics

23.3.3.1 Reciprocity in economics. The economic analysis of the relationships of reciprocity, with full economic models of the type summarized in foregoing chapters, has been proposed since the early seventies (conferences on this topic in 1974 and 1975 have been noted), and gathered in book

---

[2] See in particular the contributions to Macaulay and Berkowitz, eds. (1970), Berkowitz (1966, 1968, 1971), Berkowitz and Friedman (1967), Bryan and Test (1967), Doland and Adelberg (1967), Frisch and Greenberg (1968), Gergen, Gergen and Meter (1972), Goodstadt (1971), Goranson and Berkowitz (1966), Greenglass (1969), Handlon and Gross (1959), Harris (1967), Hornstein (1970), Hornstein, Fisch and Holmes (1968), Latané and Darley (1970), Leventhal, Weiss and Long (1969), Midlarsky (1968), Pruitt (1968), Rosenhan (1969), Wilke and Lanzetta (1970), Wright (1942), and the more recent works of Hoffman and Spitzer (1982), and Kahneman, Knetsch and Thaler (1986a, 1986b).

form in Kolm (1984a). Relying on, generalizing, and applying the social psychological analyses of labour reaction to
pay, George Akerlof (1982) presented the "efficiency wage"
explanation of involuntary unemployment (the various types
of social sentiments and conducts concerning work and pay
and the resulting best policies are analysed in Kolm 1990).
Under the name of reciprocity, Robert Sugden (1984) presented an analysis of the conditional voluntary contribution
to public goods. This was applied to the question of the depletion of a common resource by James Swaney (1990).

23.3.3.2 Labour relations. The domain of labour relations,
extending that of the labour market, is a major field of display of the various types of social relations, including the
various kinds of reciprocity. This domain is characterized
both by its intrinsic importance and by the nature of the
items transferred. It generates most of individual and overall income, occupies the largest part of people's time, and
provides their most important social relations and inser-
tions beyond the family. It consists of transfers of personal
services or of their availability, generally in durable relations. This field is studied by the various disciplines of
social science, sometimes in collaboration rarely found elsewhere. The employee's reciprocitarian reaction to pay studied by the classical equity theory of social psychology, or,
with a fuller modelling, by George Akerlof's theory of "efficiency wages", is but one case among many. The relation can
be between employer and employees or among employees
or larger groups of wage earners for whom the wage level
(and other general circumstances of labour) is a public good.
Reciprocities of all types can intervene: balance reciprocity
and notably issues of fairness, liking reciprocity especially in
steady relations, sequential exchange, solutions of the type
of domination or of equilibrium, and relations with various
durations and in particular long ones. Discussions, models,
theory, and consequences for policy can be found in Kolm

(1984a and particularly 1990 – a general analysis of the social role of wages), and discussions of the empirical evidence of some behaviours of this type are provided by Bewley (1995, 1999), Bishop (1987), Baron (1988), Simon (1991), Levine (1991, 1993), Rabin (1993), Rotemberg (1994), and in works reviewed by Fehr, Gächter and Kirchsteiger (1999b).

23.3.3.3 Interdependent utilities, inequality aversion, sequential exchange. Moreover, three issues that are not reciprocity proper but are closely related to it have been analysed by economics for a long time: interdependent preferences or utilities, inequality aversion, and sequential exchange.

As we have seen in the previous chapters, the nature and logic of the various types of reciprocity introduce a basic difference in the resulting structures of the two types of reciprocity proper, balance reciprocity and liking reciprocity; in balance reciprocity, the object of concern is the gift, transfer or service, whereas, in liking reciprocity, the object of concern is the overall situation of the other person, i.e. the initial situation with the addition of the gift or transfer, and it can notably be the other person's overall satisfaction, happiness or utility (or her overall resulting allocation) – secondarily, this opposition in the nature of the relevant items is qualified by the facts that balance reciprocity may compare gifts relative to some means of the giver or some needs of the receiver, and that gifts may have a role of information in liking reciprocity. The case of liking reciprocity – but not that of balance reciprocity – refers to a classical topic of economics, abundantly considered and analysed for a long time, the question of altruistic "interdependent utilities," or favourable concern for other people's income or situation. Indeed, the economic modelling of liking reciprocity in chapter 19 has led to individuals' utility functions including, as variables, others' utility levels or favourable aspects of others' situation which can be their income or anything else. However, there are three levels of such concerns for others' utility or situations. The first level is just this concern. The second level considers the possible mutuality of such concerns, or any other interdependence among individuals' concerns for others. The third level explains each individual's concern for items concerning others by explaining the interpersonal sentiments that elicit it, notably as a result of others' concern for the individual in a reciprocity. The first level is a simple externality, the second – the interdependence – leads to a system of interdependent relations and equations, and the third entails the relations of the first level and, hence, the system of the second. Liking reciprocity implies the concern; generally, it also implies the mutual concern; yet, its specificity is that it explains the concern. It belongs to the issue of the formation of preferences, concerning this altruism and this mutual altruism. Indeed, in equation (1) of chapter 19, individual i's utility U^i as a function of individual j's utility (or happiness or satisfaction) U^j or of any aspect of her situation S_j depends on individual i's liking of individual j, ℓ_i (moreover, items ℓ_j, x_j and x_i also intervene). Balance reciprocity explains preferences about what the other receives rather than has (although this can also intervene as a parameter of this preference).

Simply considering liking something because it is good for others is very ancient in economics; a possible mutuality then is only implicit. Adam Smith describes marvellously the pleasure derived from others' pleasure (*The Theory of Moral Sentiments*), but he stops short of considering that you may be pleased from the pleasure that other people derive from your pleasure (or pleased that they derive such a pleasure). Bentham argues that the pleasure you derive from others' pleasure should be added into the utilitarian sum. Individual utilities that depend on the "welfares" or "ophelimities" of all individuals are considered for two individuals and as a weighted sum by Edgeworth (1881) and generally by Pareto (1913). The general interdependence of utilities that are function of others' utilities or incomes or consumption is analysed in Kolm (1966). The case of incomes is also stud-ied by Hochman and Rodgers (1969) and a subsequent litera-ture (see Kolm 2000a, 2006). These interdependencies imply mutual concerns. Reciprocity (of the liking type) is one step deeper by constituting a cause of these mutual concerns.

Balance reciprocity rests on the desire to establish some kind of equality between the items received and those given in return. This desire may meet some other motive, such as self-interest, which induces giving less, and this motive may have an influence in a choice of returning less than required for balance. This choice is made by comparing the material advantage with the moral or social inconvenience resulting from the deficit and the inequality that describes it. Simi-larly, an agent who seeks a surplus in the comparison of the two gifts in order to benefit from a moral debt of the other towards herself attaches some value to the corresponding inequality. Moreover, in reciprocal fairness an agent behaves fairly towards another in reciprocity to this other's fairness towards herself; these manifestations of fairness can refer to some sharing of benefits from the acting agent; then, the reciprocated items would be some measures of inequality, with fairness attached to their being lower. These situations extend into generalized and reverse reciprocities. All these cases rest on attaching some value to lower (or sometimes higher) inequality. Now, saying when a distribution is more or less unequal – or unjustly unequal –, hence choosing the relevant index of inequality, is quite a delicate issue. Fortu-nately, this problem has been studied extensively by a well-developed branch of economics.[3] Fairness in reciprocal fair-ness can also refer to some other aspect of the agent's choice, and the vast economic literature about the various criteria of fairness and the choice of the relevant items and its meaning can be helpful for analysing these cases.

---

[3] Basic results are proposed in Kolm 1966, a full analysis is presented in Kolm 1999, and Lambert 2001 is an exhaustive survey in book form.

The reciprocal behaviour most studied by economists is sequential exchange. Most often, they consider it to be purely self-interested, and hence without the properly reciprocitarian motivations. However, such motivations are sometimes pointed out. Peter Hammond (1976) and Mordechai Kurz (1978b, 1979) enjoyed showing that "altruism is egoistic," but emphasized backward induction – which, as we have seen, can be solved by uncertainty about the end of the process or the behaviour of the other agent. Robert Axelrod's (1981, 1984) "empirical proof" of the dominance of the tit-for-tat strategy accompanied an abundant discussion of the "folk theorem" saying that repeated games (which include repeated sequential exchanges) can sustain any solution in which both parties benefit – although with rather particular hypotheses. This prompted a number of analyses such as an explanation by evolution by Güth and Yaari (1992) and Güth (1995a), the role of commitment by investment (Prasnikar and Roth, 1992) or by gifts (Carmichael and McLeod, 1993), the issue of punishment (Bolton and Ockenfels, 2000, and the studies discussed and proposed by Fehr and Gächter, 2000b), and the question of punishment as a public good in sequential contributions to public goods (Kolm 1984a, Fehr and Gächter, with different emphases on fairness and normative motives – see chapter 12, section 3.5).

In applications of this kind of process to actual economic issues, a few studies showed awareness of the possible relational aspect of reciprocities – usually from reading anthropologists – although they do not analyse this aspect. Of course, in reality both cases with and without specific relational value (or disvalue) exist – but the case in which it does not exist is a particular case of the general framework. Kimball (1988) and Coate and Ravallion (1993) model mutual insurance in which transfers are made to the participant who incurs a particular unforeseen misfortune. Rachel Kranton (1994) considers individuals' choices between using the market or such a sequential exchange, the resultant sharing of the volume of transfers between both systems, and the dynamics of this situation. This choice and its consequences are essentially determined by information costs. As a consequence, a system is more favourable when it has a larger share of the transfers. There results a tendency to extreme sharings and to the prevalence of an inefficient system. In fact, a number of different phenomena lead to such consequences in the establishment of economic systems,[4] and this study constitutes a precise example of such effects of information facilities and costs.

23.3.3.4 Good economics: realistic psychology and rational and powerful representation. Let us note here that a number of economists want to explain (and sometimes also to appraise) all social situations from the behaviour of individuals exclusively interested in the "material" outcome concerning solely themselves. This position suggests the following evaluation. If this view denied the existence, or the influence on conduct – indeed, the paramount influence in certain cases – of facts such as love, affection, duty, honour, hatred, revenge, gratitude, faithfulness, fairness and unfairness, status, superiority and inferiority, envy, jealousy, shame, guilt, pride, and so on, then it would only be absurd, as anyone can see from looking around (and, doubtless, within herself). On the other hand, this position can be valid if it consists solely in the research program of trying to investigate the scope of what the assumed simplistic motivation can explain, in particular when it is associated with more refined analyses of expectations or of strategic interactions. However, in studying a specific actual case, other motivations should not be discarded when they manifestly exist and are relevantly influential. The fact that actors commonly express reasons for their actions that are not the true ones does not imply that solely the narrowest end-state self-interest is at work

---

[4] Cf. Kolm 1984a, chapters 6 and 10.

in all cases. However, it is also clear that, in many cases, there can be much uncertainty as to which motivations are the true ones and what the actual scope of each is (individuals are even commonly confused about their own motivations, notably about the relative importance of various motivations that determine a given act). Then, the scientific position requires one to have theories for all the possible cases and not just for one. A priori "parsimony" in hypotheses (or Occam's razor) is not intrinsically justified epistemologically and can, rather, be intellectual laziness and a deficit in scientific imagination – it often also leads to hypotheses different from purely self-interested motives.

One can even use classical tools of economic analysis for the study of conducts very different from those most usual in economics, as the foregoing chapters have shown for the various types of reciprocity. Introducing other people's welfare into an individual's utility function for describing altruism is very ancient and classical, as we have seen. Other items related to other people and other motives of concern for others can be introduced similarly. One can, notably, describe comparative sentiments, such as envy or jealousy, sentiments of superiority or inferiority, a desire for conformity or distinction, and fairness either involving oneself or among others.[5] The arguments of a utility function can represent either objects of the person's choice, or parameters of this function of these variables. One can take in particular, as instrumental variables or as parameters, the actions or the transfers of any individuals, and describe various motives concerning them (as with balance or fairness for balance reciprocity). Concerning motives, there is a large difference when one passes from the classical "consequentialist" concern about end-states to the results of action motivated by duty or propriety. Nevertheless, preference orderings or utility functions can very well

---

[5] The proper modelling of comparative sentiments requires some elaboration (see Kolm 1995).

describe the latter motives too, as we have seen. In particular, one can describe in this way the case in which these
motives dictate a specific course of action (about which there
seems to be no actual choice); in fact, however, the individual also often chooses to obey more or less some norm of
conduct, and the resulting choice can be described by preferences and the tools of choice theory. Sentiments can also
be more or less explicitly described, yet as items with very
different possible statuses. They can be sentiments of the
agent or of other people. An individual's sentiment can be
a determinant of her preferences or utility function. It may in
particular be represented as a parameter of this ordering or
function. However, an individual may also have preferences
about sentiments of hers. She may then also, sometimes, more
or less influence sentiments of hers (by using attention and
sometimes reasoning). Individuals also commonly have preferences about others' sentiments, in particular when they
concern themselves, and various ways of influencing them.
Items such as sentiments, or the type of social relation, can
be properly represented by parameters or variables having
the required properties (without using arbitrary or meaningless variables). However, one goes beyond representation by
utility functions when individuals' choices introduce non-
consequentialist considerations about the choice of a solution
of a game they play (as we have seen for the "equilibrium"
solutions of reciprocities), although this can also be described
in more extended preferences.

These useful representations by preferences, utility, and
maximizing evaluation and behaviour are, therefore, very
flexible. The essential point, however, is that the representation does not introduce meaningless or arbitrary properties
and follows the obvious methodological indications noted in
section 2 of this chapter.[6]

---

[6] Unfortunately, a number of studies (including empirical ones for a long
time), have handicapped their own meaningfulness and scope by their
modelling in this respect.

23.3.4 *Game theory*

Apart from the game-theoretic analyses of reciprocities and in particular gifts/return-gifts relations with "reciprocity games" and "return-gift games,"[7] the bulk of the literature in game theory used to ignore reciprocity and reciprocation. Indeed, it used to shun social sentiments in general and their role in social interaction (with the very occasional exception of altruism). Its ethos was bound, in fact, to particularly discard deontological conduct as "irrational." This was but one aspect of an outlook ingrained in a part of economics. This view, however, runs counter to many cases of clear evidence, and it is in opposition to the central views and concerns of all the other branches of social science. Nevertheless, there now seems to be the beginning of a reversal – after early observations by Reinhart Selten – starting with works such as those of Matthew Rabin (1993), the Zurich school of Ernst Fehr and his associates (1994 and following ones), Claude Meidinger (2000), and a number of others. In Rabin's model, two players play a simultaneous one-shot game (while situations of reciprocative conducts are more typically sequential); each has a single-valued belief about the other's action and about the other's belief concerning her own action; each action's "fairness" towards the other agent is the deviation from the average of the best and worst possible payoff it can inflict on the other; and each individual prefers to be fairer when the other is towards herself. Then, Cournot-Nash equilibria are with both agents maximally benefiting or hurting the other – an extreme example of a general tendency.

23.3.5 *Recent experiments*

Recently, a number of scholars have wanted to confirm by experiments our common knowledge about a few sentiments

---

[7] Kolm 1973, 1979, 1984a, 1984b.

that intervene more or less in reciprocity, in the wake of the grand tradition of social psychology since the 1950s noted earlier. Notably, they set up experiments to confirm that people care about fairness (a term that exists in our common language), about equity (also a common term, and the very one used by social psychologists in the 1960s), or about the intentions of other people (a basis of moral sentiments and literature and of religions). Often, they use very simple devices, such as the "ultimatum game" (or even the "dictator game" – which is hardly a game), to verify that people sometimes prefer to receive nothing than to be given an unfair share. Variations enable one to see the effects of various aspects of the circumstances on behaviour. Although the existence of the sentiments in question is obvious, the comparison and dispersion of individuals' reactions can be informative about the populations studied. However, these studies emphasize the question of existence, because they generally justify themselves by their falsifying the hypothesis that motives are only narrowly self-interested, a hypothesis that is often (not always, by far) assumed in economic studies – and which is often a justified approximation for many questions. These studies also often propose particular models of their topic, and notably individuals' utility functions. In this respect, one can only refer to the methodological considerations noted earlier: only following them would give to these formulations – and to earlier ones in social psychology – their full usefulness.

These studies are reviewed by Sobel (2005), following reviews by Fehr and Schmidt (2003), Fehr and Gächter (2000a), and early ones by Güth (1995b) and Roth (1995). Levine (1998), after Rabin (1993) noted earlier, models a case of reciprocal liking (although with the modelling problems noted). Various other aspects of concern for fairness and inequity aversion are studied by Fehr and Schmidt (1999), Bolton and Ockenfels (2000), Charness and Rabin (2002), Falk, Fehr and Fishbacher (2003), Cox (2004), Dufwenberg and Kirchsteiger (2004), Falk and Fishbacher (2005), and Bereby-Meyer and Niederle (2005). As we have seen, an important domain of balance reciprocity motivated by fairness is labour reacting to pay, and this classical topic of social psychology since the early 1960s and of the field of labour relations (and of Akerlof's (1982) efficiency-wage theory generalized in Kolm (1990)) is experimentally studied by Fehr, Kirchsteiger and Riedl (1993), Fehr, Kirchler, Weichbold and Gächter (1998), Fehr and Schmidt (2002), and Charness and Haruvy (2002).

Our general knowledge of human sentiments, motives and conducts, confirmed or made more precise by all inquiries and experiments, establishes for us the existence of reciprocity and of the various related sentiments. Given these facts, three things remain to be done: explaining these sentiments; explaining, from them, action and interaction between agents; and application to specific important situations. The explanation of these sentiments consists in a psychological analysis relating them to more basic psychological items, as has been done in previous chapters for the various types of reciprocity. We have also suggested possible roles of sociological selection. The analysis of the effects of these sentiments on behaviour, and of the interactions between sentiments and acts of various individuals, can be much helped by, and often require, formal models of these relations. However, such models are actually helpful only if they respect the rational methodology noted above. Among applications, the analysis and understanding of reciprocity can complete most parts of economics, sometimes importantly or crucially, as summarized in section 4.

23.3.6 Four recent volumes

Reciprocity is one of the main topics of four volumes recently published. Three of them are collective volumes. In *The Economics of Reciprocity, Giving and Altruism* (2000) – the volume of a conference of the International Economic Association held in 1997 – and in the *Handbook of Giving, Altruism and Reciprocity* (2006), both edited by S.-Ch. Kolm and J. Mercier Ythier, reciprocity is analysed, alongside giving and altruism, in chapters by most of the economists working in these fields (and a few other scholars). The volume *Moral Sentiments and Material Interests* (2005), edited by H. Gintis, S. Bowles, R. Boyd, and E. Fehr, gathers important contributions by a number of authors, including remarkable overviews of the scope and consequences of non-interested motives in society by D. Kahan, and S. Bowles and H. Gintis, with an emphasis on a notion of "strong reciprocity" shortly discussed. Finally, J. Elster's lectures on *Disinterestedness* (2007) discuss reciprocity in the framework of the logic of non-interested rationalities.

The notion of "strong reciprocity" is defined as an individual's conduct that rewards the good behaviour and punishes the bad behaviour of other individuals, at a net cost for this "strong reciprocator," that is, not (or not only) from a motive of self-interest. The most interesting conclusion is that everybody's good behaviour can be sustained by the presence of a sufficient proportion of strong reciprocators in a society. "Strong reciprocity" is contrasted with "weak reciprocity" which means sequential exchange.

The notion of "strong reciprocity" raises conceptual and factual questions. Basically, is it sufficiently finely defined and analysed, and is it sufficiently important as a block or unit of conducts of a sufficiently important type of social characters? These questions associate with existing normative judgments and with the differences in the facts and views of different cultures in this respect.

First of all, "strong reciprocity" associates three conducts which are by no means always associated. There is "positive" reciprocity returning gift for gift or good for good (the usual and traditional definition of reciprocity in social science) and negative reciprocation returning harm for harm.

(Positive) reciprocity can have two very different types of motives, leading to balance reciprocity and to liking reciprocity. As we have seen, negative reciprocation has motives of the balance type only (revenge in the case of a direct personal reciprocity hurting people who hurt oneself), in addition to retaliation for deterrence. Many people are prone to some of these conducts in the appropriate circumstances and not to others, and they can have important consequences for society. In particular, (positive) reciprocity, or negative reciprocation, or both jointly, can be a dominant feature of social relations in a society, and this is often a main determinant of both the type of stability (the social glue) and the quality of the society.

Moreover, reciprocity refers, first of all, to a mutual relationship in a dyad (between two persons), whereas "strong reciprocity" is often presented as responses to people's actions favourable or unfavourable to a larger society. It certainly includes providing favours to people behaving favourably towards third parties (the Descartes effect) and the symmetrical punishment of people who hurt third parties (the motivating behaviour can also similarly affect the reciprocator herself). In any event, the descriptions consider behaviour favourable or unfavourable to society without further precision. In fact, "strong reciprocity" is also presented as conducts that enforce norms by individually provided gratification or punishment. This can a priori also apply to social norms that are not favourable to other people (notably that are neutral in this respect). Finally, the strong reciprocator is often seen as the individual who volunteers to reward or punish other people's behaviour at a cost for herself, in particular who endorses the role of the self-appointed little policeman self-righteously punishing or rewarding others on behalf of morals or society. She will also denounce infringements and assist repression. In many cultures, this is seen as a rather repulsive character (sometimes an ostracized one).

In fact, there is another type of character who emphasizes reciprocity, but considers "positive" reciprocity and is prone to associate it with altruism rather than with negative recipro-cation. This reciprocity also promotes pro-social behaviour, notably if it also gratifies people who act favourably towards third parties (a Descartes effect), and these reciprocators may add altruistic acts in themselves. These "strong positive" reciprocators with altruistic tendencies constitute, moreover, an intrinsically valuable type of persons in the society. Then, punishing bad acts is often better left to the anonymous enforcement of the appropriate institutions (the police and the courts). The presentations of "strong reciprocity" often praise it for enforcing good social behaviour. They should extend their evaluations to the issues of the intrinsic value of social interactions and social actors. These appraisals have consequences for education and the setting up of institutions.

In any event, all the studies in these volumes contribute in important ways to the study of what needs the most urgently to be considered for understanding and improving society and in particular its economy.

23.4 Completing economics

23.4.1 The role, values and importance of reciprocity

23.4.1.1 The place of reciprocity. The existence, importance and determinants of reciprocity are obvious to perceptive observation. The work that was needed, therefore, was to explain reciprocity, to present its general theory, to point out and explain the scope of its manifestation, and, then, to apply this theory to specific cases in which this is useful. Discover-ing reciprocity or its causes in an experiment, or imagining a particular model of it and particular variables, constitute different exercises which, however, may be introduced in the discussion. The foregoing chapters have presented the general theory of reciprocity, its scope, the particularities of its main manifestations, the psychological causes of its motives, and the comparison with other modes of realization (exchange, command, pure gift giving). They have also suggested how reciprocity could acquire its actual place, role and scope in society, notably as a result of competition in efficiency and attractiveness between various social forms and modes of realization. This latter explanation can be based on the comparisons presented between the properties and the outcomes of these various modes. This explains both the competitions and the symbioses of reciprocity with the other modes, notably exchange and organization, and the relative place of these ways of social realization – a piece of information necessary for understanding the actual scope, role and function of reciprocity (and for the organization of social betterment).

One can thus conclude with a summarized synthesis of the comparison and relations between reciprocity and the other modes of social realization and of the resulting place of reciprocity in the various parts of society and its economy. These other modes are: exchange, agreements, and markets; command and hierarchies; and pure gift giving. The comparisons are both about intrinsic relational and behavioural values and about the "extrinsic" effects of these modes – the latter including the effects on economic efficiency and distribution.

23.4.1.2 Intrinsic and extrinsic values. Intrinsically, pure altruistic giving and liking reciprocity have, on the other modes, the advantage of being founded on and manifesting social relations of particular value – altruism and benevolence – and the corresponding virtue of the givers. Balance reciprocity is founded on and manifests the intrinsically valuable relations of social balance, respect, and fairness, and the corresponding particular social virtues of the givers. Command is the only relation in which one party lacks freedom. Formally, at least, since balance reciprocity and pure gift giving also sometimes result from more or less constraining social norms which may be felt as more oppressive than simple, emotionless material constraints.

With regard to the efficiency of the realization of social actions and interactions and of economic transfers, command can have advantages provided by the centralization of information, but, conversely, exchange can have the classical virtue of markets with regard to local information and incentives. Yet, these qualities have limits due to costs and limitations in information and constraining of various types, in "transaction," setting up contracts, and so on. Constraints are a priori necessary for implementing both commands and previous agreements. There result "failures" of markets and agreements, and of hierarchies and systems of command. These obstacles are largely due to the effects of self-interest in actions and in the transmission or withholding of information. Many of them vanish if agents freely hand out items and information and obey indications or previous agreements. This saves the necessity and costs of constraints and provides or reveals needed information. However, this results from non-purely self-interested motivations which are moral or altruistic, and include duty-bound behaviour, honesty, sincerity, truth telling, promise keeping, trustworthiness, and so on.

23.4.1.3 Giving and reciprocity. Giving of all kinds can thus present a double advantage, as an appreciated intrinsic virtue of the relation and the actor, and for an extrinsic quality of efficiency in remedying failures of exchanges and commands. This holds both for pure giving and for gifts that are parts of reciprocities. However, for all the reasons previously discussed, these conducts are more likely the more they are held in reciprocity, so that people who practice them also benefit from others' such social conducts.

In particular, giving – i.e., performing acts beneficial to others at some cost to oneself –, when repeated with the same giver, tends to impoverish her, and hence may not to be sustainable for this reason. In reciprocity, by contrast, the giver also receives and this effect may not occur. By and large, reciprocity is self-sustainable altruism. Hence, the possibilities of pure giving or altruism are a priori more limited than those of reciprocity, because it can be too detrimental to the giver's self-interest. There can also be mutual altruism or giving that is not reciprocity, but such relationships would a priori be fortuitous, whereas reciprocity ties the acts together, since, among the giving and the receiving of each agent, at least one entails the other. Moreover, reciprocity in itself adds its specific further motives for giving (plus the effects of imitation). These reciprocities can also be extended ones (generalized or reverse).

23.4.1.4 Reciprocity and social systems. This is why reciprocity is the standard palliative to "failures" of exchanges, markets, or agreements, and of hierarchical organizations and systems of command. For markets, it is the decentralized palliative, an alternative to public intervention which has its own problems of information, constraining, and motives of public officials. Numerous specific examples of this role of reciprocity have been noted in the foregoing chapters.

However, sentiments and conducts of reciprocity also exist in themselves. They are the main fuel in such social forms as the family or genuine cooperatives. They have a special importance in others, notably related to communities of various kinds. They also have a place in systems mainly based on exchange or organization. There, they can have the remedying roles just noted. But they can also, on the contrary, interfere with the efficient logic of these systems by leading to conducts different from those on which this efficiency is based. For instance, the classical informational and behavioural efficiency of the price system can be disrupted when people give to each other, perhaps in reciprocity, rather than self-interestedly exchanging (even though a single gift is Pareto efficient, as we have seen).[8] Similarly, the working

---

[8] For an analysis of the disruptive effects of giving see Kolm (1984a) and Kranish (1998).

of an organization can be disrupted by reciprocitarian collusions between some of its members. However, motives of reciprocity imply preferences different from the purely self-interested ones (used in competitive markets, for instance), and such disruptions of systems may not be actually inefficient in the end (beyond the Pareto efficiency of a single giving, the analyses of chapter 22 have focused on this issue for reciprocities).

Reciprocity, therefore, has a multifarious relation with other systems such as markets and organizations (e.g., firms or the public sector). A priori, it may replace them, support them by replacing a defective sub-part, or impair their working. It often permits the working of these systems, notably by remedying their "failures" due to difficulties in constraining and information of various types. It is even necessary for them by having an important role of securing general respect – for instance of property rights in exchange. It is commonly a complement for them in activities in which they do not perform well. Nevertheless, reciprocity is also more or less a possible substitute to other systems which it can supplant or which can replace it, an alternative to them, although this implies important changes in motives and social sentiments, and a different logic raising issues of efficiency and of the nature of social relations. In particular, reciprocity can be both market-supporting and a market substitute (and even both jointly when it palliates a partial "failure"), and it has the same ambivalent relation with organizations.

There results the place of reciprocity in society and its economy which have been presented and can be subsumed here. Three roles of reciprocity should be distinguished: its pervasive manifestation in all social relations and as an indispensable agent of general peace; its being the main principle of important social systems such as the family and various communities; and its role – apparently secondary in overall concern but often dealing with crucial and critical aspects – in other social systems such as various organizations and

markets (there, reciprocity's role is often like that of a lubricant which permits the functioning of an engine).

23.4.2 Reciprocity in economic life

23.4.2.1 A basic social relation. The roles and importance
of reciprocity in the various parts of the economy have been
presented in the foregoing analyses and can be gathered and
summarized at this point. The most basic manifestation of
reciprocity is its inherent a priori presence or potentiality
in all encounters between humans, as a basic bond, glue or
cement of society and mankind (as explained, for instance, by
Hobhouse, Simmel, and many other scholars). Peace within
groups owes much to a general reciprocity of respect, since
the possibilities of private or public protection by force are
limited and costly. This permits, in particular, the working
of other modes of relations in markets and organizations –
which requires the respect for the appropriate rights or rules.
Of course, this concerns relations within groups which, at the
same time, may be at war with one another.

23.4.2.2 Reciprocitarian groups; the family. In systems
based essentially on reciprocity, the main one is the family,
in which exchange and force are often in fact moments of
a general permanent reciprocitarian relationship, based on
liking reciprocity with, however, some aspects of balance
reciprocity between members (including the noted chain
reciprocities between generations). The economic theory of
the family has shifted from a model of a benevolent dictator
with Becker's *pater familias*, to the "new economic theory
of the family" which sees it as a self-interested exchange
(Chiappori), and then to the "new new economics of the
family" based on reciprocity (e.g. Arrondel and Masson) –
although reciprocal liking should be more important than balance. Reciprocity is also the dominant and sometimes the sole
mode of relation in relatively tight groups or communities,

various traditional economies, genuine cooperatives, and so on.

23.4.2.3 Exchange, markets and reciprocity. Other systems benefit from the basic respect, which permits peaceful inter-action, and from the primal propensity to reciprocity which they use in various ways. This holds for markets, for orga-nizations (such as firms, public administration and politics, and others), and for the interface between both, notably in the labour market.

Reciprocity is both a market failure and a main corrector of market failures. It is a market failure in the sense that the acts concerning others do not result from an agreement, the proper reciprocitarian motives are not pure self-interest (as in the classical theory of markets), and an agent is directly con-cerned with aspects of the situation of the other person. This concern, however, is in part very different from the standard structure. Only the concern for the welfare (or consumption goods) of the other person in liking reciprocity is standard since this is the usual description of altruism, whereas the other concerns are not. In balance reciprocity, the concern is for an act or a transfer of the other person in themselves (and not for their effect on the allocation), and for compar-ison between them and those of the reciprocator. In liking reciprocity, the other concern is for a sentiment of the other person – and for the gift received – , and the effect is a senti-ment which leads to a formation of preferences (which may in turn induce giving).

A most common application of this reciprocitarian disrup-tion of exchange is also the oldest topic of specific reciprocity analysed in laboratory and by modelling. This is the labour reaction to pay of the social psychology of the 1960s (Adams and others), refined by George Akerlof (1982) to explain invol-untary unemployment due to "efficiency wages," and gener-alized and much developed for labour relations in general (see Kolm 1990). Note that reciprocity implies preferences about the relation (intrinsic preferences), and preferences about the transferred items (pay, labour) which are a priori different from what they would be in the case of pure self-interest alone. Moreover, the solution of the "game" may be other than a "domination" by the employer exploiting the employees' reciprocal reaction. Hence, there may be no proper "involuntary unemployment" or loss in social efficiency, or these concepts have to be further specified – an application of the analyses of chapter 22.

Moreover, the properly reciprocitarian motives – balance and fairness on the one hand and induced liking on the other – can also more or less correct other market failures. As we have seen, they can induce one to respect others' property and mutual agreements, freely provide one's part, pay for positive externalities, restrain from inflicting negative ones, freely contribute to non-excludable public goods and collective actions, provide the last service of sequential exchanges, tell the truth and reveal information, keep promises, be trustworthy and trustful, accept fair sharing, accept balanced reciprocal concessions necessary for reaching an agreement, accept a fair deal and even prefer it to a good deal. These motives can transform prisoner's dilemmas into coordination games with one solution preferred by all.

In the end, general reciprocity secures a sufficient level of respect of property rights and of general honesty. Reciprocities permit the market to survive missing contracts, incomplete agreements and asymmetric information. They permit life in society to transmute collective concerns and actions, externalities, obstacles to exclusion and information, and impossibilities in establishing contracts or implementing them, from failures of self-interested individualism to the manifestation and achievement of a reciprocitarian community. These remedies to market failures are alternatives to the use of force by internalizing the issue into a larger economic unit or by public interventions – solutions which have themselves their imperfections and shortcomings.

23.4.2.4 Organizations and reciprocity. The same conducts are helpful, and in part necessary, in the working of organizations of all types, basically for the same reason – in particular, difficulties in constraining and information which can induce "command failures." This leads to reciprocal help and exchange of information between members of the organization, reciprocities of favours and labour between members and the organization or its management, reciprocities in trust or in promise keeping, and reciprocal free contributions to collective concerns. Moreover, the frequent contacts in an organization extend the scope of reciprocal services of all types, both between colleagues and across hierarchical levels including with the management. The frequency of contacts has two effects on the reciprocitarian nature of the relations, which oppose one another in a sense. On the one hand, the recurrence tends to introduce a dimension of sequential exchange (which can be purely self-interested). On the other hand, the frequency and duration is favourable to the development of positive interpersonal sentiments, which is indeed a frequent case.

The correlation between productivity and the importance of reciprocity in trust and more or less informal help, with similar technologies, has been documented at all levels – cultures, nations, provinces, firms, branches, and teams – as we have seen.

23.4.2.5 Development and reciprocity. A vast and very important domain of substitutions between reciprocities and the market is constituted by processes of "development" which consist largely of replacements of reciprocities by markets (and command). The normative assessment of these processes cannot be summarized since there are many different types of cases and the effects are far-reaching (not only whole lives are transformed, but civilizations disappear). The conclusion for policy is to be found in the conception of a development that both respects cultures and rests on the rich potential of their solidarities and reciprocities.

23.4.2.6 Reciprocity in the public and political sector. The decentralized correction of "market failures" also makes reciprocity a substitute for the public sector, since a major role of this sector is the correction of these "failures" in a centralized, authoritarian, and political mode. However, the social place and action of the public and political sector itself is based on a number of reciprocities. One can distinguish a basic and general public reciprocity, which has various aspects, and a number of specific actual or putative reciprocities leading to various specific policies. People receive a vast amount of public services for free, but they can be good citizens in general, law abiding people and taxpayers, and voters who choose governments and taxes. There are corresponding reciprocitarian bonds and sentiments in three forms: between society as a whole and individuals (each of whom can also take the "point of view of the society" to which she belongs), between the public administration and the people's general support of the political/public system, and between politicians on the one hand and voters and political activists on the other hand.

23.4.2.7 Welfare policies. Reciprocity among citizens also intervenes in the normative foundation of a number of policies. This is in particular the case for policies that characterize the "welfare state." For instance, concepts of intergenerational chain reciprocities induce the acceptance of pay-as-you-go pension schemes or of the symmetrical public financing of education. Reasonings and sentiments of putative reciprocity (I help because I would be, or would have been, helped if I needed this assistance) lead to the support of people suffering from personal and social handicaps. As we have seen, this motive underlies the strong attachment of many to public health insurance.

23.4.3 Reciprocity in analysis

23.4.3.1 Positive theory. Although reciprocity has long been emphasized by social science, and in particular discussed and modelled for a long time by economists, these introductions of the consideration and theory of reciprocity into all branches of economics is, today, mainly an agenda for future analyses. This should be an important part of the progress towards more psychological realism and depth in the understanding and representation of the conduct of agents and interactions between them. And taking greater account of the relevant psychology of humans in society is undoubtedly a major part of the needed progress in explaining and understanding economic life. This progress in psychological realism and deepening should, of course, be more ambitious than merely pointing out examples of obvious and particular deviations from purely self-interested behaviour. Rather, it should set its aim as: back to Adam Smith's "moral sentiments" and Pareto's interpersonal concerns and "derivations" (with the addition of modern analytical tools which may compensate for difficulties we may have in matching the depth and subtlety of such authors).

23.4.3.2 Normative theory. Finally, the normative branch of economics needs progress no less than its positive branch. Four levels of issues can be distinguished here: efficiency, distribution and justice, the value and quality of social relations, and the value of the sentiments, motives and intentions of people. The important contributions of motives and conducts of reciprocity to economic efficiency have been discussed. The effects of reciprocity on the other normative levels result from its two proper motives: balance and fairness, on the one hand, and liking, altruism and benevolence, on the other. The equality in balance reciprocity implements sentiments of local justice in the distribution. Reciprocal fairness tends to establish consensus about distributive justice. The transfers or services of liking reciprocity freely implement distribution and redistribution. The sentiments of fairness and of mutual liking entail the intrinsic quality – valued both by the individuals and by morals – of the reciprocitarian relationships, of the sentiments and motives themselves, and, ultimately, of the individuals having these sentiments – that is, their virtue.

23.4.4 Reciprocity in society

23.4.4.1 Pervasive and basic. Practically all encounters between persons elicit sentiments, interactions and relations of reciprocity which can combine, in all possible degrees, norms of social balance and fairness, mutually induced affects of any intensity, and mutual interest. These relations are often visible and conspicuous, but also, very often, they are considered so obvious that they are not explicitly emphasized. Nevertheless, they are always very important, as we have emphasized, because they provide the basis and framework of and necessary conditions for relations of other types such as exchange, cooperation, or a workable and acceptable hierarchy. These most unconspicuous, yet pervasive and indispensable, reciprocities are the air of social breathing; their role also resembles that of the lubricant that permits the working of the engine or – on the contrary – of the small ruggedness that creates the friction necessary for walking. However, other reciprocities are large, conspicuous, and the major social fact, as in families, the polity, organizations and communities. The perceptive social scientists who saw reciprocity as the central social phenomenon and relation – such as Hobhouse, Thurnwald, or Simmel – were probably on the right track. There remained to analyse this relation, its various types and logic, and its consequences, and there remains to pursue this analysis in specific instances, without forgetting that the final aim may be to improve society and not only to understand it. There is no society without a good amount of reciprocity, and, a fortiori, there is no good viable society that does not rest on a dense network of reciprocal respect, esteem, gratitude and solidarity.

23.4.4.2 The relational paradigm. Acknowledging the fundamental role and the overall importance of reciprocity emphasizes the view of society as a set of relations, in contrast to both a set of individuals who may interact and a set of social structures which determines individuals and their actions. Reciprocity is, as we have seen, necessary for overall peaceful relations. It associates mutual interest, fairness and liking. It is relational not only in acts, as exchange and forcing are, but also and primarily in feeling, emotions and sentiments. It is bilateral rather than unilateral as forcing, simple giving and simple liking are. It is more deeply relational than liking, and even mutual liking, because liking reciprocity is mutually induced mutual liking. Reciprocity is both the bedrock and the keystone of the relational paradigm for understanding society. Its analysis can rest on a development of the economic analysis of individual action and interaction, and of the psychology of individuals in society, as we have seen. However, each person takes others not only as means of her satisfaction, but also as ends in themselves as being objects of affection and subjects of justice, and as mirror-persons who reciprocally bestow on her the respect, regard, fairness and affection necessary for her dignity and humanity.

Bibliography

Adam, C., and P. Tannery (eds.) (1965), *René Descartes: Oeuvres Complètes*, Paris: Vrin.

Adams, J. S. (1963), 'Wage inequities, productivity and work quality', *Industrial Relations* 3: 9–16.

(1965), 'Inequity in social exchange', in: L. Berkowitz (ed.), *Advances in Experimental Social Psychology*, vol. II, New York: Academic Press, 267–99.

Adams, J. S., and W. B. Rosenbaum (1964), 'The relationship of worker productivity to cognitive dissonance about wage inequalities', *Journal of Abnormal and Social Psychology* 69: 19–25.

Adolphs, R. (2000), 'Social cognition and the human brain', *Trends in Cognitive Science* 3: 469–79.

Akerlof, G. (1982), 'Labor contract as partial gift exchange', *Quarterly Journal of Economics* 97: 543–69.

Alesina, A., and E. La Ferrara (2000a), 'Participation in heterogeneous communities', *Quarterly Journal of Economics* 115 (3): 847–904.

(2000b), *Who Trusts Others?*, Discussion Paper no. 2646, Centre for Economic Policy Research, London.

(2002), 'Who trusts others ?', *Journal of Public Economics* 85 (2), 207–34.

Altman, I. (1973), 'Reciprocity of interpersonal exchange', *Journal of Theory of Social Behaviour* 3: 249–61.

Ames, R., and G. Marwell (1979), 'Experiments on the provision of public goods: resources, interest, group size, and the free-rider problem', *American Journal of Sociology* 84: 1335–60.

Andreoni, J. (1988a), 'Privately provided public goods in a large economy: the limits of altruism', *Journal of Public Economics* 35 (1): 57–73.

(1988b), 'Why free ride? Strategies and learning in public goods experiments', *Journal of Public Economics* 37 (3): 291–304.

(1989), 'Giving with impure altruism: applications to charity and Ricardian equivalence', *Journal of Political Economy* 97: 1447–58.

(1990), 'Impure altruism and donations to public goods: a theory of warm-glow giving', *Economic Journal* 100: 464–77.

(1995), 'Warm-glow versus cold-prickle: the effects of positive and negative framing on cooperation in experiments', *Quarterly Journal of Economics* 110 (1): 1–21.

Archibald, G. C., and D. Donaldson (1976), 'Non-paternalism and the basic theorems of welfare economics', *Canadian Journal of Economics* 9: 492–507.

Aronfreed, J. (1970), 'The socialization of altruistic and sympathetic behavior: some theoretical and experimental analyses', in: J. Macaulay and L. Berkowitz (eds.), *Altruism and Helping Behavior*, New York: Academic Press, 103–26.

Aronfreed, J., and V. Paskal (1965), 'Altruism, empathy, and the conditioning of positive affect', unpublished manuscript, University of Pennsylvania.

Arrow, K. J. (1972), 'Gifts and exchanges', *Philosophy and Public Affairs* 1: 343–62.

(1979), *Optimal and Voluntary Income Distribution*, Technical Report no. 288 (Economic Series), Institute for Mathematical Studies in the Social Sciences, Stanford University, CA., and in (1981), *Economic Welfare and the Economics of Soviet Socialism: Essays in Honor of Abram Bergson*, Cambridge: Cambridge University Press, 267–88.

Axelrod, R. (1981), 'Emergence of cooperation among egoists', *American Political Science Review* 75: 306–18.

(1984), *The Evolution of Cooperation*, New York: Academic Press.

Banks, S. (1979), 'Gift-giving: a review and an interactive paradigm', in: W. Wilkie (ed.), *Advances in Consumer Research*, vol. VI, Ann Arbor: Michigan Association for Consumer Research, 319–24.

Baron, J. N. (1988), 'The employment relation as a social relation', *Journal of the Japanese and International Economies* 2: 492–525.

Basu, K. (1977), 'Information and strategy in iterated prisoners' dilemma', *Theory and Decision* 8: 293–8.

(1987), 'Modelling finitely repeated games with uncertain termination', *Economic Letters* 23: 147–51.

Becker, G. S. (1961), *Notes on an Economic Analysis of Philanthropy*, working paper, National Bureau of Economic Research, New York.

(1974), 'A theory of social interaction', *Journal of Political Economy* 82 (6): 1063–93.

(1976a), 'Altruism, egoism and genetic fitness: economics and sociobiology', *Journal of Economic Literature* 14: 817–26.

(1976b), *The Economic Approach to Human Behavior*, Chicago: University of Chicago Press.

(1981), 'Altruism in the family and selfishness in the market place', *Econometrica* 48: 1–15.

Becker, H. (1956a), 'Empathy, sympathy and Scheler', *International Journal of Sociometry* 1: 15–22.

(1956b), *Man in Reciprocity: Introductory Lectures on Culture, Society and Personality*, New York: Praeger.

Benabou, R., and J. Tirole (2003), 'Intrinsic and extrinsic motivation', *Review of Economic Studies* 70 (3): 489–520.

Ben-Porath, Y. (1980), 'The F-connection: families, friends, and firms and the organization of exchange', *Population and Development Review* 6: 1–30.

Bentham, J. (1789), *Principles of Morals and Legislation*, Oxford: Clarendon Press.

Bereby-Meyer, Y., and M. Niederle (2005), 'Fairness in bargaining', *Journal of Economic Behavior and Organization* 56 (2): 173–86.

Berg, J., J. Dickhaut and K. A. McCabe (1995), 'Trust, reciprocity and social history', *Games and Economic Behavior* 10: 122–42.

Bergstrom, T. C. (1970), 'A "Scandinavian consensus" solution for efficient income distribution among non-malevolent consumers', *Journal of Economic Theory* 2: 383–98.

Berkowitz, L. (1966), 'A laboratory investigation of social class and national differences in helping behavior', *International Journal of Psychology* 1.

(1968), 'Responsibility, reciprocity, and social distance in help-giving: an experimental investigation of English social class differences', *Journal of Experimental Psychology* 4: 46–63.

(1970), 'The self, selfishness and altruism', in: J Macaulay and L. Berkowitz (eds.), *Altruism and Helping Behavior*, New York: Academic Press, 143–54.

(1971), 'Social norms, feelings and other factors affecting helping behavior and altruism', unpublished manuscript, University of Wisconsin.

Berkowitz, L., and L. Daniels (1963), 'Responsibility and dependency', *Journal of Abnormal and Social Psychology* 66: 429–37.

Berkowitz, L., and P. Friedman (1967), 'Some social class differences in helping behavior', *Journal of Personality and Social Psychology* 5: 217–25.

Bernheim, B. D., A. Shleifer and L. H. Summers (1985), 'The strategic bequest motive', *Journal of Political Economy* 93: 1045–76.

Bewley, T. F. (1995), 'A depressed labor market as explained by participants', *American Economic Review* 85 (2): 250–4.

(1999), 'Work motivation', *Review of the Federal Reserve Bank of St Louis* 81 (3): 35–50.

Bianchi, M. (1993), 'How to learn sociality: true and false solutions to Mandeville's problem', *History of Political Economy* 25 (2): 209–38.

Binmore, K., J. McCarthy, G. Ponti, L. Samuelson and A. Shaked (2002), 'A backward induction experiment', *Journal of Economic Theory* 104 (1): 48–88.

Bishop, J. (1987), 'The recognition and reward of employee performance', *Journal of Labor Economics* 5: S36–S56.

Boehm, C. (1993), 'Egalitarian behavior and reverse dominance hierarchy', *Current Anthropology* 34 (3): 227–40.

Bolton, G., J. Brandts and A. Ockenfels (1998), 'Measuring motivations for the reciprocal responses observed in simple dilemma games', *Experimental Economics* 1 (3): 207–19.

Bolton, G. and A. Ockenfels (1998), 'Strategy and equity: an ERC-analysis of the Güth–van Damme game', *Journal of Mathematical Psychology* 42 (2): 215–26.

(2000), 'ERC: a theory of equity, reciprocity and competition', *American Economic Review* 90 (1): 166–93.

Boudon, R. (1979), *La logique du social*, Paris: Hachette.

Boulding, K. (1973), *The Economy of Love and Fear*, Belmont, CA: Wadsworth.

Bowles, S. (1998), 'Endogenous preferences: the cultural consequences of markets and other economic institutions', *Journal of Economic Literature* 36 (1): 75–111.

Bryan, J. H., and M. A. Test (1967), 'Models and helping: naturalistic studies in aiding behavior', *Journal of Personality and Social Psychology* 6: 400–7.

Buchan, N., R. Croson and R. Dawes (2002), *Swift Neighbors and Persistent Strangers: A Cross-Cultural investigation of Trust and Reciprocity in Social Exchange*, paper presented at the Microeconomic Seminar, Universitat Pompeu Fabra, Barcelona, 17 December.

Camerer, C. (1988), 'Gifts as economic signals and social symbols', *American Journal of Sociology* 94: 5180–214.

Campbell, D. T. (1965), 'Ethnocentric and other altruistic motives', in: D. Levine (ed.), *Nebraska Symposium on Motivation*, Lincoln: University of Nebraska Press, 283–311.

Carmichael, H. L., and W. B. Macleod (1997), 'Gift giving and the evolution of cooperation', *International Economic Review* 38 (3): 485–509.

Charness, G., and E. Haruvy (2002), 'Altruism, equity, and reciprocity in a gift-exchange experiment: an encompassing approach', *Games and Economic Behavior* 40 (2): 203–31.

Charness, G., and M. Rabin (2002), 'Understanding social preferences with simple tests', *Quarterly Journal of Economics* 117 (3): 817–69.

Cialdini, R. C., and M. R. Trost (1998), 'Social influence: social norms, conformity, and compliance', in: D. T. Gilbert, S. T. Fiske and G. Lindzey (eds.), *The Handbook of Social Psychology*, Boston: McGraw-Hill, 151–85.

Coate, S., and M. Ravallion (1993), 'Reciprocity without commitment', *Journal of Economic Development* 40: 1–24.

Collard, D. (1978), *Altruism and the Economy: A Study in Non-Selfish Economics*, Oxford: Martin Robertson.

Coricelli, G., K. McCabe and V. Smith (2000), 'Theory-of-mind mechanism in personal exchange', in: G. Hotano, N. Okada and H. Tanabe (eds.), *Affective Minds*, Amsterdam: Elsevier, 249–59.

Cox, J. C. (2004), 'How to identify trust and reciprocity', *Games and Economic Behavior* 46 (2): 260–81.

Croson, R. T. A. (1999), *Theories of Altruism and Reciprocity: Evidence from Linear Public Good Games*, discussion paper, Wharton School, University of Pennsylvania.

Daly, G., and F. Giertz (1972), 'Welfare economics and welfare reform', *American Economic Review* 62 (1): 131–8.

Danner, P. L. (1973), 'Sympathy and exchangeable value: keys to Adam Smith's social philosophy', *Review of Social Economy* 34 (3): 317–31.

Darwin, C. (1871 [1981]), *La descendance de l'homme, et la sélection sexuelle* (trans. E. Barbier), Brussels: Editions Complexe.

Dasgupta, P. (2000), 'Economic progress and the idea of social capital', in: P. Dasgupta and I. Serageldin (eds.), *Social Capital: A Multifaceted Perspective*, World Bank: Washington, DC, 325–424.

Davis, J. (1975), 'The particular theory of exchange', *Archives Européennes de Sociologie* 16 (2): 151–68.

Dawes, R., and R. Thaler (1982), 'Cooperation', *Journal of Economic Perspectives* 2: 187–97.

Dawes, R. M., A. J. C. van de Kragt and J. M. Orbell (1988), 'Not me or thee but we: the importance of group identity in eliciting cooperation in dilemma situations', *Acta Psychologica* 68: 83–97.

Doland, D., and K. Adelberg (1967), 'The learning of sharing behavior', *Child Development* 38: 695–700.

Dufwenberg, M., and G. Kirchsteiger (2004), 'A theory of sequential reciprocity', *Games and Economic Behavior* 47 (2): 268–98.

Durkheim, E. (1958), *Professional Ethics and Civic Morals* (trans. C. Brookfield), Glencoe, IL: Free Press.

Edgeworth, F. Y. (1881), *Mathematical Psychics: An Essay on the Application of Mathematics to the Moral Sciences*, London: London School of Economics.

Eglar, Z. E. (1958), *Vartan Bhanji: Institutionalized Reciprocity in a Changing Punjab Village*, PhD thesis, Columbia University NY.

Ekstein, R. (1972), 'Psychoanalysis and education for the facilitation of positive human qualities', *Journal of Social Issues* 28 (3): 71–85.

Elster, J. (1989), *The Cement of Society: A Study of Social Order*, Cambridge: Cambridge University Press.

(1998), 'Emotions and economic theory', *Journal of Economic Literature* 36: 47–74.

(2007), *Disinterestedness*, Lectures at the College de France.

(forthcoming), *Le Désintéressement*, Paris: Editions du Seuil.

Falk, A., E. Fehr and U. Fischbacher (2000), *Informal Sanctions*, Working Paper no. 59, Institute for Empirical Research in Economics, University of Zurich.

(2003), 'On the nature of fair behavior', *Economic Inquiry* 41 (1): 20–6.

Falk, A., and U. Fischbacher (1999), *A Theory of Reciprocity*, Working Paper no. 6, Institute for Empirical Research in Economics, University of Zurich.

(2001), *A Theory of Reciprocity*, Discussion Paper no. 3014, Centre for Economic Policy Research, London.

(2005), 'Modeling strong reciprocity', in: H. Gintis, S. Bowles, R. Boyd and E. Fehr (eds.), *Moral Sentiments and Material Interests: The Foundations of Cooperation in Economic Life*, Cambridge, MA: MIT Press, 193–214.

Fehr, E., and S. Gächter (1998), 'How effective are trust- and reciprocity-based incentives?', in: A. Ben-Ner and L. Putterman, *Economics, Values and Organizations*, Cambridge: Cambridge University Press, 337–63.

(2000a), 'Fairness and retaliation: the economics of reciprocity', *Journal of Economic Perspectives* 14 (3): 159–81.

(2000b), 'Cooperation and punishment in public goods experiments', *American Economic Review* 90 (4): 980–94.

(2002), *Do Incentive Contracts Crowd out Voluntary Cooperation?*, Working Paper no. 34, University of Zurich.

Fehr, E., S. Gächter and G. Kirchsteiger (1996), 'Reciprocal fairness and noncompensating wage differentials', *Journal of Institutional and Theoretical Economics* 152 (4): 608–40.

(1997), 'Reciprocity as a contract enforcement device: experimental evidence', *Econometrica* 65 (4): 833–60.

Fehr, E., E. Kirchler, A. Weichbold and S. Gächter (1998), 'When social norms overpower competition: gift exchange in experimental labor markets', *Journal of Labor Economics* 16 (2): 324–51.

Fehr, E., G. Kirchsteiger and A. Riedl (1993), 'Does fairness prevent market clearing? An experimental investigation', *Quarterly Journal of Economics* 108 (2): 437–59.

Fehr, E., and K. M. Schmidt (1999), 'A theory of fairness, competition and cooperation', *Quarterly Journal of Economics* 114 (3): 817–68.

   (2002), 'Fairness, incentives, and contractual choices', *European Economic Review* 44 (4–6): 1057–68.

   (2003), 'Theories of fairness and reciprocity: evidence and economic applications', in: M. Dewatripont, L. P. Hansen and S. J. Turnovsky (eds.), *Advances in Economics and Econometrics*: 8th World Congress. Cambridge: Cambridge University Press, 208–57.

Fellner, C. H., and J.-R. Marshall (1970), 'Kidney donors', in: J. Macaulay and L. Berkowitz (eds.), *Altruism and Helping Behavior*, New York: Academic Press, 269–81.

Firth, R. (ed.) (1957), *Man and Culture: An Evaluation of the Work of Bronislaw Malinowski*, New York: Humanities Press.

Fischbacher, U., S. Gächter and E. Fehr (1999), *Are People Conditionally Cooperative? Evidence from a Public Good Experiment*, Working Paper no. 16, Institute for Empirical Research in Economics, University of Zurich.

Frank, R. H. (1988), *Passions within Reason: The Strategic Role of the Emotions*, New York: Norton.

   (1990), 'A theory of moral sentiments', in: J. Mansbridge (ed.), *Beyond Self-Interest*, Chicago: University of Chicago Press, 71–96.

Freuchen, P. (1961), *Book of the Eskimos*, Cleveland and New York: World Publishing.

Frey, B. (1997), *Not Just for the Money: An Economic Theory of Personal Motivation*, Cheltenham: Edward Elgar.

Friedrichs, R. W. (1960), 'Alter versus ego: an exploratory assessment of altruism', *American Sociological Review* 25: 496–508.

Frisch, D. M., and M. S. Greenberg (1968), 'Reciprocity and intentionality in the giving of help', in: *Proceedings of the 76th Annual Convention of the American Psychological Association*, vol. III, Washington, DC: American Psychological Association, 383–4.

Gächter, S., and A. Falk (2002), 'Population and reciprocity: consequences for the labour relation', *Scandinavian Journal of Econometrics* 104: 1–27.

Geanakoplos, J., D. Pearce and E. Stacchetti (1989), 'Psychological games and sequential rationality', *Games and Economic Behavior* 1 (1): 60–79.

Gérard-Varet, L.-A., S.-Ch. Kolm and J. Mercier Ythier (eds.) (2000), *The Economics of Reciprocity, Giving and Altruism*, London: Macmillan.

Gergen, K. J., M. Gergen and K. Meter (1972), 'Individual orientations to prosocial behavior', *Journal of Social Issues* 28 (3): 105–30.

Gergen, K. J., M. S. Greenberg and R. H. Willis (eds.) (1980), *Social Exchange: Advances in Theory and Research*, New York: Plenum Press.

Gide, C. (1905), *Economie sociale*, Paris: Librairie de la Société du Recueil général des lois et des arrêts.

Gintis, H. (2000), 'Strong reciprocity and human sociality', *Journal of Theoretical Biology* 206: 169–79.

Gintis, H., S. Bowles, R. Boyd and E. Fehr (eds.) (2005), *Moral Sentiments and Material Interests: The Foundations of Cooperation in Economic Life*, Cambridge, MA: MIT Press.

Glaeser, E. L., D. Laibson, J. A. Scheinkman and C. I. Sautter (2000), 'Measuring trust', *Quarterly Journal of Economics* 115: 811–46.

Goeree, J. K., and C. A. Holt (2000), 'Asymmetric inequality aversion and noisy behaviour in alternating-offer bargaining games', *European Economic Review* 44 (4–6): 1079–89.

Goldfarb, R. S. (1970), 'Pareto optimal redistribution: comment', *American Economic Review* 60 (4): 994–6.

Goodstadt, M. S. (1971), 'Helping and refusal to help: a test of balance and reactance theories', *Journal of Experimental Social Psychology* 7: 610–22.

Goranson, R. E., and L. Berkowitz (1966), 'Reciprocity and responsibility reactions to prior help', *Journal of Personality and Social Psychology* 3: 227–32.

Gouldner, A. (1960), 'The norm of reciprocity: a preliminary statement', *American Sociological Review* 25: 161–78.

Greenberg, J. (1978), 'Effects of reward value and retaliative power on allocation decisions: justice, generosity or greed?', *Journal of Personality and Social Psychology* 36: 367–79.

Greenberg, M. S. (1980), 'A theory of indebtedness', in: K. J. Gergen, M. S. Greenberg and R. H. Willis (eds.), *Social Exchange: Advances in Theory and Research*, New York: Plenum Press 2–26.

Greenberg, M. S., and D. Frisch (1972), 'Effect of intentionality on willingness to reciprocate a favor', *Journal of Experimental Social Psychology* 8: 99–111.

Greenglass, E. R. (1969), 'Effects of prior help and hindrance on willingness to help another: reciprocity or social responsibility', *Journal of Personality and Social Psychology* 11: 224–32.

Gregory, C. A. (1982), *Gifts and Commodities*, London: Academic Press.

(1987), 'Gifts', in: J. Eatwell, M. Milgate and P. Newman (eds.), *The New Palgrave: A Dictionary of Economics*, London: Mackmillan, 524–8.

Gui, B. (2000), 'Beyond transactions: on the interpersonal dimension of economic reality', *Annals of Public and Cooperative Economics* 71 (2): 139–68.

Gui, B., and R. Sugden (eds.) (2005), *Economics and Social Interaction: Accounting for Interpersonal Relations*, Cambridge: Cambridge University Press.

Güth, W. (1995a), 'An evolutionary approach to explaining cooperative behavior by reciprocal incentives', *International Journal of Game Theory* 24 (4): 323–44.

(1995b), 'On ultimatum bargaining experiments a personal review', *Journal of Economic Behavior and Organization* 27 (3): 329–44.

Güth, W., P. Ockenfels and M. Wendel (1977), 'Cooperation based on trust: an experimental investigation', *Journal of Economic Psychology* 18: 15–43.

Güth, W., R. Schmitterberger and B. Schwarze (1982), 'An experimental analysis of ultimatum bargaining', *Journal of Economic Behavior and Organization* 3: 367–88.

Güth, W., and M. E. Yaari (1992), 'An evolutionary approach to explain reciprocal behavior in a simple strategic game', in: U. Witt (ed.), *Explaining Process and Change: Approaches to Evolutionary Economics*, Ann Arbor: University of Michigan Press, 23–4.

Guttman, J. M. (2000), 'On the evolutionary stability of preferences for reciprocity', *European Journal of Political Economy* 16 (1): 31–50.

Guyer, P. (1993), *Kant and the Experience of Freedom*, Cambridge: Cambridge University Press.

Hamilton, W. D. (1971), 'Selection of selfish and altruistic behavior in some extreme models', in: J. F. Eisenberg and W. S. Dillon (eds.), *Man and Beast: Comparative Social Behavior*, Washington, DC: Smithsonian Institution Press, 57–91.

Hammond, P. (1975), 'Charity: altruism or cooperative egoism?', in: E. Phelps (ed.), *Altruism, Morality, and Economic Theory*, New York: Russell Sage Foundation, 115–32.

Handlon, B. J., and P. Gross (1959), 'The development of sharing behavior', *Journal of Abnormal and Social Psychology* 59: 425–8.

Hardin, G. (1968), 'The tragedy of the commons', *Science* 162: 1243–8.

Harris, L. A. (1967), 'A study of altruism', *Elementary School Journal* 68: 135–41.

Harris, M. (1970), 'Reciprocity and generosity: some determinants of sharing behavior', *Child Development* 41: 313–28.

Hartmann, H. (1960), *Psychoanalysis and Moral Values*, New York: International Universities Press.

Heider, F. (1958), *The Psychology of Interpersonal Relations*, New York: Wiley.

Helliwell, J. F., and R. D. Putnam (1999), *Education and Social Capital*, Working Paper no. 7121, National Bureau of Economic Research, Cambridge, MA.

Henrich, J., R. Boyd, S. Bowles, H. Gintis, E. Fehr, R. McElreath and C. Camerer (2001), 'In search of Homo economicus: behavioral experiments in 15 small-scale societies', *American Economic Review* 91 (2): 73–8.

Herold, F. (2003), *Carrot or Stick? Group Selection and the Evolution of Reciprocal Preferences*. Discussion Paper 2003–05, Department of Economics, University of Munich.

Hobhouse, L. T. (1906 [1951]), *Morals in Evolution: A Study in Comparative Ethics*, London: Chapman and Hall.

Hochman, H. M., and J. D. Rodgers (1969), 'Pareto optimal redistribution', *American Economic Review* 59 (3): 542–57.

Hoffman, E., and M. L. Spitzer (1982), 'The Coase theorem: some experimental tests', *Journal of Law and Economics* 95: 73–98.

Hoffman, M. (1970), 'Moral development', in: P. Mussen (ed.), *Carmichael's Manual of Child Development*, New York: Wiley.

Holesovsky, V. (1977), *Economic System Analysis and Comparison* Tokyo: McGraw-Hill, Kogakusha.

Holländer, H. (1990), 'A social exchange approach to voluntary cooperation', *American Economic Review* 80 (5): 1157–67.

Holmstrom, B., and P. Milgrom (1991), 'Multitask principal–agent analyses: incentive contracts, asset ownership, and job design', *Journal of Law, Economics and Organization* 7 (Special issue): 24–52.

Homans, G. (1958), 'Social behavior as exchange', *American Journal of Sociology* 68: 597–606.

Hornstein, H. A. (1970), *Experiments in the Social Psychology of Prosocial Behavior: Final Report*, Washington, DC: National Science Foundation.

Hornstein, H. A., E. Fisch and M. Holmes (1968), 'Influence of a model's feelings about his behavior and his relevance as a comparison on the observers' helping behavior', *Journal of Personality and Social Psychology* 10: 222–6.

Isaac, M. R., K. F. McCue and C. Plott (1985), 'Public goods provision in an experimental environment', *Journal of Public Economics* 26: 51–74.

Isaac, M. R., and J. M. Walker (1988a), 'Communication and free-riding behavior: the voluntary contribution mechanism', *Economic Inquiry* 26: 585–608.

(1988b), 'Group size effects in public goods provision: the voluntary contribution mechanism', *Quarterly Journal of Economics* 103: 179–99.

Isaac, M. R., J. M. Walker and S. H. Thomas (1984), 'Divergent evidence on free riding: an experimental examination of possible explanations', *Public Choice* 43 (2): 113–49.

Isaac, M. R., J. M. Walker and A. M. Williams (1994), 'Group size and the voluntary provision of public goods: experimental evidence utilizing large groups', *Journal of Public Economics* 75: 1–36.

Isen, A. M., and P. F. Levin (1972), 'Effect of feeling good on helping: cookies and kindness', *Journal of Personality and Social Psychology* 21: 384–8.

Kahneman, D., and J. L. Knetsch (1992), 'Valuing public goods: the purchase of moral satisfaction', *Journal of Environmental Economics and Management* 22 (1): 57–70.

Kahneman, D., J. L. Knetsch and R. H. Thaler (1986a), 'Fairness as a constraint on profit seeking: entitlements in the market', *American Economic Review* 76 (3): 728–41.

(1986b), 'Fairness and the assumptions of economics', *Journal of Business* 59: S285–S300.

Kant, I. (1790 [1952]), *Critique of Judgement* (ed. and trans. J. C. Meredith), Oxford: Clarendon Press.

(1797 [1991]), *The Metaphysic of Morals* (trans. M. J. Gregor), Cambridge: Cambridge University Press.

Keser, C., and F. van Winden (2000), 'Conditional cooperation and voluntary contributions to public goods', *Scandinavian Journal of Economics* 102 (1): 23–39.

Kim, O., and M. Walker (1984), 'The free rider problem: experimental evidence', *Public Choice* 43 (1): 3–24.

Kimball, M. (1988), 'Farmer's cooperatives as behavior toward risk', *American Economic Review* 78 (1): 224–32.

Knack, S., and P. Keefer (1997), 'Does social capital have an economic payoff? A cross-country investigation', *Quarterly Journal of Economics* 112: 1251–88.

Kolm, S.-C. (1959), *Les hommes du Fouta-Toro*, Saint-Louis, Senegal: MAS.

Kolm, S.-Ch. (1966), 'The optimal production of social justice', International Economic Association Conference on Public Economics, Biarritz, proceedings, H. Guitton and J. Margolis, eds. Reproduced in (1968), *Economie Publique* (Paris: CNRS) 109–77, and (1969), *Public Economics* (London: Macmillan) 145–200.

(1971), *Justice et équité*, Paris: CEPREMAP. (Reprint 1972, Paris: CNRS). [Published in English 1998, *Justice and Equity* (trans. H. F. See), Cambridge, MA: MIT Press.]

(1973), *La théorie de la réciprocité*, Paris: CEPREMAP.

(1975), *La réciprocité générale*, Paris: CEPREMAP.

(1976), 'Unequal inequalities', *Journal of Economic Theory*, Part I, 12: 416–42; Part II, 13: 82–111.

(1977), 'Multidimensional egalitarianism', *Quarterly Journal of Economics* 91: 1–13.

(1979), *Fondements de la théorie du don, de la réciprocité, et du choix des systèmes économiques*, Paris: CEPREMAP.

(1980), 'Psychanalyse et théorie des choix', *Social Science Information* 19 (2): 269–339.

(1981a), 'Altruisme et efficacité: le sophisme de Rousseau', *Social Science Information* 20: 293–344.

(1981b), 'Efficacité et altruisme: le sophisme de Mandeville, Smith et Pareto', *Revue Economique* 32: 5–31.

(1982), *Le Bonheur-Liberté* (*Bouddhisme Profond et Modernité*), Paris: Presses Universitaires de France.

(1983a), 'Altruism and efficiency', *Ethics* 94: 18–65. Reprinted in S. Zamagni (ed.), *The Economics of Altruism*, op. cit.

(1983b), 'Introduction à la réciprocité générale', *Social Science Information* 22 (4–5) 569–621.

(1984a), *La Bonne Economie: la Réciprocité Générale*, Paris: Presses Universitaires de France.

(1984b), 'Théorie de la réciprocité et du choix des systèmes économiques', *Revue Economique* 35: 871–910.

(1985), *Le Contrat Social Liberal*, Paris: Presses Universitaires de France.

(1986), 'Is only egoism productive?', *Development* 3.

(1987), 'Public economics', in: J. Eatwell, M. Milgate and P. Newman (eds.), *The New Palgrave: A Dictionary of Economics*, London: Macmillan, 1047–55.

(1989), 'Le devoir général de réciprocité', *Revue d'Ethique et de Théologie Morale* 168 (supplement: *Les Devoirs de l'Homme*): 135–46.

(1990), 'Employment and fiscal policies with a realistic view of the social role of wages', in: P. Champsaur, M. Deleau, J.-M. Grandmont, R. Guesnerie, C. Henry, J.-J. Laffont, G. Laroque, J. Mairesse, A. Monfort and Y. Younes (eds.), *Edmond Malinvaud: Essays in His Honor*, Cambridge, MA: MIT Press, 226–86.

(1992), 'Reciprocity', *Political Economy of the Good Society Newsletter* 2 (Summer): 1–6.

(1994), 'The theory of reciprocity and of the choice of economic systems', *Investigaciones Económicas* 18 (1): 67–95.

(1995), 'The theory of social sentiments: the case of envy', *Japanese Economic Review* 1 (46): 63–87.

(1996a), *Modern Theories of Justice*, Cambridge, MA: MIT Press.

(1996b), 'The theory of justice', *Social Choice and Welfare* 13: 151–82.

(1998), 'Une introduction à la théorie de la réciprocité et du choix des systèmes économiques', in: F.-R. Mahieu and H. Rapoport (eds.), *Altruisme: Analyses Economiques*, Paris: Economica 17–50.

(1999), 'Rational foundations of income inequality measurement', in: J. Silber, *Handbook on Income Inequality Measurement*, Boston: Kluwer Academic, 19–94.

(2000a), 'Introduction to the economics of reciprocity, giving and altruism', in: L.-A. Gérard-Varet, S.-C. Kolm and J. Mercier Ythier (eds.), *The Economics of Reciprocity, Giving and Altruism*, London: Macmillan, 1–44.

(2000b), 'The theory of reciprocity', in: L.-A. Gérard-Varet, S.-C. Kolm and J. Mercier Ythier (eds.), *The Economics of Reciprocity, Giving and Altruism*, London: Macmillan, 1115–41.

(2000c), 'The logic of good social relations', *Annals of Public and Cooperative Economics* 72 (2): 171–89.

(2004), *Macrojustice: The Political Economy of Fairness*, New York: Cambridge University Press.

(2005), 'The logic of good social relations', in: B. Gui and R. Sugden (eds.), *Economics and Social Interaction: Accounting for Interpersonal Relations*, Cambridge: Cambridge University Press, chap. 8.

(2006), 'Introduction to the economics of giving, altruism and reciprocity', in: S.-C. Kolm and J. Mercier Ythier (eds.), *Handbook of the Economics of Giving, Altruism and Reciprocity*, 1–122.

(2008), 'The paradox of the alleviation of poverty, joint giving and efficient transfers', mimeo.

Kolm, S-Ch., and J. Mercier Ythier (eds.) (2006), *Handbook of the Economics of Giving, Altruism and Reciprocity*, Amsterdam: North Holland Publishing Company.

Kolpin, V. (1993), 'Equilibrium refinements in psychological games', *Games and Economic Behavior* 4 (2): 218–31.

Kranich, L. J. (1998), 'Altruism and efficiency: a welfare analysis of the Walrasian mechanism with transfers', *Journal of Public Economics* 36: 369–86.

Kranton, R. E. (1996), 'Reciprocal exchange: a self-sustaining system,' *American Economic Review* 86 (4): 830–51.

Kreps, D. M. (1997), 'Intrinsic motivation and extrinsic incentives,' *American Economic Review* 87 (2): 359–64.

Kreps, D. M., P. Milgrom, J. Roberts and R. Wilson (1982), 'Rational cooperation in the finitely repeated prisoners' dilemma', *Journal of Economic Theory* 27 (2): 245–52.

Kropotkin, P. (1892), *La conquête du pain*, Paris: Tresse and Stock.

(1896), 'Co-operation: a reply to Herbert Spencer, part 1', *Freedom* 13 (12).

(1897), 'Co-operation: a reply to Herbert Spencer, part 2', *Freedom* 14 (1).

(1902 [1972]), *Mutual Aid: A Factor of Evolution*, London: Penguin.

(1913), *La Science Moderne et l'Anarchie*, Paris: Stock.

(1927), *L'Ethique*, Paris: Stock.

Kurz, M. (1978a), 'Altruism as an outcome of social interaction', *American Economic Review* 68 (2): 216–22.

(1978b), 'Altruism as an outcome of social interaction', *Journal of Public Economics* 36: 369–86.

(1979), 'Altruistic equilibrium', in: B. Balassa and R. Nelson (eds.), *Economic Progress, Private Values and Policy*, Amsterdam: North-Holland, 177–200.

Lambert, P. (2001), *The Distribution and Redistribution of Income*, Oxford: Basil Blackwell.

Landa, J. T. (1994), *Trust, Ethnicity and Identity: Beyond the New Institutional Economics of Ethnic Trading Networks, Contract Law, and Gift-Exchange*, Ann Arbor: University of Michigan Press.

Latané, B., and J. Darley (1970), *The Unresponsive Bystander: Why Doesn't He Help?*, New York: Appleton-Century-Croft.

Ledyard, J. (1995), 'Public goods: a survey of experimental research', in: A. Roth and J. Kagel (eds.), *Handbook of Experimental Economics*, Princeton, NJ: Princeton University Press, 111–94.

Leeds, R. (1963), 'Altruism and the norm of giving', *Merrill-Palmer Quarterly* 9: 229–40.

Lenrow, P. (1965), 'Studies in sympathy', in: S. S. Tomlins and C. E. Izard (eds.), *Affect, Cognition, and Personality: Empirical Studies*, New York: Springer, 264–94.

Leventhal, G. S., and D. Anderson (1970), 'Self-interest and the maintenance of equity', *Journal of Personality and Social Psychology* 15: 57–62.

Leventhal, G. S., T. Weiss and G. Long (1969), 'Equity, reciprocity and reallocating rewards in the dyad', *Journal of Personality and Social Psychology* 13: 300–5.

Levine, D. K. (1991), *You Get What You Pay for: Tests of Efficiency Wage Theories in the United States and Japan*, Working Paper no. 1054, University of California, Berkeley, Institute of Industrial Relations.

(1993), 'Fairness, markets, and ability to pay: evidence from compensation executives', *American Economic Review* 83 (5): 1241–59.

(1997), 'Modeling altruism and spitefulness in experiments', *Review of Economic Dynamics* 1 (3): 593–622.

Lévi-Strauss, C. (1949), 'The principle of reciprocity', in: L. A. Coser and G. Rosenberg (eds.), New York: Macmillan, *Sociological Theory: A Book of Readings*, 84–94.

Lindbeck, A., and J. Weibull (1988), 'Altruism and time consistency: the economics of the fait accompli', *Journal of Political Economy* 96: 1165–82.

Lindbeck, A., S. Nyberg and J. Weibull (1999), 'Social norms and economic incentives in the welfare state', *Quarterly Journal of Economics* 116 (1): 1–35.

Macaulay, J., and L. Berkowitz (eds.) (1970), *Altruism and Helping Behavior*, New York: Academic Press.

Malinowski, B. (1932), *Crime and Custom in Savage Society*, London: Paul, Trench, Trubner.

Mandeville, B. (1705), *The Grumbling Hive, or: Knaves Turn'd Honest*, London.

  (1714), *The Fable of the Bees, or: Private Vices, Publick Benefits*, London.

Margolis, H. (1981), *Selfishness, Altruism and Rationality*, Cambridge: Cambridge University Press.

Marwell, G., and R. Ames (1979), 'Experiments on the provision of public goods: resources, interest, group size, and the free-rider problem', *American Journal of Sociology* 84: 1335–60.

  (1981), 'Economists free ride, does anyone else? Experiments on the provision of public goods, IV', *Journal of Public Economics* 15: 295–310.

Mauss, M. (1924), 'Essai sur le don, forme archaïque de l'échange', *Année Sociologique* n.s. 1: 30–186. (English trans., *The Gift: Forms and Function of Exchange in Archaic Societies*, 1967, New York: Norton).

McCabe, K. A., S. J. Rassenti and V. L. Smith (1996), 'Game theory and reciprocity in some extensive form experimental games', *Proceedings of the National Academy of Sciences of the United States of America* 93 (23): 13,421–8.

  (1998), 'Reciprocity, trust, and payoff privacy in extensive form bargaining', *Games and Economic Behavior* 24 (1–2): 10–24.

Mead, G. H. (1934), *Mind, Self and Society*, Chicago: University of Chicago Press.

Meidinger, C. (2000), 'Equity, fairness equilibria and coordination in the ultimatum game', in: L.-A. Gérard-Varet, S.-C. Kolm and J. Mercier Ythier (eds.), *The Economics of Reciprocity, Giving and Altruism*, London: Macmillan, 142–52.

Mercier Ythier, J. (1993), 'Equilibre général de dons individuels', *Revue Economique* 44 (5): 925–50.

  (1998), 'The distribution of wealth in the liberal social contract', *European Economic Review* 42: 329–47.

Merton, R. (1957), *Social Theory and Social Structure*, New York: Free Press.

Midlarsky, E. (1968), 'Aiding responses: an analysis and review', *Merrill-Palmer Quarterly* 14: 229–60.

Miller, A. A. (ed.) (1970), *Selected Writings on Anarchism and Revolution*, Cambridge, MA: MIT Press.

Miller, D. (1988), 'Altruism and the welfare state', in: J. Donald Moon (ed.), *Responsibility, Rights, and Welfare: The Theory of the Welfare State*, Boulder, Co, and London: Westview Press, 163–88.

Mishan, E. J. (1972), 'The futility of Pareto-efficient distribution', *American Economic Review* 62 (4): 971–6.

Morelly (1755 [1953]), *Code de la Nature*, Paris: Editions sociales.

Morris, W. (1890 [1993]), *News from Nowhere and Other Writings*, London: Penguin.

Musgrave, R. A. (1970), 'Pareto optimal redistribution: comment', *American Economic Review* 60 (5): 991–3.

Nagel, T. (1970), *The Possibility of Altruism*, Oxford: Oxford University Press.

   (1986), *The View from Nowhere*, Oxford: Clarendon Press.

Neuberger, E., and W. Duffy (1976), *Comparative Economic Systems: A Decision-Making Approach*, Boston: Allyn and Bacon.

Nicole, P. (1675), *Essais de Morale*, Paris.

Offer, A. (1997), 'Between the gift and the market: the economy of regard', *Economic History Review* 50 (3): 450–76.

Olsen, E. O. (1971), 'Some theorems in the theory of efficient transfers', *Journal of Political Economy* 79: 166–76.

Orbell, J., and L. A. Wilson (1978), 'Institutional solutions to the N-prisoners' dilemma', *American Political Science Review* 72: 411–21.

Orbell, J. M., R. M. Dawes and A. J. C. van de Kragt (1978), 'Explaining discussion induced cooperation', *Journal of Personality and Social Psychology* 54: 811–19.

   (1983), 'The minimal contributing set as a solution to public goods problems', *American Political Science Review* 77: 112–22.

Ostrom, E., and J. M. Walker (1991), 'Cooperation without external enforcement', in: T. P. Palfrey (ed.), *Laboratory Research in Political Economy*, Ann Arbor: University of Michigan Press 287–322.

Pantaleoni, M. (1898), *Pure Economics*, Clifton, NJ: Kelley.

Pareto, V. (1911), *Le mythe vertuiste et la littérature immorale*, Paris: Rivière.

(1913), 'Il massimo di utilità per una colletività', *Giornale degli Economisti* 3: 337–41. [Reprinted as a long footnote in *A Treatise on General Sociology*.]

(1916), *A Treatise on General Sociology*, New York: Dover.

Parsons, T. (1951), *The Social System*, Glencoe, IL: Free Press.

Piaget, J. (1932), *La Naissance du Sentiment Moral chez l'Enfant*, Geneva: Payot.

Polanyi, K. (1944), *The Great Transformation: The Political Origin of Our Time*, Boston: Beacon Press.

Prasnikar, V., and A. E. Roth (1992), 'Considerations of fairness and strategy: experimental data from sequential games', *Quarterly Journal of Economics* 107 (3): 865–88.

Proudhon, P. J. (1853), *Manuel du spéculateur à la bourse*, Paris: Garnier Frères.

Pruitt, D. G. (1968), 'Reciprocity and credit building in a laboratory dyad', *Journal of Personality and Social Psychology* 8: 143–7.

Pryor, F. (1977), *The Origins of the Economy*, New York: Academic Press.

Putnam, R. O. (1993), *Making Democracy Work: Civic Traditions in Modern Italy*, Princeton, NJ: Princeton University Press.

Rabin, M. (1993), 'Incorporating fairness into game theory and economics', *American Economic Review* 83 (5): 1281–302.

(1998), 'Psychology and economics', *Journal of Economic Literature* 36: 11–46.

Radner, R. (1980), 'Collusive behavior in noncooperative epsilon-equilibria of oligopolies with long but finite lives', *Journal of Economic Theory* 22 (2): 136–54.

Rose-Ackerman, S. (1996), 'Altruism, nonprofits, and economic theory', *Journal of Economic Literature* 34: 701–28.

Rosenhan, D. L. (1969), 'Some origins of concern for others', in: P. Mussen, J. Langer and M. Covington (eds.), *Trends and Issues in Developmental Psychology*, New York: Holt, Rinehart and Winston, 134–53.

(1970), 'The natural socialization of altruistic autonomy', in: J. Macaulay and L. Berkowitz (eds.), *Altruism and Helping Behavior*, New York: Academic Press, 251–68.

Rosenhan, D. L., and G. M. White (1967), 'Observation and rehearsal as determinants of prosocial behavior', *Journal of Personality and Social Psychology* 5: 424–31.

Rotemberg, J. (1994), 'Human relations in the workplace', *Journal of Political Economy* 102 (4): 684–717.

Roth, A. E. (1995), 'Bargaining experiments', in: J. H. Kagel and A. E. Roth (eds.), *Handbook of Experimental Economics*, Princeton, NJ: Princeton University Press, 253–348.

Sacco, P. L., and S. Zamagni (1996), 'An evolutionary dynamic approach to altruism', in: F. Farina, F. Hahn, and S. Vannucci (eds.), *Ethics, Rationality, and Economic Behaviour*, Oxford: Clarendon Press, 265–300.

(eds.) (2002), *Complessità Relazionale e Comportamento Economico*, Bologna: Il Mulino.

Sahlins, M. (1968), *Tribesmen*, Englewood Cliffs, NJ: Prentice-Hall.

(1977), *The Use and Abuse of Biology. An Anthropological Critique of Sociobiology*. London: Tavistock.

Sawyer, J. (1966), 'The altruism scale: a measure of cooperative, individualistic, and competitive interpersonal orientation', *American Journal of Sociology* 71: 407–16.

Schneider, F., and W. Pommerehne (1981), 'On the rationality of free-riding: an experiment', *Quarterly Journal of Economics* 96: 689–704.

Schwartz, B. (1967), 'The social psychology of the gift', *American Journal of Sociology* 73: 1–11.

Schwartz, R. (1970), 'Personal philanthropic contributions', *Journal of Political Economy* 78 (6): 1264–91.

Scott, R. H. (1972), 'Avarice, altruism, and second party preferences', *Quarterly Journal of Economics* 86 (1): 1–18.

Segal, U., and J. Sobel (1999), *Tit for Tat: Foundations of Preferences for Reciprocity in Strategic Settings*, Discussion Paper 99–10, University of California, San Diego.

Selten, R., and A. Ockenfels (1998), 'An experimental solidarity game', *Journal of Economic Behavior and Organization* 34 (4): 517–39.

Service, E. R. (1966), *The Hunters*, Englewood Cliffs, NJ: Prentice-Hall.

Sethi, R., and E. Somanathan (2001), 'Preference evolution and reciprocity', *Journal of Economic Theory* 97: 273–97.

(2003), 'Understanding reciprocity', *Journal of Economic Behavior and Organization* 50 (1): 1–27.

Silber, J. (ed.) (1999), *Handbook on Income Inequality Measurement*, Boston: Kluwer Academic.

Simon, H. A. (1990), 'A mechanism for social selection and successful altruism', *Science* 250: 1665–8.

(1991), 'Organization and markets', *Journal of Economic Perspectives* 5: 27–44.

Smale, S. (1980), 'The prisoner's dilemma and dynamic systems associated to non-cooperative games', *Econometrica* 48: 1617–34.

Smith, A. (1759 [1966]), *The Theory of Moral Sentiments*, New York: Kelly.

(1776 [1937]), *An Inquiry into the Nature and Cause of the Wealth of Nations*, New York: Random House.

Sobel, J. (2005), 'Interdependent preferences and reciprocity', *Journal of Economic Literature* 43: 392–436.

Solow, J. L. (1993), 'Is it really the thought that counts? Toward a rational theory of Christmas', *Rationality and Society* 5: 506–17.

Solow, R. M. (1979), 'Another possible source of wage stickiness', *Journal of Macroeconomics* 1 (1): 79–82.

Stark, O. (1995), *Altruism and Beyond: An Economic Analysis of Transfers and Exchanges within Families and Groups*, Cambridge: Cambridge University Press.

Stark, W. (ed.) (1952–4), *Jeremy Bentham's Economic Writings* (3 vols.), New York: Franklin.

Stein, E. (1964), *On the Problem of Empathy* (trans. W. Stein), The Hague: Martinus Nijhoff.

Stotland, E. (1969), 'Exploratory investigations of empathy', in: L. Berkowitz (ed.), *Advances in Experimental Social Psychology*, New York: Academic Press, 271–314.

Sugden, R. (1984), 'Reciprocity: the supply of public goods through voluntary contribution', *Economic Journal* 94: 772–87.

(1993), 'Thinking as a team: towards an explanation of nonselfish behavior', *Social Philosophy and Policy* 10: 69–89.

(2000), 'Team preferences', *Economics and Philosophy* 16: 175–205.

(2002), 'Beyond sympathy and empathy: Adam Smith's concept of fellow feeling', *Economics and Philosophy* 18: 63–88.

Swaney, J. A. (1990), 'Common property, reciprocity, and community', *Journal of Economic Issues* 24: 451–62.

Thurnwald, R. G. (1916), 'Bánaro society: social organization and kinship system of a tribe in the interior of New Guinea', *Memoirs of the American Anthropological Association* 3 (4): 251–391.

(1921), *Die Gemeinde der Bánaro*, Stuttgart: Ferdinand Enke.

(1932a), *Die Menschliche Gesellschaft*, 5 vols., Berlin and Leipzig: Walter de Gruyter.

(1932b), *Economics in Primitive Communities*, London: Oxford University Press.

Titmuss, R. M. (1971), *The Gift Relationship*, London: Allen and Unwin.

Tognoli, J. (1975), 'Reciprocation of generosity and knowledge of game termination in the decomposed prisoner's dilemma game', *European Journal of Social Psychology* 5: 297–313.

Tönnies, F. (1972), *Gemeinschaft und Gesellschaft*, Darmstadt: Wissenschaftliche Buchgesellschaft.

Tournier, P. (1963), *The Meaning of Gifts*, Richmond, VA: John Knox Press.

Trivers, R. L. (1971), 'The evolution of reciprocal altruism', *Quarterly Review of Biology* 46 (1): 35–58.

Uhlaner, C. J. (1989), 'Relational goods and participation: incorporating sociability into a theory of rational action', *Public Choice* 62: 253–85.

Van de Kragt, A. J. C., J. M. Orbell and R. M. Dawes (1983), 'The minimal contributing set as a solution to public goods problems', *American Political Science Review* 77: 112–22.

Vickrey, W. S. (1962), 'One economist's view of philanthropy', in: F. Dickinson (ed.), *Philanthropy and Public Policy*, New York: National Bureau of Economic Research.

Von Furstenberg, G. M., and D. C. Mueller (1971), 'The Pareto optimal approach to income redistribution: a fiscal application', *American Economic Review* 61 (3): 628–37.

Waller, W., and R. Hill (1951), *The Family: A Dynamic Interpretation*, New York: Dryden Press.

Walras, L. (1865 [1969]), *Les associations populaires de consommation, de production et de crédit*, Rome: Bizzarri.

Warr, P. G. (1982), 'Pareto optimal redistribution and private charity', *Journal of Public Economics* 19: 131–8.

Weisbrod, B. A. (1988), *The Nonprofit Economy*, Cambridge, MA: Harvard University Press.

Westermarck, E. (1908), *The Origin and Development of the Moral Ideas*, vol. II, London: Macmillan.

Wicksteed, P. H. (1888), *The Alphabet of Economic Science*, London: R. H. Hutton.

(1933), *The Common Sense of Political Economy*, London: Robbins Edn.

Wilke, H., and J. Lanzetta (1970), 'The obligation to help: the effects of prior help on subsequent helping behavior', *Journal of Experimental Social Psychology* 6: 466–93.

Winter, S. J., Jr. (1969), 'A simple remark on the second optimality theorem of welfare economics', *Journal of Economic Theory* 1: 99–103.

Wintrobe, R. (1981), 'It pays to do good, but not to do more good than it pays', *Journal of Economic Behavior and Organization* 2: 201–13.

Wispe, L. (1968), 'Sympathy and empathy', in: D. L. Sills (ed.), *Encyclopedia of the Social Sciences*, vol. XV, New York: Macmillan, 441–7.

Wolff, K. H. (ed.) (1950), *The Sociology of Georg Simmel*, trans. K. H. Wolff, Glencoe, IL: Free Press.

Wright, B. (1942), 'Altruism in children and the perceived conduct of others', *Journal of Abnormal and Social Psychology* 37: 218–33.

Zak, P. J., and S. Knack (2001), 'Trust and growth', *Economic Journal* 111: 295–321.

Zamagni, S. (ed.) (1995), *The Economics of Altruism*, Cheltenham: Edward Elgar.

Zeckhauser, R. (1971), 'Optimal mechanisms for income transfer', *American Economic Review* 61 (3): 324–34.

Index